D1785699

Environmental Education in a Climate of Reform

Environmental Education in a Climate of Reform

Understanding Teacher Educators' Perspectives

Sylvia Christine Almeida
Monash University, Australia

SENSE PUBLISHERS
ROTTERDAM/BOSTON/TAIPEI

A C.I.P. record for this book is available from the Library of Congress.

ISBN: 978-94-6300-215-8 (paperback)
ISBN: 978-94-6300-216-5 (hardback)
ISBN: 978-94-6300-217-2 (e-book)

Published by: Sense Publishers,
P.O. Box 21858,
3001 AW Rotterdam,
The Netherlands
https://www.sensepublishers.com/

All chapters in this book have undergone peer review.

Printed on acid-free paper

All Rights Reserved © 2015 Sense Publishers

No part of this work may be reproduced, stored in a retrieval system, or transmitted in any form or by any means, electronic, mechanical, photocopying, microfilming, recording or otherwise, without written permission from the Publisher, with the exception of any material supplied specifically for the purpose of being entered and executed on a computer system, for exclusive use by the purchaser of the work.

TABLE OF CONTENTS

SECTION 1

BUILDING THE STORIES

INTRODUCTION

We are responsible for whatever we are, and whatever we wish ourselves to be, we have the power to make ourselves. If what we are now has been the result of our own past actions, it certainly follows that whatever we wish to be in the future can be produced by our present actions; so know how to act.

Swami Vivekananda

As we work our way on this earth there are numerous experiences that we go through. What sense we make of these journeys, how we imbibe the various experiences ultimately lies with us and our perceptions. My own life experiences have shaped this book, which I see as a 'taking stock of my journey so far' point on this travel. In writing about environmental education and teacher education particularly in the Indian context there will be different colours thrown in, many of which will lie slightly to the left or right of the actual plot of this book but all of them will add together to help tell my story and through me the story of the teacher educators who have participated in the study that frames this book. This is as much my story as it is theirs.

It is important to document some background information on what prompted me to tell this story? Why did I want to tell this story or this book? And what were some of the triggers that put me on this path.

BACKGROUND

In December 2003, the Supreme Court of India mandated the teaching of environmental education across all years of formal schooling (Supreme Court of India, 2003). At the time, this appeared to provide a much needed impetus in raising the awareness of environmental issues in India; a phenomenon that has been growing significantly alongside the rapid growth of the Indian economy (Rangarajan, 2009; Ravindranath, 2007).

While the education community welcomed the mandate, the mode of implementation raised many concerns. As a teacher at the time, I too was concerned about the modalities of implementation, such as how the government would support teachers in implementing the mandate and how it would be translated into everyday teaching practice. On a more fundamental level, the question as to whether or not teachers were comfortable with the mandate and shared the same environmental concerns in India is ever present.

This significant national policy development reignited my longstanding interest in environmental education (EE) and particularly my thinking about the role of EE in teacher education. My Research interests in EE originated when I was a student for my Master's degree in Education, in the United States. My scholarship was funded by GLOBE (Global Learning and Observation to Benefit the Environment), which is a NASA initiative designed to build student/scientist partnerships. As part of that project I was involved in assessing biodiversity (loss of species) in a chain of Metro Parks in the city of Cleveland, Ohio. My project was aimed at involving school children in the program, developing long-term student-scientist partnerships, and encouraging teachers/school districts to include such initiatives as part of their school curriculum.

The Personal Connection

I have lived outside India for almost fifteen years. However, each yearly visit back to India has left me with a gnawing realisation that a lot needs to be done towards stemming the environmental concerns that have been growing disproportionately to the colossal economic strides that India has been taking in recent times. The changes have come with dizzying speed and as Kamdar (2007, p. 3) notes, it feels like "watching time-lapse photography".

Two incidents in particular stand out as main sparks that jumpstarted the thought process. One of them was a visit to Juhu beach after a break of almost 10 years. The degradation on the beach, the amount of rubbish strewn on its once beautiful sand and the almost blackish coloured water moved me to tears. The place was especially dirty as I had visited after a festival when numerous idols are immersed into the sea. The second event was the devastating floods of 2005 that brought the entire city to a halt. Numerous lives were lost and there was extensive damage to property. Most of my family members that travel to work were trapped – in fact we did not have any news from my niece for two days. While Mumbai did receive unprecedented rainfall in the 24 hours leading up to the flood this was not necessarily the main cause for the floods. The city's main natural drainage systems – namely the Mithi River and its extensive mangrove systems had been completed clogged leaving very little room for the water to leave the city thereby causing the floods.

While I had been thinking and reading about research in EE these two events provided the necessary impetus to take some action towards making a difference. There seems to be a growing acknowledgement that education – both formal and informal- in so many ways is key to societal change. However any attempt to reform the formal education system is futile unless it is accompanied by widespread support to teachers and teacher educators. Conversations with colleagues and eminent personalities in the field of teacher education have led me to believe that EE in formal teacher education institutions is still in a nascent stage and that there is a perceived gap in research about EE in teacher education. This study has been an attempt in understanding the ground realities and with the intention to help towards bridging this gap.

RATIONALE

> In the course of history, there comes a time when humanity is called to shift to a new level of consciousness, to reach a higher moral ground. At a time when we have to shed our fear and give hope to each other. That time is now. Those of us who have been privileged to receive education, skills and experiences and even power must be role models for the next generation of leadership. (Maathai, 2009, p. 16)

There has been no other time in history where environmental issues have been so prevalent (Cuff & Goudie, 2009; Diamond, 2005; Earth Summit, 2012; Krapivin & Varotsos, 2007; Nielsen, 2005; Pretty et al., 2007). Nielson (2005) identified seven broad issues – population explosion, diminishing land resources, diminishing water resources, destruction of the atmosphere, the approaching energy crisis (climate change), social decline, and conflicts and increased killing power. The explosion in world population has placed inordinate stress on the limited and finite resources of the earth, which have led to serious consequences such as destruction of natural habitats (Cuff & Goudie, 2009), increased levels of pollution and colossal losses in biodiversity.

Correcting these environmental imbalances requires a complete change in the general attitude towards treatment of the environment. Quoting a proverb by Chinese poet Kuan Tzu, 500 BC, Swaminathan outlines the impact that education can have in changing the future: 'If you are planning one year ahead – plant rice, if you are planning ten years ahead – plant trees, if you are planning a hundred years ahead – educate the people' (Swaminathan, 1987, p. 23).

Education is an important tool of change because it has the ability to bring about a shift in attitude. The 2007 International Conference on Environmental Education in Ahmedabad declared that, 'Through education, human lifestyles can be achieved that support ecological integrity' (K. Sarabhai, 2008, p. 2). The importance of education in bringing about a change in attitudes towards the environment that is sustainable was also emphasized in UNESCO's (United Nations Educational, Scientific and Cultural Organization) Guidelines and Recommendations for Reorienting Teacher Education to Address Sustainability – 'Education is essential for moving toward a more sustainable future. We cannot imagine how the people of all nations could move toward a more sustainable world without the contribution of educators from around the globe' (UNESCO, 2007, p. 10).

Despite the fact that the concept of EE has been in existence for some time, there is no single agreed upon definition. Stapp coined the first formal definition in 1968 however the most commonly used definition was created by the International Union for Conservation of Nature and Natural Resources in 1971. According to the IUCN, EE is:

> ... the process of recognizing values and clarifying concepts in order to develop skills and attitudes necessary to understand and appreciate the inter-relatedness among man, his culture, and his biophysical surroundings. Environmental education also entails practice in decision-making and self-formulation of a code of behaviour about issues concerning environmental quality. (IUCN, 1971, p. 7)

UNESCO has been central to the development of EE. The Belgrade Charter in 1975 and the Tbilisi conference in 1977 (which was the first UNESCO conference involving different governments) provided the most commonly used aims, objectives, and guiding principles for EE used to this day in international and national policy documents (UNESCO, 1975; UNESCO & UNEP, 1977). In recent years there has been extensive debate surrounding EE. There has been a dramatic shift toward education for sustainable development since the World Summit on Sustainable Development held in Johannesburg in South Africa. The general reason for this shift is the perception that EE lacked a holistic approach – one that also takes into account the developmental needs of society (Tilbury, 2004). Further to this, there has been a call to find a balance between the conservation of resources and meeting human needs in a sustainable manner. The World Conservation Strategy launched in 1980 first highlighted the need for sustainable development (International Union for Conservation of Nature and Natural Resources (IUCN), 1980). The Bruntland Commission devised the most commonly used definition for sustainable development

> development that meets the needs of the present without compromising the ability of future generations to meet their needs. (World Commission on Environment and Development, 1987, p. 43)

The advent of the concept of sustainable development in some respects has pushed EE to the background. Major conferences and international literature appears to increasingly focus on education for sustainable development. Often sustainable development is considered an end purpose of EE. This can be problematic especially as the term is still fluid in its meaning and a universally accepted definition as yet, does not hold sway. Another cause for concern is that the notion of sustainable development has tended to push environment, nature and its study way from the centre of the issue and blur the focus somewhat. However, there can be no education for sustainable development without the environment being an integral part of it (Lotz-Sistika, 2009). Despite this situation, EE policy tends to adopt characteristics of ecological sustainability, thus further highlighting the lines of difference and concern that exist in the field (Cutter-Mackenzie, 2010).

It has been argued that the practice of EE in schools has been seriously lacking. In Australian schools, a growing culture of sustainability is prevalent (Cutter-Mackenzie, 2010). The depth and breadth of practice varies markedly, although even ten years ago EE was considered to be a failing in school systems. While progress in teacher education has been slow, this area is now increasingly becoming an area of focus in some teacher education faculties (McKeown-Ice, 2012). Globally, education for sustainable development in the higher education sector is becoming increasingly important (Cotton, Warren, Maiboroda, & Bailey, 2007). In Australia EE is integrated across the curriculum and is beginning to be taught in more systematic ways in some teacher education institutions (Cutter-Mackenzie & Tilbury, 2002). In India, although teaching EE has been mandated across all schools, it does not appear to be mandatory in teacher education.

In 1991 UNESCO labelled teacher education as the 'priority of priorities' in relation to environmental education. This has been further emphasised through an international effort to reorient teacher education to EE (McKeown-Ice, 2005; Tilbury, 1992). The rationale for this approach is multifaceted.

In 1996 (Oulton, 1996, p. 1) argued that 'only limited progress has been made at the school and teacher education levels' to incorporate EE into the formal education system. An earlier study undertaken by the Organization for Economic Cooperation and Development (OECD) in five countries saw teacher education as the weakest aspect of EE programs in all these five countries (Organisation for Economic Co-operation and Development, 1995). Additionally the study also found that very few teachers thought that teacher education institutions are doing enough to prepare teacher for teaching environmental issues. The main impediments for this seem to be the traditional disciplinary structure and pedagogical practice of higher education. An Australian study (Miles & Cutter-Mackenzie, 2006, p. 148) also found that:

> ... despite national and international policy rhetoric about the importance of pre-service teacher preparation in environmental education, the present study has shown that there are still inadequate levels of environmental education provision at the teacher education level and that pre-service teachers' preparedness for teaching environmental education is overwhelmingly low.

It has now been 15 years since the OECD study. Research undertaken since that time (Cutter-Mackenzie, 2009; McKeown-Ice, 2000, 2012; Oulton, 1996; Tilbury, 2004) has significantly aided in explaining existing patterns of EE provision and identified reasons as to why teacher education programs have typically failed to adequately prepare teachers in EE. Major impediments/barriers to this include: inadequate provision for EE in teacher education programs; inadequate preparation of teachers such that they do not have the requisite knowledge, skills and experience to teach EE (Cutter, 1998; Cutter-Mackenzie & Tilbury, 2002; Ferreira, Ryan, & Tilbury, 2006; Miles, Cutter-Mackenzie, & Harrison, 2006);

- lack of commitment from teacher education institutes;
- lack of awareness about the environment;
- lack of motivation; and,
- lack of disposition of the individual student teachers and teacher educators.

Miles, Cutter-Mackenzie and Harrison (2006) contend that 'little has changed in the adequate provision of environmental education in pre-service teacher education over the last twenty years.' They challenge teacher education providers to consider 'new ways and approaches to better prepare future teachers in the area of environmental education' (p. 57). Such conclusions have tended to be based upon pre-service teachers' (student teachers') course experiences (McKeown-Ice, 2000; Plevyak, Bendixen-Noe, Henderson, & Wilke, 2001; Tilbury, 1992, 1994). Teacher educators themselves have seldom featured in such studies, which makes this thesis particularly significant in advancing the field of EE from a teacher education perspective.

Significance of the Study

> If education has to be an effective tool of change, in the general attitude towards the treatment of environment, teacher education will have to respond to this effectively at all levels. The content and processes of teacher education will have to equip teachers with a proper understanding of and love for the nature around and the skill of inculcating these among their students. This may result not only in a healthier society, both physically and mentally, but also the much needed replenishment and sustenance of natural resources notwithstanding all the material and industrial development. (National Council of Teacher Educators, 2005, p. 57)

While there are a growing number of research studies investigating pre-service teachers' thinking and experiences in EE, teacher educators themselves and the culture and organisation in which they operate have tended to be overlooked. There is a lack of research concerning teacher educators' understandings of, and attitudes in, the field of EE (Cotton et al., 2007). UNESCO's key Reorientation Policy emphasised that:

> Institutions of teacher education fulfil vital roles in the global education community; they have the potential to bring changes within educational systems that will shape the knowledge and skills of future generations. Often, education is described as the great hope for creating a more sustainable future; teacher-education institutions serve as key change agents in transforming education and society, so such a future is possible. Not only do teacher-education institutions educate new teachers, they update the knowledge and skills of in-service teachers, create teacher-education curriculum, provide professional development for practicing teachers, contribute to textbooks, consult with local schools, and often provide expert opinion to regional and national ministries of education. Institutions of teacher education also perform similar services for school principals who have significant impact on what occurs in schools. Because of this broad influence in curriculum design and implementation, as well as policy setting within educational institutions, faculty members

of teacher-education institutions are perfectly poised to promote education for sustainable development (ESD). By working with the administrations and faculties of teacher education institutions, governments can bring about systematic, economically effective change. For these reasons, nations should include teacher education institutions in their national sustainability plans. (UNESCO, 2005b, pp. 11–12)

Fien and Maclean (2000) identify a special commitment from teacher education institutions as a necessity for reorienting teacher education towards sustainability. It is important to note that UNESCO-UNEP made an urgent request two decades ago for the preparation of teachers to be considered as 'the priority of priorities', yet little seems to have changed in practice.

As Ravindranath (2007) pointed out, there is need for the development of an integrated approach towards teacher education, which brings together modern and traditional approaches and retains the basic Indian philosophy of respect for the environment and all creatures that live within it. The National Council for Teacher Education (NCTE, 2005) India's top governing body for teacher education clearly recognised the crucial role of teachers and teacher educators in creating environmental consciousness amongst all sections of society. While it recognised the importance of EE in teacher education it also acknowledged the lack of work in the sector. The NCTE also highlighted the need for EE to be made compulsory and taught as an integral component of teacher education (National Council of Teacher Educators, 2005). However, there appears to be little evidence that this recommendation is being implemented and, that is where the significance of this study lies; in understanding teacher educators' experiences in implementing EE.

ENVIRONMENTAL EDUCATION &
TEACHER EDUCATION

A Review of Literature Review

INTRODUCTION

Satellite pictures in the sky show a denuded landscape where mangroves, wetlands and forests are vanishing. Negative trends seem to overwhelm positive ones. Yet, the signs of hope, the spirit of enquiry beckons equally strongly. In our capacity to master the means, ignorance is a luxury nobody can afford. (Rangarajan, 2009, p. xxii)

While a complete comprehensive review of research is beyond the scope of this chapter it does aim to provide a snapshot existing literature pertaining to major concepts pertaining to this study. It starts by looking at research spanning global and local environments and contexts highlighting some of the key environmental concerns. I first begin by discussing the major global and national (Indian) environmental issues and challenges. It is important the threats and concerns for the environment serve as a background towards laying down the importance of this book. Overtime there has been a push towards education as a means to bring about change. The next section therefore provides a historical analysis of these global and national trends in Environmental Education especially with an emphasis on policy. Any change in the education sector needs to be supported by sound understanding of the role of teachers and teacher educators in implementing Environmental Education. Current trends in this field are presented in the third section. The final section of this chapter focuses on existing literature that helps understand the teacher preparation and environment education in India.

GLOBAL – LOCAL: ENVIRONMENTAL CONCERNS AND CHALLENGES

Global Issues

Latest reports from the biannual Living Planet (2014) reveal that our demands on the planet are 50 per cent more than what it can sustain. There has been a rapid loss in biodiversity with sharp declines in the representative populations of all species. In particular the Indo-Pacific region shows a dramatic decline in freshwater species – about 76 per cent.

It can well be argued that the planet is facing an environmental crisis. Lester Brown, President of the Earth Policy Institute aptly describes the situations as follows:

> We are liquidating the earth's natural assets to fuel our consumption. Half of us live in countries where water tables are falling and wells are going dry. Soil erosion exceeds soil formation on one third of the world's cropland, draining the land of its fertility. The world's ever-growing herds of cattle, sheep, and goats are converting vast stretches of grassland to desert. Forests are shrinking by 13 million acres per year as we clear land for agriculture and cut trees for lumber and paper. Four fifths of oceanic fisheries are being fished at capacity or overfished and headed for collapse. In system after system, demand is overshooting supply. (Brown, 2011, pp. 3–4)

Humans have caused more changes to the ecosystems in the past 50 years than any comparable period in history mainly to meet rapidly growing demands for food, fresh water, timber, fibre and fuel leading to large and irreversible loss to diversity of life on Earth (Millenium Ecosystem Assessment Board, 2005). Environmental concerns are currently at unprecedented levels worldwide and continue to escalate and are presently one of the most important issues facing humanity today. Global ecosystems have undergone massive changes, especially over the past 50 years (Matthews et al., 2012). India and China have been growing at an unprecedented rate since 2001 – China at a nine-year doubling time and India at a seven-year doubling time. Consequently environmental pressures have also been growing at the same rate. If these two economic giants fail to improve their environmental footprint they will be responsible for the 37% of the increase in global environmental footprint by 2015 (UNEP, 2012b). If the entire world adopted U.S.'s current resource consumption and waste production patterns (Bryner, 2011) points out that it would amount to having the worlds population suddenly grow to 72 billion.

Diamond (2005), Krapivin and Varotsos (2007), Nielsen (2005), Palmer (1998) and the most recent GEO 5 report (UNEP, 2012a) amongst others have described and categorized the global environmental problems in detail. For the purpose of this review, global environmental problems will be discussed by placing them in the following categories.

a. Population and Unsustainable development: The world's population has increased from 2.8 billion in 1950 to around 7 billion in the year 2011 (Rajagopalan, 2011). In this century, the world has experienced the highest rate of population growth (averaging 2.04% per year) in the 60s, and the largest increment to the world population (86 million people every year) in the 80s (U.S. Bureau of Census , 2009). Neilsen (2005) termed this explosive growth- growth that is sudden and very fast. Naturally, this sudden and fast increase placed a tremendous burden on the limited and finite resources of the Earth particularly food, freshwater, wood, fibre and fuel (Palmer, 1998; Pretty et al., 2007).

The increasing population has led to a 2.5-fold increase in food production from 1980–2000, more than doubled the freshwater consumption, tripled the use of wood for paper and doubled the power of hydroelectric stations' (Krapivin & Varotsos, 2007, p. 46). These needs are met by intensifying activities using modern technology to harvest resources. It is suggested that in the next 50 years the need for food will grow by 70–85% and the need for water will increase by 30–85%, and this will lead to further ecosystem degradation. Such intensified usage often leads to the outbreak of diseases, decrease in water quality especially coastal waters – leading to collapse of fisheries and climate change amongst other changes. In short, as continuing rapid population growth leads to scarce cropland, dry wells, disappearing forests, increased soil erosion, rising unemployment and spreading hunger (Brown, 2011).

b. Loss of forests: Three issues, namely – loss of biodiversity, scarcity of fresh water, and disruptive climate change have been identified as particularly difficult and emblematic of the environmental problems facing humanity (Bryner, 2011). Loss of forests at the rate of 15–20% since pre-agricultural times has led to a rapid loss of biodiversity (Cuff & Goudie, 2009). Most deforestation is happening in the tropics with countries like Indonesia losing large tracts of forests for farming (Gornall, Wiltshire, & Betts, 2012). Globally forest cover declined at the rate of 200 kms^2 per day between 2000–2005 (Gornall et al., 2012). An estimated 45 million hectares of forests is lost annually and foreshadows the loss of all biologically productive land in 200 years (Nielsen, 2005). In India the forest cover has declined from 40% a century ago to 19% – in other words it lost more than half its forests (Rajagopalan, 2011). In the past 30 years, larger amounts of land were transformed into agricultural lands, 20% of global coral reefs have been lost and 20% have been damaged, 35% of mangroves have been destroyed. About 50% of the worlds wetlands have disappeared since 1900 (Bryner, 2011). It is estimated that about one species every 20 minutes or approximately 30,000 species every year are lost on Earth which is about 1000 times higher than normal (Edwards, 2010). In an interview Vandana Shiva points to the expedited loss of genetic diversity particularly of cultivated species due to genetic manipulation/ engineering (Mazur & Miles, 2009). Overall it is estimated that at this rate half of the existing species in the world will be wiped out in the next 70 years (Krapivin & Varotsos, 2007).

c. Desertification and drought: Desertification impacts approximately one-sixth of the worlds population, about 70% of all dry lands and about a quarter of the entire land area of our planet (Bryner, 2011). This is caused by natural processes like soil erosion but accelerated due to human activities. Removal of forests or grazing pastures for agriculture, large-scale logging and clearing for timber or fuel wood along with agricultural mismanagement, land conversion, industry and urbanization (including roads and highways) are causes for rapid desertification (Kemp, 2004). While drought and famine have been long standing issues these seem to have exacerbated in recent times. Additional desertification, which is mainly man-made, has emphasised human contribution to the problem. Land management is also a serious issue that impacts the environment with a plateau reached in nitrogen use efficiency. This translates to farmers having to use increasing levels of fertilisers which adds to the problem of runoff of nitrogen into the biosphere creating hazardous water and atmospheric pollution (Gornall et al., 2012).

d. Fresh Water: Growing demand for fresh water and declining water quality due to increasing pollution. As described earlier the increasing population has placed a tremendous burden on the water systems of the Earth. Only 0.3% of the Earth's water resources are found in renewable resources like lakes, rivers, marshes, and wetlands – which are becoming increasingly polluted and affecting water quality. Global water withdrawals have increased 7 fold in the past 100 years. Water availability has decreased by 40% in industrialized nations and 70% in developing countries, it is estimated to decline further to only 80–90% of the 1950s level (Nielsen, 2005). According to the World Bank (World Bank, 2003) there will be a 50% increase in water consumption over the next thirty years and about half the worlds population will live under conditions of severe water stress by 2025.

e. Oceans: Degradation of oceans, coast and marine resources due to pollution and over exploitation. The number of large predatory fish in the oceans has decreased by ninety per cent the beginning of industrial fishery (Orr, 2007). Excessive pollution and oil spills from shipping accidents lead to the formation of 'dead zones' – parts of the oceans that cannot support any form of life (Nielsen, 2005).

f. Atmosphere: Atmospheric pollution, climate change, ozone layer depletion and acid deposition are pressing environmental issues directly influenced by human contributions. Air pollution mainly causes by the use of fossil fuels has harmful effects on human health. It kills about 1.9 million people each year in developing countries. India and China have the highest levels of air pollution in the world – cities like Delhi, Calcutta and Mumbai are amongst the most polluted (Nielsen, 2005). These pollutants have thinned and caused holes in the ozone layer and along with increased amounts of greenhouse gases are adding to the global warming process. Bryner (2011, p. 25) summarises the evidence that clearly documents the effects of global warming like the almost two fold increase in average Arctic temperatures over the past hundred years or the widespread changes in extreme temperatures over the past fifty years. 'Climate change threatens, among other things, food security and biodiversity' and people in 'developing regions are especially vulnerable to the effects of climate change' (UNEP, 2012a, p. 33). It is expected that by the end of the century warming could be up to 5°C compared to pre-industrial times and this would lead to a world with 'more extreme weather events, most ecosystems stressed and changing, many species doomed to extinction, and whole nations threatened by inundation' (World Bank, 2010).

g. Energy: Growing demands for energy coupled with unsustainable use and pollution of the environment are pressing problems. Energy consumption has increased nearly 70% since 1971 and is projected to increase by approximately 2%

annually over the next fifteen years (Bryner, 2011). The approaching energy crisis is caused mainly by the exhaustion of fossil fuel supplies, which have already fallen to half and are expected to fall further. As demands for these fuels continues to rise there is an ever widening gap between supply and demand (Nielsen, 2005).

h. Waste: Population growth, new lifestyles and rapidly changing technology create serious waste disposal problems (Kemp, 2004). Managing exceeding levels of solid waste and use of non-biodegradable products particularly plastics. Disposal of hazardous substances including nuclear waste is also a serious point of contention.

i. Global Security: Global security is threatened due to increasing conflicts over sharing (or lack thereof) of resources. The World Commission on Sustainable Development points out that historic responses to the above mentioned scarcity of resources has often been the source of conflict (Barrow, 2012; World Commission on Environment and Development, 2004).

Apart from the challenges briefly noted above, other issues such as decreasing levels of photosynthetic ceiling – the amount of sunlight fixed by plants to produce food, the introduction of 'alien species' or non-native species, and the production of greenhouse gases by the burgeoning human population are also cause for concern (Diamond, 2005). Orr (2007) predicts that these issues bode a trouble future for the signature accomplishments of the fourth 'design revolution' namely the creation of an homogenised industrial civilisation through science and technology.

The World Wildlife Fund (WWF) cites the loss of a third of the planet's wildlife in the past 35 years and argues that humans will need the equivalent of two planets if current lifestyles continue unabated (World Wide Fund (WWF), 2008). Neilsen (2005) affirms that the increasing population is putting enormous stress on the environment, and human needs are now reaching or exceeding the planet's ecological limits. If current consumption levels continue there will be a surplus of 3 billion people on the planet by 2020, and six Earth-like planets will be needed to accommodate the surplus population.

Neilsen (2005) also categorizes social decline as key environmental issue and lists the gap between the "haves and the have-nots" and the disparity in their GDP's as a leading cause for concern. China and India for example account for 76 per of the world's population but for only 29 per cent of its income. Krapivin & Varatsos (2007) point out that about 1.1 billion people live on daily income of less than a dollar a day. This poverty is particularly acute in Asia and Africa with 29 sub-Saharan African countries forming the bottom rung of the Human Development Index (HDI) – an index developed to rank 177 countries based on their level of socio-economic welfare, health and education (Human Development Report Office, 2011). In countries like Ethiopia 98 per cent of the population live on less than $2 a day. This disparity is evident even locally within countries, for example, on the one hand India is home to some of the richest billionaires in the world, but on the other hand 60 per cent of India's poor live on Rupees 35 (approx. half a dollar) a day and nearly as many in the cities who live on Rupees 66 (approximately one dollar) a day. Overall 30% of India's population lives on less than $1 a day (National Survey Sample Organization, 2012; World Bank, 2012).

It is this poverty and disparity in wealth that triggers Nobel Peace prize winning Kenyan environmentalist Wangari Muta Maathai (see, World Commission on Environment and Development, 2004, p. 100) to say, 'If you want to save the environment you should protect the people first, because human beings are part of the biological diversity. If we can't protect our own species, what's the point of protecting tree species?' She points to the irony of the poor, who depend most on the environment, yet are also often the ones who are responsible for its destruction. She attributes that situation to the fact that the poor are often 'so preoccupied with their survival that they are not concerned about the long-term damage they are doing to the environment simply to meet their most basic needs' (p. 100). This contention, although credible in its own right, also raises the question of long-term vision – if the poor are the most dependent on a resource then that should also impel them to act to save it. However, the issue often goes beyond poverty to the distribution and unequal distribution and overconsumption of natural resources. Industrialized nations containing 20% of the global population shared 86% of global wealth while the 20% living in poor countries shared only 1% of the global wealth, by the end of the 20th century. China, India, Indonesia, Brazil and Russia accounted for 50% of the world's population but shared only 9% of its wealth (Nielsen, 2005). Krapivin and Varotsos (2007, p. 49) highlighted the disparity between global consumption and population (see Table 2.1).

Table 2.1. Shares of global consumption and population (%) in different regions

Region	Consumption	Population
USA and Canada	31.7	5.3
Western Europe	28.9	6.5
Eastern Asia and Pacific Ocean Region	21.6	32.9
Latin America and Caribbean Region	6.9	8.7
Eastern Europe and Central Asia	3.7	8.2
South Asia	2.2	22.5
Australia and New Zealand	1.8	0.6
Near East and North Africa	1.7	4.4
Sub-Saharan Africa	1.5	10.9

An average American consumes natural resources dozens of times greater than an average individual in developing countries. Despite a history and obvious evidence of over consumption, wealthy countries have not even begun to contemplate the concept of "consumption policy". The Western countries, and the U.S.A. in particular, have contributed to two-thirds of greenhouse gases, which are responsible for global warming; yet the brunt of this is being borne most by the developing countries (Cuff & Goudie, 2009). Paradoxically, developing countries are often unwilling to share any responsibility for the mistakes of the Western world yet would like to achieve industrialization and wealth despite the environmental cost. They do not want to sacrifice their right to development in order to protect the environment especially as they view the current environmental crisis as largely the doing of the economic growth patterns and 'footprints' of the Northern countries (Young, 2002). In general, there is a greater emphasis on economy rather than environment and a lack of consensus between North and South over which environmental issues are of major global concern (Young, 2002). The developing countries also disagree with the hegemony of developed countries over solutions to environmental problems and their unwillingness to consider the significance of cultural aspects in seeking alternative solutions (Smyth, 2008).

In his speech at the Rio Earth Summit, then Malaysian President Mahathir Mohammed was quoted as saying:

> We know that 25% of the world's populations who are rich consume 85% of its wealth and produce 90% of its waste. Mathematically speaking, if the rich reduce their wasteful consumption by 25%, worldwide pollution will be reduced by 22.5%. But, if the poor 75% reduce consumption totally and disappear from this earth altogether, the reduction in pollution will only be by 10%. It is what the rich do that counts, not what the poor do, however much they do it. The rich will not accept a progressive and meaningful cutback in their emissions of carbon dioxide and other greenhouse gases because it will be a cost to them and retard their progress. Yet they expect the poor people of the developing countries to stifle even their minute growth as if it will cost them nothing ... Malaysia will do what can reasonably be expected of it for the environment. (Conca & Dabelko, 2004, p. 334)

There is no doubt about the fact that environmental change is a risk to human security. Global environmental change brings new and often unprecedented threats to human security raising important questions about equity and sustainability. However environmental change goes hand in hand with other social factors like poverty and discrimination in creating these insecurities (Barnett, Matthew, & O'Brien, 2010). This conflict of assets, attitude and interests between the haves and have-nots increases immigration pressures, breeds resentment against richer countries, encourages terrorism and is causing further delays in stemming the environmental decay (Nielsen, 2005). As Barnett (2010, p. 4) state global environmental change is 'inherently a question about the capacity to respond to new challenges and to reconcile the growing disparities that undermine human security'. Young (2002) suggested there was real value in an equal and participatory approach in helping local people manage local environmental issues with the help of international expertise, without having this help imposed on them.

In the Asian context given the population densities and the rapid economic development particularly of India and China, it is imperative that they take environmental sustainability into account failing which they will export their suffering to the rest of the world (Luce, 2006). The blurring between local and global environmental problems and challenges has become omnipresent, increasingly with governments referring to current issues in a *'glocal'* sense. The tensions between developed (rich) and developing (poor) countries are likewise omnipresent. However, for the purpose of this review, each concept is considered individually before identifying the tensions and relations between local and global (or glocal) keeping in mind the arguments concerning developed and developing nations.

Nielsen (2005) conceded that one could argue about the unimportance of a small, seemingly insignificant species and its extinction. But this response would then miss the point, that even the smallest creature is a link in the web of life and regular loss of such 'small' and 'inconsequential' species disturbs the natural equilibrium, which humans cannot replace. The interactions between different ecosystems, species and genes is absolutely critical in determining the overall health of the system and of individual species – humans being one of those (Bryner, 2011)

Atmospheric pollution is of particular concern due to climate change, global warming, ozone layer depletion and acid deposition to which it leads. Global impacts of these changes are expected to have widespread effect on the populace with estimates that natural disasters killed more than 120,000 people per year in the past decade, which was almost double of the toll in the 1990s. 174 million people were affected annually by natural disasters in the mid-1980s to the mid-1990s. This number rose to 254 million a year in the decade from 1995–2004 and in 2007 just the floods in Asia had affected 250 million people. These numbers show the exponential increase of global impact by natural disasters driven in part by climate change (Hunter Lovins & Cohen, 2011, p. 9). There are predictions that the environment is reaching its threshold level and any further increase could lead to dramatic and perhaps irreversible changes.

The disparity in GDP's between developed and developing countries is a major cause of concern; only 11% of countries containing 16% of the global population are rich. It is estimated that the richest 20% of the world's population accounts for 86% of total private expenditure while the poorest 20% consume only 5% or less of these resources (Khoshoo, 2010). China and India account for 76% of the global population but for only 29% of its income. Approximately 1.1 billion of the world's population currently live on a daily income of less than $1/day (Krapivin & Varotsos, 2007). This poverty is particularly acute in Asia and Africa with 35 sub-Saharan African countries forming the bottom rung of the Human Development Index (HDI) – an index developed to rank 177 countries based on their level of socio-economic welfare, health and education (Human Development Report Office, 2011). In countries like Ethiopia 98 per cent of the population lives on less than $2/day. Often the most populated countries are also amongst the poorest and most environmentally stressed.

While current environmental problems are due to the detailed physical and scientific issues noted above, these are also a result of deeper underlying issues around social change in society brought about by greater change in culture and personal lifestyles. According to Lacey (2011, p. 86) 'our destiny and thriving are bound up with the land, in the city as well as in the countryside. We are learning too that equity and autonomy are vital in the human community and that these too are bound up with the health of the biosphere.' As discussed earlier poverty and discrimination are often at the heart of our interactions with the environment.

As with other contemporary issues there are objections as to the seriousness of these environmental issues. The veracity of some of the environmental challenges have been challenged as myths that have been created by distorting facts and drawing biased conclusions about a few scientific facts (Bennett, 2012). Cutter-Mackenzie (2009) discusses some of these including claims that the environmental problems are getting smaller not bigger, and that environmentalists are basically anti-modernization in their attitudes. Commonly cited objections range from arguments such as: 'Technology will solve our problems' and, 'If we exhaust one resource, we can always switch to some other resource meeting the same need'.

For some, there is also a sense of over simplification of the entire environmental issue, as reflected by statements such as:

> There is no food problem; there is already enough food; we only need to solve the transportation problem of distributing that food to places that need it. Look at how many times in the past the gloom-and-doom predictions of fear mongering environmentalists have proved wrong. Why should we believe them this time? (Diamond, 2005, p. 169)

The above arguments are short sighted, simplistic and highly technocentric views of the world and the environment. For example while relying heavily on technology to solve our problems we overlook the fact that most of the current environmental problems have been caused by technology. In suggestion the transfer of food to so called Third world countries the logistics and politics of the matter is overlooked. Shiva (2005) further points out to the dangers of globalisation and biopiracy that developing nations face in dealing with food security/insecurity. There is a serious lack of studies and research articles that counter the arguments of these critics. Cutter-Mackenzie (Cutter-Mackenzie, 2003, p. 37) made an important observation that 'to date the arguments of environmental critics have not been analysed in the environment literature'.

India faces several of the problems highlighted above so it comes as no surprise that many of these environmental concerns have a direct impact on the country. The next section considers the nature of environmental issues as applicable to India.

Local (India)

No other country matters more to the future of our planet than India. There is no challenge that we face, no opportunity we covet where India does not have critical relevance (Kamdar, 2007, pp. 3–4). India is the second fastest growing economy in the world and with a population of 1.2 billion is also the second most populous nation. Between 2001–2011 the addition to India's population is slightly less than population of Brazil – which is the fifth most populous nation in the world. At 1.2 billion people, India's population is almost equal to that of six other populous nations put together – namely Brazil, Indonesia, Bangladesh, Pakistan and Japan. India has only 2.4% of the world's surface area but accounts for 17.5% of the world's population. In contrast a country like U.S.A. covers 7.2% of the world's surface area but accounts for only 4.5% of the world's population (Census of India, 2011).

India is hugely diverse both in terms of its population and ecosystems. Kamdar (2007, p. 4) describes it as a world in a microcosm, a nation that is 'at once an ancient Asian civilisation, a modern nation grounded in Enlightenment values and democratic institutions, and a rising twenty-first century power'. This is where diversity is found in almost everything and centuries harmoniously coexist (Khoshoo, 1987). With approximately 1652 languages and numerous dialects spoken, a myriad mixture of religions and traditions exist in India (Ravindranath, 2000). Its land and population size, unprecedented growth and immense diversity make India's environment and environmental management vital to the entire world. What happens in India will have deep, long-range consequences for the entire planet (Rangarajan, 2009, p. xx).

The rapid growth, both in terms of its population and development especially in the last two decades has simultaneously raised major environmental concerns. The Environmental Performance Index ranks India at a dismal 125 amongst all nations – it has the unhealthiest air quality in the world compared to the other 133 nations (Yale University, 2012). Unlike Western nations where industrialization was a comparatively slow process, India has seen tremendous growth in just three decades. Kamdar (2007) contends that the magnitude or velocity of India's transformation has been unparalleled. This has led to an increase in population and rapid development, which in turn has placed tremendous demands on its resources (Joshi, 2005; Luce, 2006; Rangarajan, 2009; Ravindranath, 2002a; K. Sarabhai, 2008). For example India's rivers, which were once symbols of purity and linked to deep spiritual beliefs have been reduced to mere receptacles of sewage and toxic waste (Sharma, 2010). India's future; its possibilities and perils reflect globally for according to Kamdar (2007, p. 3) 'as goes India, so goes the world'. It holds the key to the emerging new world, which has been recalibrated due to Asia's phenomenal rise. This newfound power has serious environmental implications. One example is the rise in energy consumption in India – it is the 'fifth largest consumer of energy in the world' even though about '57% of its rural population have no access to electricity' (Srivastava, 2009, p. 33). Given the economic growth that it has been witnessing, India is expecting to join the league of 'developed' nations by 2020. It is not hard to imagine the kind of energy usage India will reach if every Indian household is to access energy and electricity to the same level as those in 'developed' countries. If India along with China does not stem rapid deterioration of their environment then they will export their suffering to the rest of the world (Luce, 2006).

Extreme poverty remains a significant concern in India. Nearly half of India's urban population lives in slum-like conditions. About 10% of the global population (and half of India's) live in the Ganges valley and is also the concentration of the world's greatest poverty (Cuff & Goudie, 2009). The disparity of wealth between richer states/people and the economically underprivileged ones is great. This region is also prone to the most severe effects of climate change – the drying up of the rivers, soil erosion, frequent flooding, and earthquakes. Water shortages are also a growing area of concern. Brown (2011, p. 14) states that the 'water bubble' that India lives in – over pumping aquifers to grow grain to feed over 175 million Indians – could burst anytime leading to mass food shortages.

Cuff and Goudie (2009, p. 358) raise and consequently answer four major questions about environmental problems and challenges in India:

Does the size of the population alone create damaging environmental pressures?

Population size alone has "prompted major schemes with both negative and positive impacts, and a potentially damaging agrochemical form of agriculture" (Cuff & Goudie, 2009, p. 358). A large population places increasing demands for resources. This in turn stresses the environment especially since the demands are unsustainable. For example, huge dams have been built in India and China to meet fresh water and energy requirements of the increasing in population. These dams while solving some problems also create new social, political and ecological problems. They contribute to global warming, destroy productive land areas, disturb habitat of species, contribute to deforestation, and displace people creating 'ecological refugees'. They also add to international disputes over water sharing treaties (Nielsen, 2005). The Narmada Dam in India is a glaring example of one such disaster.

Does poverty of large areas create environmental pressures?

Indian Prime Minister Indira Gandhi while addressing the first UN Conference on Environment in Stockholm in 1972 stipulated 'poverty and need' to be the greatest polluters of the environment:

> We do not wish to impoverish the environment any further and yet we cannot for a moment forget the grim poverty of large numbers of people. Are not poverty and need the greatest polluters? The environment cannot be improved in conditions of poverty. Nor can poverty be eradicated without the use of science and technology. (as cited in, Rangarajan, 2009, p. xviii)

Poor and dense rural/urban populations in India are often unable to maintain sustainable development. This could be due to inadequate training and lack of education in sustainable development and procurement of livelihoods (Cuff &

Goudie, 2009). Rangarajan (2009) emphasizes the need to alleviate poverty in order to secure the future of the planet.

Do the new large cities have damaging ecological footprints?

25 of the 100 fastest growing urban cities in the world are in India. This is in contrast to China that has only 8 of them (Barta & Pokharel, 2009). 60% of India's population lives in these cities (World Bank, 2012; World Bank, 2009) in slum-like conditions. These cities place a huge demand on natural resources like food, water and building materials which affects not only the immediate urban, but also the distant rural environments.

Is India's unique environment particularly 'difficult' or 'fragile'?

India's environment is as diverse as the country and consists of different biomes. From windy, wet lengthy coastlines to the dry hinterlands of Central India that lack both wind and rain, from the snow-covered alpine regions in the Himalayan foothills to the desert of Rajasthan, different ecosystems and climates exist within the country. Each of these poses a different kind of challenge in terms of the environmental issues it raises (Joshi, 2005).

The next section considers the disparities and tensions between global and local.

Glocal

> How the earth will fare may be a distant concern for a person who is unsure of the next meal. But how that meal and that person are made secure will have a lot to do with the fate of the earth. How poverty will be tackled may have little immediate relevance to anyone with a credit card. But riches cannot fully guard against contaminated water and air anymore than they can against the return of diseases once thought to have been eradicated. In contrast to 'purely' economic issues, those with an ecological edge or an environmental dimension can help trace the threads that bind us in a common future. (Rangarajan, 2009, p. xxi)

The Asian Development Bank has identified Asia as the world's most polluted and degraded region with a range of potentially dangerous environmental problems and a high economic cost attached to these problems (Yencken, Fien, & Sykes, 2002). Environmental problems often transcend boundaries as water, air and nature as such does not honour manmade borders (Rangarajan, 2009). Issues concerning India are not confined locally and are most likely to have global repercussions.

As identified earlier, unlike Western nations where industrialization was a relatively slow process (in comparison to India and China), India has seen tremendous growth in just three decades. India's booming growth, both in terms of its population and economy, has led to unprecedented demands on its resources thereby adding to its environmental problems and challenges. These problems are transposed to neighbouring nations and to the planet. Luce (2006) identified India, China and the United States as the three most important obstacles to international consensus in tackling global warming. International agencies like the UNESCO, UNDP (United Nations Development Program) and World Bank are attempting to have a strong presence in India and are actively involved in improvement and creating awareness through education. The World Bank (2009) for example, stresses the need for long-term vision and urgent action in dealing with India's environmental issues which have made it exceptionally vulnerable to effects of climate change – namely cyclones, floods and droughts. They believe that growth has led to a higher toll on India's natural resources and emphasise the need for sustainable development and reduction of the burden that environmental degradation imposes on the most vulnerable population group.

On the other hand it can be observed that the World Bank is also the major funding agency for many of the development projects that have been environmentally unfriendly. A case in point is the Narmada Dam, which was labelled as the world's greatest planned environmental disaster (Gadgil, 2007), which even according to conservative estimates directly displaced 100,000 people, a majority of which were landless tribes, and affected millions more. These double standards often send out mixed messages and further push developing countries such as India into struggles between environmental protection and economic development. The interests and policies of these international agencies can be in direct contrast to their actions and practices.

The path to projects that are environmentally conducive, and aim at long-term economic progress, can only be achieved through support of initiatives that are sustainable. The one essential tool towards sustainability of any sort is Education with public awareness, education and training as the key factors for moving society towards sustainability (McKeown, Hopkins, Rizzi, & Chrystalbridge, 2002).

The following sections examine the role of education in the environmental context, and begin to provide a background on the state of EE, both globally and in relation to India.

A HISTORICAL ANALYSIS OF EE (FROM GLOBAL TO LOCAL)

The origins of EE may be found in what started out as a Nature Study movement in the early 1900s. This was followed by a phase of the conservation movement in the mid-1900s (Palmer, 1998). The original emphasis was on getting students out into nature to be able to admire and consequently develop a desire to pursue preservation. Increasing environmental deterioration led to the development of an awareness of human impact on the environment and the need to reduce those affects. This increasing environmental consciousness was fuelled by scientists and authors like Carson (Carson, 1964) and Gough (Gough, 2006).

Table 2.2 offers a timeline of the landmark events and developments in the field of EE from the 1970s to the present. Although the term 'EE' was first used in 1965, the EE movement started gaining momentum around 1960. The 'classic' definition of the term was developed and adopted in 1970. According to the International Union for Conservation of Nature and Natural Resources EE is:

> ... the process of recognizing values and clarifying concepts in order to develop skills and attitudes necessary to understand and appreciate the inter-relatedness among man, his culture, and his biophysical surroundings. Environmental education also entails practice in decision-making and self-formulation of a code of behaviour about issues concerning environmental quality. (IUCN, 1971, p. 7)

Table 2.2. Chronology of landmark developments in EE

Year	Event	Development
1972	The United Nations Conference on the Human Environment, Stockholm, Sweden.	The International Environmental Development Program (IEEP) 1975
1975	The United Nations Belgrade Workshop.	The Belgrade Charter Statement
1977	The UNESCO Intergovernmental Conference on Environmental Education, Tbilisi, Former USSR.	'Tbilisi Declaration'
1980	The International Union of Conservation of Nature (IUCN), Natural Resources, The United Nations Environment Programme and World Conservation Foundation.	'World Conservation Strategy' (1980).
1988	World Commission on the Environmental Development.	Our Common Future – most commonly used definition of Sustainable Development.
1992	The United Nations Conference on Environment and Development, Rio De Janeiro, Brazil.	'Agenda 21'
1997	The United Nations International Conference on Environment and Society, Thessaloniki, Greece.	'Thessaloniki Declaration'
2002	World Summit on Sustainable Development, Johannesburg, South Africa.	'Plan of Implementation' and the 'Key Outcomes Statement'
2007	4th International Conference on Environmental Education, Ahmedabad, India.	'The Ahmedabad Declaration 2007'
2012	United Nations Conference on Environment and Development, Rio De Janeiro, Brazil.	Rio + 20 Declaration

The first Conference on the Human Environment was held in 1972 at Stockholm and was the first attempt at bringing together higher-level government officials and discussing ways to deal with the environmental situation and raise the issue at an international level (Tilbury, 1994). It was a significant achievement as it marked the first attempt towards international cooperation and commitment to environmental conservation. It was also vital in highlighting the importance of education and training in environmental problems as the means of creating awareness and practical action (Gough, 2006, p. 23). This conference also led to the formation of the United Nations Environment Program (UNEP) which plays an important role in negotiating global environmental treaties by bringing all concerned parties together (Cuff & Goudie, 2009).

The establishment of the UNESCO-UNEP International Environment Programme (IEEP) with the goal of furthering EE through a cooperative international programme was in 1975 (Gough, 2006). In that year, IEEP organised the Belgrade International Workshop on EE, which formulated The Belgrade Charter – A Global Framework for EE, a strong policy statement that was endorsed by 64 countries. It has been hailed as the greatest landmark in EE history where there was a call for the establishing a harmonious relationship between humanity and the environment, as well as a call for the eradication of poverty, illiteracy, pollution and exploitation (UNESCO, 1975).

The 1977 the Tbilisi Conference (UNESCO & UNEP, 1977) that followed provided goals and objectives that went on to be the basis of EE globally. These included amongst others the provision of 'opportunities to every individual to acquire knowledge, values, attitudes, commitment and skills to protect the environment' (Gough, 2006, p. 73).

The World Conservation Strategy was published in 1980 by the IUCN in collaboration with the UNEP and the World Wildlife Fund (WWF) and was the first to discuss the interdependence of conservation and development and was the first to call for the need for 'sustainable development' (International Union for Conservation of Nature and Natural Resources (IUCN), 1980).

The 1982 Nairobi conference – a decade after the landmark Stockholm conference- called for the setting up of United Nation's World Commission on Environment and Development. The WCED came up with its report 'Our Common Future' also known as the Bruntland Report (World Commission on Environment and Development, 1987) which placed the concept of sustainable development in the realm of international environmental policy. It also provided the most commonly used (although still not universally accepted) definition for sustainable development namely:

> development that meets the needs of the present without compromising the ability of future generations to meet their needs. (p. 43)

In 1992, the United Nations Conference on Environment and Development (UNCED) called the 'Earth Summit' was held in Rio de Janeiro and led to a 'tremendous surge' in environmental consciousness among the general public (UNESCO-UNEP, 1992). It resulted in the following actions:

Agenda 21, a plan for action into the twenty-first century;

- the Rio Declaration on the Environment and Development;
- the 1992 United Nations Framework Convention of Climate Change, which was to provide a framework for the negotiation of detailed protocols on further issues such as controls on the emissions of greenhouse gases – particularly carbon dioxide-and deforestation;
- the 1992 Convention on Biological Diversity, which was aimed at arresting the alarming rate at which species were disappearing through pollution and habitat destruction; and,
- a legally nonbinding Declaration on Forests (Cuff & Goudie, 2009; Gough, 2006).

As noted earlier, *Agenda 21* highlighted education as a priority and as being significant in promoting sustainable development. It stressed participation from everyone involved in education – teachers, teacher educators, curriculum developers, education policy makers and authors of educational materials (UNESCO, 1992).

Since 1980 sustainable development has infiltrated the field of EE. The Earth Summit in Johannesburg (UNESCO-UNEP, 1992) was crucial in furthering the idea of education for sustainable development:

Education is critical for promoting sustainable development and improving the capacity of the people to address environment and development issues. It is critical for achieving environmental and ethical awareness, values and attitudes, skills and behaviour consistent with sustainable development and for effective public participation in decision-making. (Cutter-Mackenzie, 2009, p. 44)

The 1997 Thessaloniki (International Conference Environment and Society: Education and Public Awareness, 1997) conference was held to celebrate the 20th anniversary of the Tbilisi conference with an underlying aim of reorienting education for sustainability for the 20th century. It was also considered to be the beginning of the end for EE with even a call to rename EE as education for sustainability. The World Summit on Sustainable Development forwarded the cause of education for sustainable development and sought to rename EE with education for sustainable development. It also proposed a Decade of Education for Sustainable Development from 2005–2014 (UNDESD, 2007). None of the key indicators that were listed by the summit mentioned the term EE; instead it was replaced with education for sustainable development.

Although education for sustainable development and education for sustainability have permeated the field of EE, there are those that see this change as problematic. Cutter-Mackenzie (2009) identified some of these issues and highlighted their importance in shaping the debate. For example, heavily resource dependent economies can look at environmental protection as an antithesis to development. In this case without a universally accepted definition, terms like 'need' and 'development' are subject to multiple meanings. In countries like India, it may be difficult to justify how much 'development' is sufficient to satisfy the 'needs' of the people. It is a profoundly moral question to then ask 'How much should a person consume' (Guha, 2006). Since there is no real agreement on what sustainable development really constitutes, there is no real agreement on how it should be taught. Jickling and Spork (1998) suggested that students of EE needed to study and critique the ideologies pertinent to their societies rather than be indoctrinated into one particular ideology. In other words, ideologies should be accepted or rejected based on their relevance to the context rather than on origin. (This idea is discussed further in the Chapter Three: Conceptual Framework.)

The Bruntland Commission Report (World Commission on Environment and Development, 1987) places emphasis on the need to link environment and development. This is more readily accepted by many developing countries, which are often of the view that industrialisation can help alleviate poverty and lead to economic growth and that environment and development are not pitted against each other (Rangarajan, 2009). However the underlying message that comes across seems to be that development will lead to economic growth and prosperity. The major criticism here is that economic growth by itself may or may not be successful in alleviating poverty or increase sustainability (Goueli, 2003). Again, although the Commission's definition of Education for Sustainable Development has been more widely accepted – there is no consensus and hence no universal accepted definition for sustainable development. Since there is no agreement on what sustainable development really constitutes there is no real agreement on how it should be taught. For example countries like India may find it difficult to define what 'development' is and how much of it is 'sustainable', as also the ability to quantify or justify the 'needs' of the country. It could therefore be very easy to fall into the trap of mass consumption as a sign of growth and development.

There is also the danger of the environment being considered as a mere resource to meet human needs. Putting a monetary or economic value on the environment and the services it provides undermines the role that these resources play in society, history and culture. However the disposition to put an economic value to the environment is on the rise mainly because it fits into most capitalist approaches. For example Hunter-Lovins and Cohen (2011) define the current era as an era of 'climate' and 'capitalism' both intertwined as the cause and the cure for each other. Valuation of environmental resources continues to be common for three main reasons:

- It provides a mechanism to help maintain a record of society's management of environmental resources often providing a sense of accomplishment to otherwise poorly managed stewardship of these resources.
- Economic development and human interventions are now central to policy debates with a need to provide direct effects and opportunity costs of development.

- Issues of sustainability have gained more prominence in terms of being mindful of needs of future generations in decisions made today about resource use. This means the trade-off between current and future demands on the environment and the economic valuation that permit these intertemporal comparisons have become increasingly important (Pretty et al., 2007, p. 5).

Laying emphasis on the environment as a resource reeks of apathy and a lack of engagement with the environment. Khoshoo (2010, p. 152) for example echoes this sentiment while comprehending sustainability as 'the rate of harvest from a renewable system which must not exceed the rate of annual increment'. EE is considered to merely reflect on the quality of the environment and raising awareness and understanding. In contrast sustainable education is considered to deal with the ecological (environmental) dimension and also look into economic and social issues such as the social, economic and political aspects of change. The ultimate objective of sustainable development is then to improve the quality of life of people living on the planet (Khoshoo & Moolakkattu, 2009). This "self-centric" view completely overlooks the well-being of the environment and the quality of life for anything other than humans. Orr (2002)sees sustainable growth as an unachievable oxymoron while terming sustainable development as much more achievable. He argues for a change that transcends mere superficial levels if genuine sustainability is to be attained.

There are benefits and constraints attributed to both pathways. Fien and Trainer (1993) believe that often EE and education for sustainable development are intertwined and there are many times, particularly in science and social science fields, EE is also education for sustainable development. Another advantage as Selby (2006, p. 354) recounts is the opportunity to 'loosen the clutches of natural science' on the field paving the way for greater cross disciplinary influences from ethical, political, social and economic lenses. In India though there has not been a clear demarcation between the two and both EE and education for sustainable development have often (not necessarily appropriately) been interchangeably used. As Chhokar and Chandrasekharan (2006) suggest, in India it is often EE for Sustainability – a mixture of both terminologies and ideologies.

The United Nations World Summit on Sustainable Development (UNWSSD) held in 2002, in Johannesburg also emphasized the role of education, but it broadened the vision to include not just respect and nurture for the environment but also social justice and the fight against poverty. UNWSSD urged all nations to unite and work towards increasing access to basic requirements and to use modern technology in training and education to banish underdevelopment (UNESCO, 2002).

The 2007 International Conference on EE in Ahmedabad declared, 'Through education, human lifestyles can be achieved that support ecological integrity, economic and social justice, sustainable livelihoods and respect for all life. Through education we can learn to prevent and resolve conflicts, respect cultural diversity, create a caring society and live in peace' (K. Sarabhai, 2008, p. 1). It encouraged a shift from viewing education as a delivery mechanism to a lifelong, holistic and inclusive process.

As mentioned earlier, 2005–2014 has been declared as the Decade of Education for Sustainable Development (UNESCO, 2005c) in recognition of the need for commitment and skills to strengthen education systems across the world and to integrate ESD (Education for Sustainable Development) in national education plans across all sectors (J. Fien, 2006). The UNDESD's main aim is to increase and encourage initiatives that raise the importance of education in achieving sustainable development (UNESCO, 2005c).

Gough (2006) made an interesting comparison between the Belgrade Charter-1975 and current policies framing the UNDESD, and found that the same spirit underlies both the documents. She commented that maybe the path travelled over the past 40 years remains the same, but for a few curves, detours and potholes. Reading Gandhi's thoughts on 'Education for life; through life; throughout life' his perceptions of 'education as a life-long process which involves harmony of the head, heart and hands' (Sarabhai, 2007, pp. 2 & 109) and his Basic Education Framework, it is safe to assume that the path has not changed in over 60 years.

History of EE in India

O Earth, whenever I am compelled to create cavities on you they may be filled again soon. May I not inflict any injury on your bosom and cause Nammyn in your heart. (Atharvaveda XII- I, as cited in Sharma, 2010, p. 48)

EE is not new to India. Protection and improvement of the natural environment including forests, lakes, rivers and wildlife; and living harmoniously with the environment is embedded in the Constitution of India in Articles 48A and 51G. It is in fact deeply rooted in the religious and cultural traditions of India where nature is perceived as an all-encompassing entity that needs to be protected and revered (Baez, 1987; Bussey, Inayatullah, & Milojevic, 2008; Ravindranath, 2000, 2002a, 2007; K. Sarabhai, 1995). Scriptures ranging from the *Vedas, Upanishads, Smritis, Puranas* and the *Bhagavadgeeta,* which describe the Hindu-way of life uniformly sanction the environment as an integral and inseparable part of humans. The *Rigveda* for example considers the entire creation as one and indivisible; and the entire universe constitutes a life unto which every aspect of creation, including the human, is integrated (Sharma, 2010). This is echoed by Tagore who said, 'the same stream of life that runs through my veins … runs through the world' and 'the world is a living thing, intimately close to my life, permeated by the subtle touch of kinship, which enhances the value of my own being' (Haigh, 2008, p. 49).

Unlike Europe where the past is the past, in India not only does the past continue to be visible in the present, it is in many ways also the future (Luce, 2006). India's esoteric traditions continue to survive despite the onslaught of modern consumerism. Sacredness of living things has been a basic tenet of Hindu philosophy for thousands

29

of years with 'ahimsa permo dharma' – 'non-cruelty to animals the supreme religion' advocated by sages centuries ago (Wali, 1987, p. 28). Many Indians inherit nature awareness, as part of their culture; worship of trees, tigers, elephants, snakes, monkeys and other creatures is considered part of religious/social observations with an ecological meaning. For example a tree is called 'Dasputra' or 'ten sons' because it provides for ten important needs, namely food, fodder, fertilizer, fibre, fuel, air, water, soil, shade and beauty (Parthasarthy, 1987). Strict instructions on the need to preserve the environment and protect it from degradation are part of this ethos and have been laid down in ancient Hindu scriptures like the Vedas, Puranas, and the Upanishads (Baez, 1987; Khoshoo, 1987; Ravindranath, 2000, 2007; Wali, 1987). Protection of the environment and its connections with daily communal life has always been an integral part of the social fabric of Indian society (Ravindranath, 2002b). It has been laid down as one of the five *Yagnas* or daily duties that a man has to perform and is on par with duties to the Gods, teachers, ancestors and fellow human beings (Sharma, 2010). This ethos has been very simplistically echoed by Gandhi's words 'Live simply so that others may simply live' (Bussey et al., 2008, p. 243).

India's first attempt at incorporating environment in education was initiated by Mahatma Gandhi in a movement called 'Nai Taleem' or Basic Education in 1937. The essential elements of Basic Education policy were productive activity in education, correlation of curriculum with the productive activity and the physical and social environment, and intimate contact between the school and the local community (Chhokar & Pandya, 2005). The aim was to create freethinking individuals with relevant skills to be able to act locally and aspire transcendentally for liberation (Haigh, 2008).

This movement ended once India achieved independence and Gandhi died. It has been replaced by the current conventional model based on colonial methodologies of thinking and limited to the learning by rote techniques, where 'free thinking' is neither sought nor encouraged. Local and regional issues are neglected and the main aim seems to be the production of 'able' individuals who could contribute 'economically', meet the needs of rapid 'industrialization' and 'globalization' of the country.

Landmark Policies/Developments that Shaped EE in India

Table 2.3 presents the influential landmark developments that shaped EE in India. As is outlined, the field of EE has recently received major impetuses in the form of the Federal Court mandate and development of curriculum policies.

In December 2003, the Supreme Court of India passed a ruling that was hoped would change the EE scenario in India. The direction No. 4 issued by the Court reads thus:

> We accept on principle that through the medium of education awareness of the environment and its problems related to pollution should be taught as

Table 2.3. Chronology of key developments in EE in India (adapted from, K. Sarabhai, Raghunathan, & Kandula, 2000, p. 130)

1964–1966	*Report of the Education Commission – the Kothari Commission.*	*Considered the root of Environmental Education (EE) in India.*
1975	Curriculum for the Ten-Year School: An Approach Paper and Curriculum for the Ten-Year School: A Framework.	First framework to explicitly indicate teaching of EE.
1984 1986	Establishment of the Centre of Environment Education (CEE) as a National Centre for Excellence in EE under Ministry of Environment and Forests. Adoption of the National Policy on Education. The National Environmental Awareness CamNammygn of the Ministry of Environment and Forests.	CEE worked with different sectors – particularly education- to spread environmental awareness. First National policy indicated including EE in schools.
1988–89	Environmental Orientation to School Education Scheme of the Ministry of Human Resources Development.	Called for orientating curriculum to include EE.
1989	C.P. R. Chennai established as a second Centre of Excellence.	Works towards promoting EE in south India.
1991	First Supreme Court of India mandate requiring the University Grants Commission to prescribe courses on the environment at all levels of higher education.	The judiciary steps in to help control environmental problems – a first of its kind step.
2003	Second Supreme Court judgment mandating EE to be taught across all formal education institutions.	Requires every school in every state of India to teach EE.
2005	National Council for Teacher Education provides the EE curriculum framework for teachers and teacher educators. National Curriculum Framework is drafted – clearly specifies the role of EE.	A major step providing national level impetus for the inclusion of EE in teacher education. School curriculum now includes EE and has to be mandatorily taught.

a compulsory subject. Learned Attorney General pointed out to us that the Central Government is associated with education at the higher levels and University Grants Commission can monitor only the under graduate and post graduate studies. The rest of it, according to him, is a state subject. He has agreed that the University Grants Commission will take appropriate steps immediately to give effect to what we have said, i.e., requiring the Universities to prescribe a course on environment. They would consider the feasibility of making this a compulsory subject at every level in college education. So far as education up to the college level is concerned, we would require every State Government and every Education Board connected with education up to the matriculation stage or even intermediate college to immediately take steps to enforce compulsory education on environment in a graded way. This should be so done that in the next academic year there would be compliance with this requirement. (Supreme Court of India, 2003, p. 1)

This was a follow up to a 1991 ruling which had directed that 'through the medium of education, awareness about the environment and its problems related to pollution should be taught in all schools and this should be implemented by the State authorities' (Supreme Court of India, 2003, p. 1). The National Commission for Education, Research and Training (NCERT) was also directed to prepare the syllabus/curriculum for EE for all grades. This directive was not uniformly adhered to and hence was followed up by the 2003 directive that provided the government only one year to comply. In 2003 the Supreme Court also reviewed a curriculum framework prepared by the NCERT under its directions. The State governments were asked to develop textbooks using this framework and EE was made mandatory across all grades, in schools all over the country, from the year 2004–05. This directive, while giving a much-needed boost to the cause of EE concerns, also added to the strains of an already over-burdened educational system. While the mandate was of critical importance, it is still unclear whether or not it is being implemented and how effective the implementation has been.

The Supreme Court intervention seems to have provided a much-needed impetus to the cause of EE in India. The National Curriculum Framework drafted in 2005 attempted to bridge the gap in EE (National Commission for Education Research and Technology, 2005). Section 3.9 of the Framework is devoted entirely to Habitat and Learning, which in substance and spirit is equated to EE. In that Section it was acknowledged that formal education had largely become alienated from the students' 'habitats', which in turn implies that the current education system is far removed from the current lifestyles of students. The section of the NCF goes on to assert that environmental degradation is happening at an unprecedented pace. It substantiates the role of education in helping to comprehend the roots and re-establish the links between education and habitat. Overall issues and concerns pertaining to the environment were designed to better inform the different school subjects and experiences. The main focus of the Section was based on the principle that children learn in relation to their encounters with nature and the environment (National Commission for Education Research and Technology, 2005).

While establishing the necessity of EE in India, the Supreme Court (2003) ruling however also placed large responsibility on the State Education boards to adapt the syllabi from NCERT to their respective education systems. How this was to be done was not clearly spelt out, therefore the policy was open to numerous interpretations and loopholes. On paper India has done everything to ensure that EE is a major part of the school curriculum. However, as Weiner states, laws and policies in India are 'often seen as a kind of modern talisman which will bring results by the magical power of words themselves unrelated to the action (Weiner, 1991). There is currently little information available on how the different agencies interpret and implement this policy. This study tackles this situation by investigation one teacher education institution and exploring how its teacher educators interpret this federal mandate.

This section of the chapter explored the evolution of EE and some landmark developments and policies that have influenced the field – both globally and locally. The next section reviews the relationship between teacher education and EE.

TEACHER EDUCATION AND ENVIRONMENTAL EDUCATION: A ROCKY MARRIAGE

Developments/initiatives in EE with respect to its reorientation to teacher education

Teacher Educators train new teachers, provide professional development for practicing teachers, consult with local schools, and provide expert opinion to regional and national ministries of education. Teacher educators write and teach not only pre-service teacher-education curriculum, but also contribute to committees that create teacher-education standards and officially mandated curriculum for primary and secondary education. They also write textbooks and sit on advisory committees from local to national levels. Because of this broad influence in curriculum design, implementation, and policy setting, faculty members of teacher-education institutions can bring about far-reaching educational reform – even beyond training the teachers in the world. (McKeown-Ice, 2005, p. 3)

The role of teachers and hence teacher education has been widely recognised by the international community. There have been numerous efforts to highlight the role of teacher education programs in developing EE. The first efforts were made at the European International Union for the Conservation of Nature and Natural Resources (IUCN) Conference in Switzerland in 1971, which raised international concerns for adequate teacher education. This conference recognised teacher education as one of the most important and significant aspects of EE programs and recommended that all teachers be taught the basic knowledge required to implement EE.

We recognize that teacher training forms one of the most important and significant aspects in the development of environmental education programmes and we recommend that:

the training of teachers provide them with essential basic knowledge of ecological facts and an adequate background of sociology and its relationship to human ecology; efforts should be made to develop in teachers a critical

33

awareness of environmental problems to enable them to provoke responsible attitudes concerning environmental matters in their pupils;

environmental conservation is recognised as an essential part of the teacher training and that developments started in pre-service training should be continued by in-service training;

as teacher training in environmental education involves the use of many techniques and methods, all prospective teachers should be given training in the use and evaluation of pedagogic methods, including those relating to inter-disciplinary approaches to team teaching; media banks be established at the national and international level for exchange of information, training aids and teaching materials. (IUCN as cited in Tilbury, 1992, p. 270)

The 1972 Stockholm conference called for teacher education to move towards creating environmental awareness and practical action (UNEP, 1972). The Belgrade Charter in 1975 identified teachers as the principle audience of EE and recommended well-designed programs to educate teachers and set the stage for revamping the teacher education curriculum (UNESCO, 1975). The next major conference held at Tbilisi in 1977 clearly prioritized the need for in-service and pre-service teacher education. It provided the goals and objectives that went on to be the basis of EE globally. These included amongst others the provision of opportunities to every individual in order to acquire knowledge, values, attitudes, commitment and skills to protect the environment (UNESCO & UNEP, 1977).

The 1992 UNCED held at Rio de Janeiro played a pivotal role in bringing environmental consciousness to the forefront. 'Agenda 21' which was formulated at the this conference clearly lists education as a priority and called for involvement from everyone involved in the process – the teachers, teacher educators, curriculum developers, education policy makers and authors of educational materials (UNESCO, 1992).

The Thessaloniki Declaration as part of the International Conference on Environment and Society: Education and Public Awareness for Sustainability also sought to elevate education as a fourth pillar of sustainability in the 21st century. It stressed that educational messages for sustainability must also be emphasized in pre-service and in-service programmes for teacher training (International Conference Environment and Society: Education and Public Awareness, 1997). In 2002, the United Nations World Summit on Sustainable Development (UNWSSD) re-emphasised the role of teacher education to help nurture the environment. It urged nations to unite in improving access to basic requirements and training and education in order to banish underdevelopment (UNESCO, 2002).

In its Guidelines and Recommendations for Reorienting Teacher Education to Address Sustainability, UNESCO clearly highlights teacher educators as having a 'broad influence in curriculum design and implementation, as well as policy setting within educational institutions' and 'being perfectly poised to promote education for sustainable development' (UNESCO, 2005b, pp. 10–11).

The 2007 Ahmedabad Declaration continued to stress the importance of education in achieving sustainable development goals and the need to focus on teacher education (Center for Environment Education, 2007–2008; UNESCO, 2007). As outlined above there has been a strong call for reform in teacher education at an international level with respect to EE. This focus was carried forward with the Earth Summit in 2012 in Rio de Janeiro which continued the emphasis on teacher education and putting education at the centre of any significant change (Earth Summit, 2012).

Research in Teacher Education: Teacher Educators' Identities

While a lot of attention has been paid to what teachers ought to know and be able to do, there has been much less attention on teacher educators and the knowledge and subject matter appropriate for them (Cochran-Smith, 2003). Loughran (2011, p. 279) pointed to 'superficial/simplistic views of teaching and learning' and 'learning as listening' as one of the major problems with Teacher Education. 'High stakes testing and approaches to teaching standards which, because of the implicit need for simple solutions to complex situations again reinforce ingrained views of practice as the delivery of information' (p. 279) further worsen this. While discussing the situation in Australia he explains how economic imperatives undermine expectations of quality learning making it difficult to bridge the theory-practice gap and 'creates binaries that mask the real issues associated with the complexity of teaching and learning about teaching' (p. 282). This discussion could easily be extended to India given the larger economic imperatives at stake there where there is an appalling lack of qualified teachers and teacher education institutions (UNESCO, 2011). This creates pressures to shorten the length of Teacher Education courses (Currently most Bachelor of education courses are one year courses completed post Bachelors in any other discipline) and increase the student intakes. As a result class sizes can often swell to up to 100 students per class seriously impacting the quality of learning and teaching quality. Examinations – often conducted by external bodies – are the main form of assessment and teaching is often centred on how to help students perform well in these exams (Batra, 2005).

Darling-Hammond (2012, p. 3) refers to teaching quality as 'strong instruction that enables a wide range of students to learn. Such instruction meets the demands of the discipline, the goals of instruction and the needs of students in a particular context.' While strongly related to teacher quality, namely teacher's knowledge, skills and dispositions, context of instruction plays a major role in determining teaching quality. 'Curriculum and assessment systems that support teachers' work and the "fit" between teachers' qualifications and what they are asked to teach, and teaching conditions' (p. 3) are key considerations to this context. No matter how high the teacher quality, flawed curriculum, poor teaching conditions, inappropriate teaching materials and assessment, substandard space, lack of time and large classes all negate the effectiveness of a high-quality teacher. Developing teaching contexts that enable good practice is crucial in order to enable good practice. In short 'if teaching is to be effective, the policies that construct the learning environment and the teaching context must be addressed along with the qualities of individual teachers' (p. 4). Teacher quality is also vital particularly in the teaching of EE.

In an interview with Hungerford and Simmons (2003, p. 7) Paul Hart put forth the argument that 'whether teachers' actions (and intentions) originate in significant early life experiences or not, they have a historical embeddedness in personal experiences as well as sociocultural practices in which the deeper values are implicated.'. Extending this to teacher educators it might be argued that their life experiences, the culture and societal influences play a large role in their enacting of environmental actions. According to Hart, EE happens in Canada mainly because teachers have made the 'moral/ethical leap of consciousness from assuming traditional pedagogical responsibility for the construction of personal and social values to encorporate environmental values' (p. 8). They have done this even in the absence of sophisticated content knowledge of environmental issues and environmental science. This provides hope in India where teachers/teacher educators could draw from rich knowledge based on local, cultural and traditional traditions irrespective of the access to sophisticated (content) knowledge about the environment.

Hart strongly recommends that we acknowledge and pay respect to teachers' personal practical ideas as teachers' thinking and practice are mutually informing processes; it is impossible to study either of them without considering the other. Cochran-Smith asserted that what makes a successful teacher depends heavily on who they are as individuals, what experiences they have had before they started to teach and the type of education – in particular the type of teacher education program they have had (Wilson, 2008). By extension, their personal stories and theories build teachers' and teacher educators' identities and influence teacher quality in education. Teacher Quality being 'the bundle of traits, skills, and understandings an individual brings to teaching, including dispositions to behave in certain ways' (Darling-Hammond, 2012, p. 2).

Developing an identity as a teacher (and teacher educator) is essential in ensuring commitment and adherence to professional norms of practice (Darling-Hammond et al., 2005, p. 382). Identity according to Payne (2001, p. 68) is an often neglected but crucial and relevant aspect of understanding EE practices. He defines identity as 'how I view myself, how others portray me and how I perceive those others who understand me, the practices of identity relate to how I present myself in various circumstances and settings, make some sense of them, and how others relate to the various ways I present myself.' Identities are complex, deeply grounded in and shaped by everyday experiences – how individuals act, interact and communicate in relation to 'various social and environmental sensibilities'.

An individual's embodiment in everyday experiences is integral to understanding his/her identification with the environment and the nature of its 'crisis' (p. 70). For a teacher educator identity shapes his/her interactions and engagement with EE in their professional practice. While Payne discusses this in terms of pre-service teachers' ongoing struggles and predicaments 'in relation to forming or sustaining an identity as an environmental educator' (p. 70), this can easily be extended to teacher educators and their struggles in finding their identity as Environmental Educators. It is important to understand the 'local, historical, social, cultural and global 'shapers' of self, social and environmental consciousness and personal identity' and the 'politics of development' of these identities as they significantly influence teacher educators and their work. Generating 'local knowledge of practice' by linking their work to larger social, cultural and political issues helps teacher educators to be better at their work. Teacher educators who regard teaching as 'a political activity and embrace social change as part of the job' are the ones who join other educators, parents, and communities in ushering major reforms and are agents of change – like the ones needed in India right now (Cochran-Smith, 2003; Cochran-Smith & Lytle, 1999). An important consideration in building Teacher Educator Quality would be providing opportunities to 'articulate their principles of practice and see the value in so doing', which would help, minimise the 'discord associated with mixed messages so common when action and intent are at odds' (Loughran, 2011, p. 288). Teacher educators need to be able to move beyond the tacit and make their pedagogical purposes explicit in order to be able to understand the 'why' – the 'fundamental pedagogical underpinnings inherent in supporting meaningful learning' (p. 287). Their identities are 'entwined with the how and why of teaching about teaching (and that is what constitutes a pedagogy of teacher education' (p. 290). Articulating this would mean reflecting on their approaches and conceptualisation of their own practice (Loughran, 2008a). (An issue that emerges as being at the heart of the learning inherent in the study of the teacher educators involved in this project.)

Teacher education and EE.   Teacher Education has been claimed to be the 'priority of priorities' and there have been numerous recommendations seeking reorientation of teacher education toward EE (Cutter-Mackenzie, 2009; McKeown et al., 2002; McKeown-Ice, 2000; Nemerov & Agardy, 2005; Pepper & Wildy, 2008; Tilbury, 1992, 1994, 2004; Yencken et al., 2002). Such recommendations have come from UNESCO through various documents and directives chiefly the 'Guidelines and Recommendation for Reorienting Education to Address Sustainability' (UNESCO, 2005b). That document validates the influential role teacher education institutions and teacher educators' play and highlights the need to address a number of themes. It recommends the need to reorient teacher education curricula, programs, practices and policies so that they match the environmental, social, and economic conditions and goals of their respective communities, regions, and nations. The report advocates greater participation by teacher educators in the intellectual lives of their respective faculties, institutions, and the broader community as necessary in bringing about change. It also lays some onus on individual faculty members urging them to work within their own sphere of influence and exert individual authority to bring about change. The policy clearly spells out the crucial role of teacher educators recognising them as key change agents and the ones who bridge gaps between theory and practice (UNESCO, 2005b).

Although there has been an increasing emphasis on the role of teacher educators and teacher education in promoting EE and the need to implement EE, there seems to be a significant gap in actual practice. Ferreira, Ryan, Cavanagh, and Thomas (2009, p. 1) claim that 'recent research indicates that pre-service teacher education institutions and programs are not doing all they can to prepare teachers for teaching education for sustainability or for working within sustainable schools'. They summarise a body of research to identify 'teacher education as a key strategy that is yet to be effectively utilised to embed education for sustainability in schools' (p. 2).

Due to this under-utilisation – namely inadequate training – pre-service teachers have problems teaching EE (Cutter-Mackenzie, 2009). One of the main reasons teachers are not teaching EE is because they are not being well-prepared to integrate it into their classrooms (Gabriel, 1996). Since there is a lack of EE embedded in the teacher education programs, very little is written about it (J. Fien & Maclean, 2000). When EE is embedded in teacher education programs the teachers are better placed to implement it in their classroom as advocated by Plevyak, Bendixen-Noe, Henderson, and Wilke (2001). They stressed the need for teacher preparation and development of positive teacher attitudes in order for successful implementation of EE. This lack of pre-service teacher preparation was also found in a nationwide study in the U.S. which concluded that 'pre-service teacher education programs are not systematically preparing future teachers to effectively teach about the environment' (McKeown-Ice, 2000, p. 10).

Including EE in pre-service education can be a challenging task (Powers, 2004). Amongst other factors, a lack of vision or awareness of the role education can play in achieving sustainability is seen as an impediment in EE. One of the main problems documented in doing any work on education and learning about sustainability in institutions 'were lack of awareness and understanding of the concept of sustainable development among faculty members' (UNESCO, 2005b, p. 29).

There has been very little research on the role/perceptions/preparedness of teacher educators to teach EE. McKeown-Ice (2000) found most institutions lacking in commitment with the EE program (which was often driven by one person) and recommended the hiring of more faculty specialized in teaching EE. A study interviewing 18 professors of education about their perspectives on EE revealed that:

- limited time was the biggest constraint to infusing EE;
- student disposition, in particular an aversion to science was a concern;
- there was infusion of EE into existing courses rather than EE being a separate course; and,
- the use of pre-packaged, nationally disseminated curricula was common rather than developing more locale-specific curricula (Powers, 2004)

Summers, Childs and Corney's (2005) study on interdisciplinary collaborations points to the gaps in understanding of ESD. While extolling the virtues of whole-school approaches they suggest limiting collaborations to only a couple of subjects as being more reasonable to begin with rather than attempting whole school approaches. They also highly recommend professional development. Qablan (2009) uncovered a clear mismatch between teacher educators' attitudes and practice and recommended special training courses to enhance their pedagogical knowledge, and to encourage them to build learning communities that would advance their awareness, attitudes, and pedagogical knowledge relating to EE.

UNESCO (2005b) made the following recommendations to encourage teacher educators to reorient their teaching to address EE:

- create awareness amongst administration and faculty leaders about the need for reorienting teacher education programs;
- provide education opportunities to faculty members so that they understand the need for EE, its relevance in improving educational standards and how they can contribute to the overall effort of reorientation;
- set up participatory and democratic process involving the entire faculty;
- move quickly to institutionalise EE so that it continues irrespective of faculty, administration or funding changes; and,
- recognise and reward efforts especially if they are voluntary.

As the above makes clear, teacher educators are viewed as having a clear role in EE. However, there is a significant gap in the research literature on how teacher educators may come to better understand this role. Few studies have delved into the perspectives of teacher educators and how they currently integrate EE or Education for Sustainability into their teaching of pre-service teachers as pointed out by Fien and Trainer about two decades ago (1993). The paucity continues to exist with limited empirical studies about teacher educators' implementation of EE. There is also a need for studies that look into the organisational culture that influences teacher educators and their implementation of EE. UNESCO (2005b) spells out a need for concerted efforts and resources to institutionalise EE into programs, practices and policies of teacher education. Having reviewed international perspectives on teacher educators and their importance in furthering the cause of EE, the next section discusses the relationship between teacher educators and EE within teacher education in India.

THE CASE OF INDIA: TEACHER PREPARATION AND EE

While introducing the new 'EE Curriculum Framework for Teachers and Teacher Educators' Shardindu, Chairman of National Council for Teacher Education (NCTE) – India's apex body for Teacher Education remarked:

Education, especially teacher education has obviously to play an increasingly vital role towards mitigation of continuing environmental degradation and the complexities of pollution, which pose a great menace to the survival of human life and other species on this planet. (National Council of Teacher Educators, 2005, p. i)

The National Council for Teacher Education – India's central body and policy maker on teacher education clearly states:

Teachers occupy a crucial position in the system of education. Through them its message is conveyed to society, ideas are disseminated and behaviour is shape. (National Council of Teacher Educators, 2005, p. 1)

The NCTE maintains that the importance of EE is being widely recognised but 'it is yet to get its rightful place in education, much more so, in teacher education' (National Council of Teacher Educators, 2005, p. 1). The NCTE also asserts that unless EE is prescribed as a compulsory and integral component of education and teacher education its message will not be conveyed to all.

EE is taught as a compulsory core module on Environmental Studies in all undergraduate courses developed by the University Grants Commission which is a six-month course taught through both classroom and field activities. Evaluation of the course is through exams at the end of the semester with 25 out of the 100 marks allotted to fieldwork. India's largest Open University – The Indira Gandhi National Open University – also has some awareness level courses and also a Post Graduate Diploma in Environment and Sustainable Development. The Centre for Science and Environment offers a two-day training program for teachers, educators and others interested in EE (Kaur & Bhati, 2012). These possibilities are indicative of the limited efforts being made towards educating/training teachers in EE.

There have been efforts towards introducing EE in schools; but they have been few and far in between (Chhokar & Pandya, 2005; Joshi, 2005; Pande, 2001; K. Sarabhai, 1995). Pandya (2000, 2004) claims that efforts towards preparing pre-service teachers to teach EE have been made. But these efforts have been few or are unreported and hence unnoticed. Khirwadkar and Pushpanadam (2007) maintain that most teacher education programs merely train teachers to adjust to the current system of education by transmission of information.

Organisations such as the Centre for EE (CEE) have played a pivotal role in preparing teachers to teach EE. Since its inception in 1984 it has worked tirelessly to promote EE through various programs some of which have involved teachers. It has established regional centres, which often act as resource centres for school students, teachers and teacher educators. It offers the Green Teacher – a one year diploma course in EE for practicing teachers and educators offered through both online and offline modes (Center for Environment Education, 2012). CEE has been working with teachers in conjunction with the government and other Non-Governmental Organisations (NGOs) to help implement EE in schools. However, there has been no research conducted to gauge the effectiveness of these programs or to help identify the core needs of those working in the field – so that future programs could be tailored to meet those needs. CEE has been instrumental in publishing India's first international journal in the field, The Journal of Education for Sustainable Development. However, its annual report does not feature any programs directly working with the teacher educators (Center for Environment Education, 2007–2008).

Research on EE in India is still in its nascent stages. Very little research is available into that which has been conducted and published in the field of EE and particularly in the field of Teacher Education in India.

Patil (2006) in a review of research studies undertaken between 1990 and 2004 contended that the themes for research until that period included environmental awareness, developments of teaching methodology and learning styles, and curricular aspects of EE. In separate studies, she noted a number of authors that had all tried to evaluate environmental awareness amongst students. Further to this, in separate studies she also found that video instruction, field trips and 'conducive classroom environments' influenced students' learning styles. Finally, in another set of separate studies she looked at the curricular aspects of EE and found that multi-disciplinary approaches including activity based instruction helped improve student learning. Unfortunately, none of these studies involved the teachers or teacher educators. It has only been in recent times that endeavours have been made to study teacher educators and their role in EE; this study does so in India and offers insights into the field that sheds new light on the issues and concerns associated with such development.

Overall there is a well-established concern for the state of the environment, which is echoed at the global level as well as at the local level (India). Historically, the emphasis on EE was consistent with nature studies. Concurrent with the changing environment, EE has likewise changed particularly with the advent of sustainable development. This is especially true in India where the increase in environmental concerns has given rise to numerous calls for developing environmental consciousness. Education is widely seen as a means of responding to these calls.

Over the past decade in particular, efforts from national and state governments to implement EE have redoubled. The Supreme Court directives and the National Curriculum Framework have attempted to provide a jolt to the field. Policies and directives however, will only make a difference if matched by efforts to put them into practice.

EE in India as part of formal education is relatively new, although EE has been part of Indian culture for over 5000 years; it is only just becoming visible in education. It seems apt that any approach to EE in India should build on the cultural and traditional ethos so embedded in Indian culture. Varma (2005) echoes these sentiments by highlighting the antiquity of Indian culture and the need to dip into this culture – taking it to a global level. Immersing EE practices into Indian culture and using it to frame policies seems to be a logical move.

Recent developments and federal initiatives have managed to put the policies like the National Curriculum Framework and the National Curriculum for teachers and teacher educators into place. These policies are an attempt to provide direction and address the future requirements of EE. What needs to be determined is whether or not these polices are being put into practice.

In India there is a danger of using words as magical talismans that are seen to do away all evil (Luce, 2006). For example despite numerous laws to deal with such things as child labour, dowry and child marriage, such practices are still quite widespread (and sometimes flourishing) across India. Unfortunately, it is quite evident that there is limited research into the practice of EE in teacher education in India. This study responds to that need and attempts to bridge the gap by establishing a beginning point in understanding teacher educators and their experiences in teaching EE in India.

CHAPTER 3

TEACHER EDUCATORS' PRACTICES
AND IDENTITIES

Developing the Study

There are numerous factors that affect the work of teacher educators. Some stand out as crucial in understanding their experiences in implementing environmental education (EE). Outlining these factors and their influence on teacher educators' practices and identities provides the necessary scope to frame this study. Efforts to understand ways in which EE is understood, negotiated, determined and implemented by teacher educators have been based on teacher educators everyday practices and varying identities that influence these. It is noteworthy that while there are numerous factors that influence teacher educators everyday lives and practices this study only takes into account those some that appeared to be crucial in the cultural context at this time. Also to be taken into account is the attempt to frame this study with the plethora of national and international policy reforms and the climate of change in EE as a constant backdrop (Supreme Court of India, 2003; UNESCO, 1992, 2005a, 2005c; UNESCO & UNEP, 1977; UNESCO-UNEP, 1992; United Nations Educational Scientific and Cultural Organization, 1997).

CONCEPTUALISING THE STUDY

Teachers Who Teach Teachers: Teacher Educators' Practices

In education, teacher education institutes can be the point where educational reforms are first implemented. This is particularly true 'in times of major significance, change or crisis in the wider society' (Rosean & Florio-Ruane, 2008, p. 717) when teacher education institutions are especially focused on, or sometimes relied upon, to lead the reform both on the inside and outside. Teachers and academics (teacher educators) – particularly in societies such as India – are looked up to for guidance and leadership. Teacher educators are held in deep respect and looked upon as eminent members of the society. However, large class sizes, overcrowded curriculums and busy teaching schedules place heavy and consistent demands on teacher educators' time and energy.

In India, where the burgeoning population places undue stress on the education system, centralised directives replace autonomy of both school and teacher education institutions, those directives impact their curriculum and programmes (R. Heilbronn, 2008). Laws, policies and regulations, although helpful, can also seem superficial,

43

bureaucratic and/or distant (Babbage, 2008). As explained through Babbage's case study, a state education department employee designated to go to schools, listen to educators and identify real issues, presented some insightful thoughts in her end of year report:

> A mistake has been made ... the mistake was to think that school would improve if only the educational bureaucracy, laws, regulations, policies, task forces, committees, study groups, procedures, rules, and reforms could be perfected. Education is not about all of those organisational endeavours. Education is about students, teachers and what they do in classrooms. (Babbage, 2008, p. 27)

The recent Federal government thrust towards implementation of EE in India could be seen by many as a burden by already overworked teacher educators. Traditional teacher education often provides students with some coursework and a dollop of teaching practice often in classrooms that 'did not model the strategies that had previously been described in abstraction' (Darling-Hammond, 2008, p. 1321). In India there is a heavy reliance on textbooks and rote memorisation to pass examinations. Yet at the heart of teacher education practices is the 'personal take of education', which is what students remember and which influences approaches to lifelong learning (Batra, 2005). The nature of that 'personal take of education' is dramatically shaped by the way in which teacher education practices are understood to be 'authentic' because, 'authenticity [is] an issue for our students and one [that] needs to [be] effectively manage[d] (Garbett & Ovens, 2012).

Teacher educators' personal and professional experiences are strongly influenced by their beliefs (Chin, 1997; Gu, 2007).[1] Loughran (1997) maintains that beliefs serve as the foundation that informs one's practice as he/she designs curriculum for students, therefore 'Learning to articulate, question and understand our beliefs ... is the first step to improving our practice' (Chin, 1997, p. 123). A major challenge that teacher educators face then lies in recognising their own beliefs and the influence that those beliefs have on their practices.

Hart (2003, p. 207) contends that:

> Environmental issues, like politics or religion, are ethical issues. Environmental education depends not only on credible, reliable knowledge and understanding of the issues but also on the politics of human decision making, which includes emotional understanding, cultural understanding, and many other capabilities and beliefs.

As Hart (above) suggests, teacher educators need to believe that EE is important enough to be included in their curriculum. Otherwise, as mentioned earlier, given the rigours of being a teacher educator in India and the numerous competing interests in an already over-crowded curriculum, there is a strong possibility that EE could be neglected. Hart's (2003) study of teachers' thinking about EE demonstrated that positive experiences lead teachers to form positive beliefs about the environment. Therefore, it is not difficult to see how there is a need to believe in the cause of EE if it is to genuinely be implemented. Such knowledge and belief can be viewed as a productive way of providing teachers with the 'voice' and 'agency' they require to be 'expert' teachers of EE who might create 'authentic' situations through which their student teachers might learn about EE.

Teacher educators' identities are complex and shaped by all the different ways in which they 'construe themselves in social relationships as manifested in personality, values, actions, and sense of self' (Thomashow, 1996, p. 3). Three major determinants (amongst numerous others) that influence their role as environmental educators are their: professional identities as teachers; cultural identities; and, eco identities. The study outlined in this thesis focuses largely on these three determinants. Together they influence the development and understanding of EE and in turn how teacher educators might negotiate their teaching. These three major areas then combine to create a framework within which this study (of a particular group of teacher educators in an Indian Teacher Education institution) has been conceptualized and conducted. Each is examined in detail below.

Teachers/Professional Identities

Teachers are people who bring themselves into the classroom and the formation of their identities involves interplay between external and internal forces. (Rodgers & Scott, 2008, p. 732)

Research clearly demonstrates that events and experiences in personal lives are intimately linked to the performance of professional roles (Day, 2007). According to Rodgers and Scott (2008, p. 739) such experiences are critical in the formation of self and identity; with self being thought of as the 'meaning maker' and identity the 'meaning made.' Identities subsume beliefs, attitudes, life history and personal narrative and there is a strong correlation between identity and emotions. However, there is a lack of clear distinction between one's self and one's identity. This necessitates a need for teachers to become aware of their identities and the 'political, historical and social forces that shape them' and to, 'assume agency, find their voice, and take authority to shape their own professional paths and identities' (Rodgers & Scott, 2008, pp. 732–733).

Identities can also be seen to be shifting – or being constructed over time. Individuals' views and experiences of learning impacts the nature of their learning experiences in numerous ways (Loughran & Northfield, 1996), and these experiences also impact them as teachers and teacher educators. Berry (2004) similarly demonstrated the powerful influence of personal experience in prospective teachers' understanding of teaching. Thus, along the lines of Lortie's Apprenticeship of Observation (Lortie, 1975), it is not difficult to see how teacher educators' experiences as students themselves, combined with their experiences as students teachers and the kind of learning situations they experienced, have a major impact on their professional identities.

Beijaard et al. (2004, p. 122) identified four features that are essential to identity formation:

- Professional identity formation is an ongoing process of interpretation and re-interpretation of experience.
- Professional identity implies both person and context.
- A teacher's professional identity consists of multiple sub-identities (or 'selves') that more or less harmonize. The more central a sub-identity is, the more costly it is to change or lose that identity.
- Agency is an important element of professional identity, meaning that teachers have to be active in their processes of professional learning.

Identities are clearly shaped by various life experiences. Identity formation is also seen as a fluid process, which can undergo transformation with time and further experience. Teacher educators' professional identities are then not set in stone but can be influenced by future events and emerging experiences and understandings. However, current professional identities lie at the heart of how teacher educators might negotiate, determine and implement EE in their daily teaching practices.

Cultural Identities

Teachers' cultural identities are influenced by their culture, religion, traditions, personal beliefs and values. As Hart (2003) argued, these cultural understandings play a major role in teacher educators' decision making in teaching EE. The educational narrative in India is still largely dominated by the 'guru-shishya' (teacher-student) tradition. The mythos then of a teacher as an important, exemplary, inspiring figure imparting essential values for personal transformation still exists. Given this scenario a teacher's 'personal theories and understanding' play a significant role in establishing lifelong learning (Batra, 2005, p. 4350).

In trying to understand identity formation of teachers in India there is a need to delve into aspects of cultural influence. That conservation ethics was part of the Vedic times is evident from the first stanza of the Isho-Upanishad which says, 'the whole universe, together with its creatures, belong to the Lord (Nature). No creature is superior to any other, and human beings should not have absolute power over Nature. Let no species encroach upon the rights and privileges of other species. However, one can enjoy the bounties of Nature by giving up greed' (Khoshoo & Moolakkattu, 2009, p. 21).

In his lifetime, Gandhi furthered this ethos as imbued in these traditional Hindu beliefs. He believed that every living creature had a soul which was eternal and indestructible. Not only did the soul give continuity to the life processes over generations, but also imparted divinity to different living creatures. He (as do all practicing Hindus) believed there was 'transmigration of souls, and birth and rebirth in human or non-human forms' (Khoshoo & Moolakkattu, 2009, p. 47). The most enlightened souls are the only ones that can break free of this cycle of birth-rebirth. This 'together with the doctrine of ahimsa or non-violence, makes Indians inherently respectful, reverent, and conservation-oriented towards life' (Khoshoo & Moolakkattu, 2009, p. 47). All life forms therefore are worshipped as manifestations of the Almighty and treated with compassion.

The advent of globalisation and economic changes has led to massive disturbances in the environment. Ramchandra Guha (2006) emphasised the high rates of deforestation, species loss, land degradation, and air and water pollution in India as an ecological disaster zone. Inequity directly attributed to this abuse of nature is massive with glaring inequalities of consumption *within* the society of the nation. Regularly channelling natural resources from its countryside to meet the increasing needs of its urban population has caused this inequality. Globalisation and/or westernisation have further created a distancing from one's own cultural identity in order to pursue economic liberalisation. However, despite this situation, there still remains a strong influence of childhood traditions and cultural influences (especially on these particular teacher educators who grew up at a time when globalization had not yet fully gripped India.)

Cultural identity and how it is manifested in the teaching of EE is therefore at the heart of how the teacher educator participants in this study negotiate, determine and then implement EE in their classrooms.

Eco Identities

And in our time the great question is how we will live in light of the ecological fact that we are bound together in the community of life, one and indivisible. (Orr, 2012, p. 1)

Teacher educators' eco identities (Cutter-Mackenzie, 2009) can range between the dominant 'technocentric' and 'anthropocentric' views to the 'ecocentric' (R. Eckersley, 1992). The technocentric view is grounded in the belief that the environment is a resource to be used and is often claimed to be an overarching environmental belief in Western capitalist culture. In direct contrast, 'ecocentric' views are based on a consideration that the environment has to be valued for 'its own sake' and that, humans need to adjust their economies and aspirations to live in harmony with nature (Cutter-Mackenzie, 2009).

Understanding these factors can provide deeper understandings about how identities are developed. Eco literacy or the ability to ask "What then?" is an influential factor in the formation of eco identities. David Orr stresses that ecoliteracy is a belief system that encapsulates a eco identities. He contends that a failure to focus on eco literacy not only means that students lack a deeper knowledge of the earth and how it works (1992, p. 85), but that they are also being taught a 'lot of wrong stuff' when teaching is practiced as training or inculcation of rote habit; which is often the case in India (Batra, 2005). Orr (1992, p. 1) suggests that although 'training' might be viable while instructing animals; humans need to engage in learning which is a life-long process. He argues that providing surface level learning and rudimentary curriculum amounts to offering 'aspiring level solutions to potentially terminal illnesses.' Failing to take a holistic and integral approach to teaching EE and failing to integrate humanity and social sciences can be seen as a major cause of the lack of eco literate citizens. Orr (1992, p. xiii) describes the situation as a 'failure that can be ultimately traced to our schools and to our proudest universities.'

There are three main reasons why eco literacy has been difficult to develop in Western cultures according to Orr (1992, pp. 87–88):

- The lack of ability to think broadly or in other words being highly specialized. This makes it difficult to see the interconnections between things or how our actions can directly impact someone else's life elsewhere.
- Education is seen as a solely indoor activity with ecology becoming highly specialised and remote from its subject matter, the outdoors.
- The decline in aesthetic appreciation with 'ugliness' and 'sameness' becoming the norm in current times.

Although Orr pointed to the above difficulties in western cultures, the same can be applied to India. There is an increased emphasis on specialization in education, which makes it difficult to see the direct implications of an individual's actions and decisions on the surroundings. Large class sizes, expansive curriculum and high demands have made it difficult to take education beyond the four walls of the classroom. Over years this has led to a demarcation, a boundary between the classroom, home and community. In teacher education, all of this has led to a reduction in direct experiences with nature; especially for urban students.

Orr describes the outcome of this process as leading to a lack of aesthetic appreciation and acceptance of mass culture as the 'heart of the matter'. The loss of individuality is fast enveloping India. Indian cities, towns and villages all had a special flavour, culture and food. This individuality is being lost to a melting pot, assimilating into 'one huge fabric' characterised by the spread of 'shopping malls' to most parts and the spread of English as a language of choice. In such an evolving environment, developing an eco literate citizenry is increasingly difficult while enhancing technocentric identities increasingly easy.

Technocentric approaches can lead to a situation where the need for eco literacy is not felt. Under such circumstances EE can be regarded as an extra job to be done, not a core requirement or an integral part of the entire educational process. In Orr's (1992, p. 90) words, 'it all comes down to if the general public understands the relation between its well being and the health of its natural systems.' My own belief is that the day this kind of public awareness is generated, there will be greater impetus towards halting the rapidly deteriorating environmental degradation.

Working towards creating an eco literate citizenry requires an understanding of ecological or eco identities that individuals already carry. According to Thomashow (1996, p. 3):

> Ecological identity refers to all the different ways people construe themselves in relationship to the earth as manifested in personality, values, actions, and sense of self. Nature becomes an object of identification. For the individual, this has extraordinary conceptual ramifications. The interpretation of life experience transcends social and cultural interactions. It also includes a person's connection to the earth, perception of the ecosystem, and direct experience of nature.

Understanding teacher educators' ecological worldviews (and reflecting on their ecological identities) can be used to interpret their personal experiences and practices as environmental educators. It can help to explain the drive (or lack of it) that teacher educators carry for environmentalism. Common experiences often motivate people to take action and to think carefully about the moral foundations of their everyday decisions (Thomashow, 1996). This study aims to understand how teacher educators' experienced EE themselves and how those experiences and how they influence their teaching (i.e., if they 'find nature everywhere' they might encourage their students to do the same).

Eckersley (1992) suggests that teacher educators who carry a predominantly technocentric or anthropocentric eco identity are likely to transfer their beliefs to their teaching which means their student teachers are likely to be exposed to the belief that India's rampant economic growth is an absolute necessity; and it can be sustained despite ecological limits – mainly due to the ingenious use of technology to counter environmental imbalances. In contrast, teacher educators with a more eco centric identity are likely to foster the notion that the environment needs to be preserved for its sake and that there are serious limits to what technological advances can achieve when it comes to restoring environmental health. These eco identities also lie at the heart of how teacher educators negotiate, determine and implement EE in their daily teaching practices.

Conceptual Framework

Figure 3.1 details the conceptual framework for this thesis built around the three determinants that shape teacher educators' overall identities – namely their professional identities, their cultural identities and their eco identities (as outlined in detail above). These factors have a significant impact on teacher educators' identities. Teacher educators' identities influence how they understand, determine and negotiate EE, which ultimately impact their practice as environmental educators. The conceptual framework illustrates how these factors interact and influence the

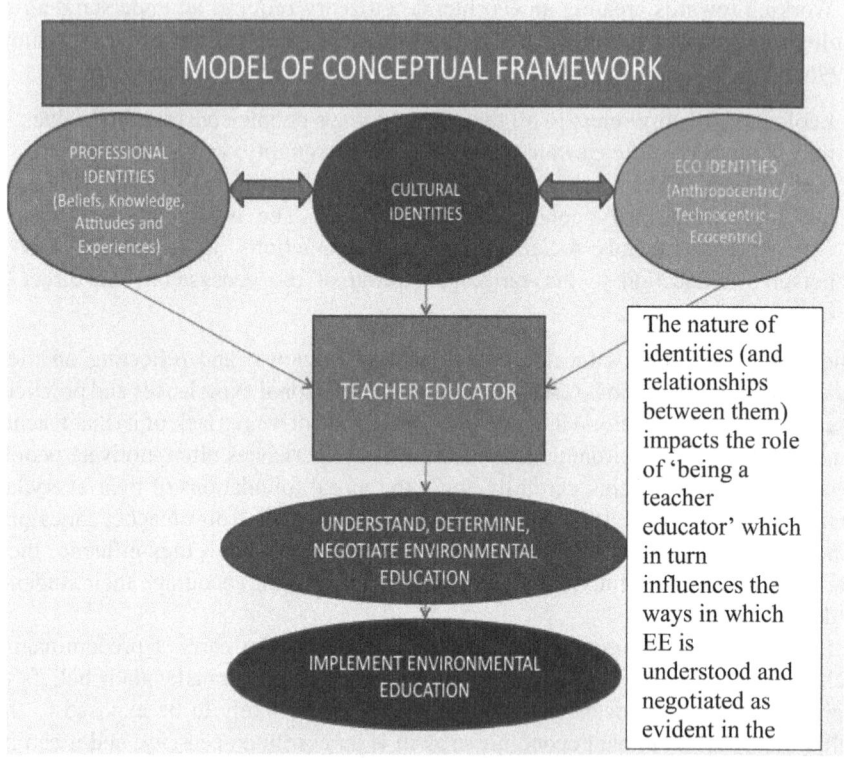

Figure 3.1. Conceptual framework

nature of teaching about teaching EE for the teacher educators who are participants in this research project.

In the light of the above discussion it is pertinent to state that understanding teacher educators' implementation of EE needs to be scaffolded by aims at understandings the extent to which teacher educators' identities influence their practice of EE in the organisational culture of teacher education.

METHODOLOGY

What is the most difficult of all?
That which seems to you the easiest,
To see with one's eyes, what is lying before them.
(Goethe – Xenienausdem Nachlass # 45 – cited in Bronfenbrenner, 1979, p. 37)

Teacher educators' identities are complex and their impact on their practices harder to study on a deeper level. This called for a methodology that would lend itself to uncovering the layers of complexities to uncover the underlying perspectives and influences. Therefore this study was based on qualitative, revelatory approaches using ethnography as a means to highlight the stories of the participant teacher educators as they unfolded.

Qualitative Research

Creswell defines qualitative research as 'a type of educational research in which the researcher relies on the views of participants; asks broad general questions; collects data consisting largely of words (or text) from participants; describes and analyses these words for themes; and conducts the inquiry in a subjective, biased manner' (Creswell, 2008, p. 46). According to Bogdan and Bilken (2007) qualitative research can be defined as research that is naturalistic, has descriptive data, is concerned with the process, is inductive and adds meaning to the daily situations of peoples' lives.

The research methodology adopted for this study is naturalistic and involves working with teacher educators. As such it fulfils most of the criteria Bogdan and Bilken (2007) use to describe qualitative studies. The research takes place in the natural contexts and daily work lives of teacher educators with special attention to the data and the processes of that work. An ethnographic approach within the naturalistic, interpretative framework of a qualitative research methodology has been used.

Ethnography

Creswell (2008, p. 473) terms ethnographic studies as qualitative research procedures that are used for 'describing, analysing, and interpreting a culture-sharing group's shared pattern of behaviour, beliefs, and languages that develop over time'. Ethnography entails documenting 'knowledge and beliefs' (Cutter-Mackenzie, 2003) within a particular culture-sharing group or individuals representative of a group (Bullough R. V. Jr., 1997; Creswell, 2007). According to Wolcott (2008), ethnographers tell the stories of people and the single most defining feature of ethnography is that it is the study of 'others'. The ethnographer is however an integral part of the study, immersed in the study for, there can be no ethnography without an ethnographer as Bohannan (1995) notes.

According to Hammersley and Atkinson (2007, p. 3) ethnography 'involves the researcher participating, overtly or covertly, in people's daily lives for an extended period of time, watching what happens, listening to what is said, and/or asking questions through informal and formal interviews, collecting documents, and artefacts – in fact, gathering whatever data are available to throw light on the issues that are the emerging focus of inquiry.' Bogdan and Biklen (2007, pp. 30–31) see it as a 'thick description' that attempts to describe cultures or aspects of culture.

Access to participants in this study was mainly through two 'gatekeepers' and considerable effort was made to gain the trust and confidence of participants – in line with that recommended by Creswell (2007). As such, the study is directed at understanding the ways in which teacher educators understand, negotiate, determine and implement environmental education (EE) in the organisational culture of teacher education.

Ethnographic research is characteristically exploratory which means that, 'it will not be clear where, within a setting, observation should begin, which actors need to be shadowed' 'what sampling strategies will be worked out' 'who will be interviewed and under what circumstances' (p. 4). Data has been collected in the everyday natural settings of the participants with analysis designed in ways that attempt to make sense of their daily lives to produce research knowledge (Hammersley & Atkinson, 2007).

The researcher spent time getting to know the institution and its participants before formally collecting data. Making the time and effort to get to know participants and putting them at ease about the research intentions was an important step in the process. While it was clear that the research process would require teacher educators to be interviewed most other details were variable and not so immediately obvious. The structure of interviews was purposely informal and the interview face sheet and small talk before interviews was used to put participants at complete ease. Classroom observations did not involve any video/audio recording and all attempts were made for the researcher to be as inconspicuous as possible in order to minimize attention from students and teacher educators and to allow the classes to proceed as normally as possible.

Ethnographic research helps understand not only individuals but also the social meanings that they interpret. This was of particular significance when trying to study these individual teacher educators who, although they belonged to the same 'culture' group, could have had very diverse life-experiences and beliefs about EE. Using an ethnographic approach allowed the researcher to delve deeply into this one teacher education institution in order to garner a rich understanding of that particular situation. It brought into sharp focus the multi-faceted workings of the institution, its teacher educators, its policies and efforts towards EE and its perceived successes and failures in implementing EE.

It is important to restate that the aim of the study was not to produce results that could be generalised to all teacher education institutions in India but to study one teacher education institution in detail and draw valuable lessons from that particular experience in implementing EE in order to be informative for other institutions.

Research Design and Data Generation

Data generation was designed to address the three aims suggested by Lofland, Snow, Anderson and Lofland (2006), that being to:

- Collect the richest possible data.
- Become intimately familiar with the setting.
- Involve and engage the participants in face-to-face interactions.

Participating in the daily work lives of the participants, in this case the teacher educators, helped best fulfil these aims. Lofland et al. (2006) recommend careful consideration of the role one has to play as a researcher in the field and the importance of 'getting along' with the participants. In this study, this was pursued by taking a 'non-threatening learner' stance in line with what Lofland et al. (2006, pp. 67–68) suggested:

> the investigator who assumes the role of socially acceptable incompetent is likely to be accepted. In being viewed as relatively incompetent ... the investigator easily assumes the role of one who is to be taught. Such persons have to be told and will not take offense at being instructed about 'obvious' things or at being 'lectured to.'

A clear brief about the study and its research objectives was presented to all participants. Hammersley and Atkinson (2007) emphasise the importance of overcoming initial suspicions and building trust. They maintain that participants are often more concerned with what kind of person the researcher is more than the research itself. Participants were also assured of complete confidentiality in this study. These measures were taken to help participants understand the study and encourage them to be supportive of the process. Most importantly it helped establish trust by making the researcher's intentions transparent.

The Principal of the institution is a scholar and avid writer. He was very keen for the research to be conducted at his institution. He personally introduced the researcher to all staff members and despite the Principal's power relation, it did not appear that the prospective teacher educators were coerced into participation; all appeared keen to participate in the study.

Being an 'Insider outsider' provided me with a unique advantage. It made it easier for the participants to talk to me as I understood the language and culture – for example when one of them invited me to go to a village function for a local deity – I was able to go and participate in the functions. At the same time having not lived in the region or the country for over 12 years provided me with the crucial 'Outsiders' perspective on things too. It gave me a unique advantage to remove myself from the situation and have an outsider's view of the situation.

Method of Recruitment

I had not lived in India for over 12 years and therefore had limited first-hand, in-field knowledge of the current status of environmental education in India. Through an exploratory visit to The Centre for Environmental Education (CEE), a leading semi-government organisation in India working in the field of EE for over three decades, I met with CEE representatives from across India. At this time, a journey was conducted to the CEE headquarters in Western India – Ahmedabad, the Delhi office in Northern India - for a meeting with the editor of India's first international journal on sustainable development (operated under the aegis of CEE) as well as to one of their offices in Southern India to meet one of India's leading teacher education experts who acted as a 'gatekeeper' and recommended teacher education faculties to initially approach about being involved in the study.

Lofland et al. (2006, p. 42) indicates the importance of gatekeepers as "connections" that help gain access to research settings. They identify two strategies to develop such facilitative connections, 'one is to exploit existing social ties ... the other is to identify key gatekeepers and develop such ties with them.' In this case the second strategy was the modus operandi with the 'gatekeeper.' As a teacher educator with over 25 years of experience in the in the field, he had a deep understanding of the need for research in EE in India and helped gain access to teacher education institutions and settle on one that expressed interest in participating in the study. It is also crucial to mention here that while there were quite a few institutions willing to fill in a survey as part of the institution none of them were willing to be involved in a longer qualitative study that allowed me to visit, interview and engage with the faculty. They saw this as time consuming and an encroachment on their valuable time, which understandably is quite short.

Research Site

As highlighted in the literature review earlier, there is a pressing need for research in EE in India – particularly in the field of teacher education. In determining how to proceed there was an inevitable trade-off between breadth and depth of investigation (Hammersley & Atkinson, 2007). Given the time and resource constraints of this study, an in-depth study focusing on one teacher education institution in India was decided upon rather than trying to cover a larger sample across a broader range. In so doing, the project therefore explicitly aimed to provide a 'thick description' of an institution and its teacher educators, and 'soft' data is rich in description of people, places and conversations (Bogdan & Bilken, 2007, p. 2).

The participating institution is a small, semi-government institute situated in one of India's few 'university towns' and is part of a larger cohort of Engineering, Medical and Science institutions. It is managed by one of India's best and very well known private institutions. It was selected for two reasons. It is a reputed institution in India and is highly recommended by leading teacher educators as an institute of repute that has been working in EE. It was also selected due to the willingness of the Dean to participate in the study (This is of special importance because in India one often has to go through excessive bureaucratic red tape to gain access to study sites thus prolonging the time taken to prepare for, and conduct, a project).

The teacher education institute was located in a university town in India. It is a semi-aided institution, which means that part of the money to run the institution comes from the government and part of it has to be 'earned' by the institution. This funding mix places a number of restrictions on the administration – the biggest being a lack of personnel. The government is responsible for recruiting new teacher educators but for this institution it had not hired a single individual in the last 10 years. There were only 3 staff members on the University Grants Commission (UGC) pay roll, the rest of the staff had been recruited by the management and were highly underpaid compared to the UGC staff.

Management was also responsible for funding the resources and there was evident tension between what the teacher educators deemed as important and what the management was willing to spend. As a consequence, very limited resources were provided. For example staff had very limited access to computers, Internet and audio visual aids. The college library was poorly resourced with limited access to the latest research journals and books and no computers or Internet was available for students.

The classrooms were very old and set up in a traditional manner. Some of the classes observed were conducted in sweltering heat with temperatures hovering above 40 degrees Celsius. There were two fans to cool the classroom and there were about 4–5 students sitting on one bench with barely any elbowroom between them. The teacher educator had to teach a class of up to 100 students, standing in the front of the class on a raised platform with a chalkboard and an overhead projector as the only tools available. The physical environment was truly challenging.

The institute was an 18-hour train journey from the city of Bombay in a semi rural district with barely adequate facilities for a visitor in terms of infrastructure. Lofland et al. (2006, p. 27) suggested that, 'Even if it [the difficulty] is real, difficulty does not necessarily equal impossibility … if the setting or situation is an especially significant or interesting one, even a partial study of it will be better than none at all.' This particular teacher education site was of particular significance because, as stated above, it was attached to one of India's most well known and prestigious educational institution groups.

Participants

It is important to note though that all teacher educators were invited to participate. There were 11 teacher educators in the institution all of who volunteered to participate in the study following the initial invitation. Following is the list of the teacher educators (refer to a detailed tabulated profile in Chapter 5). The names provided here are pseudonyms selected by the participants themselves (coding allocation and explanations are offered in the following sections of the chapter):

Anjalie 1
Medha 2
Nammy 3
Poornima 4
Axmi 5

Arya 6
Chidambar 7
Leena 8
Bhargava 9
Blue 10
Kala 11

Data Collection Procedures

The data collection phase included three steps as illustrated in Figure 3.2. Data was collected by immersion at three progressively deeper levels. The first step involved the researcher being introduced to the Principal and faculty of the Teachers' College. After a presentation to all teacher educators detailing the nature of the study, participants were invited to express interest in participating in the study. Documentary analysis involved working in the library at the research site. It involved collecting the curriculum and syllabus documents and the modules or 'unit guides' that were in use in the institution for the teaching of EE. The second phase involved individually interviewing the participants (all of whom volunteered to be involved). The final deeper immersion phase involved observing participants in their classes. Field notes, observations and reflections were carefully and diligently recorded.

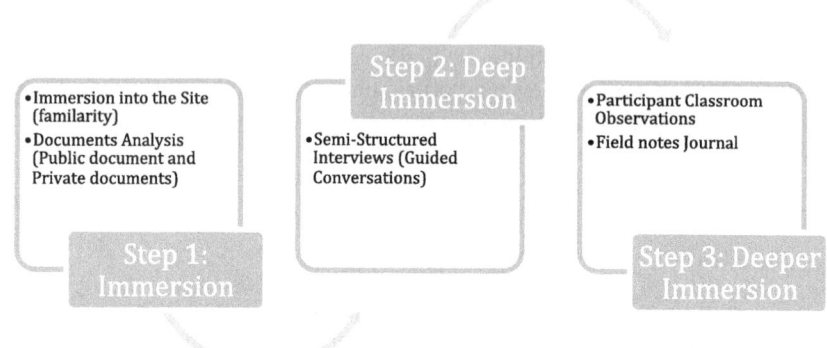

Figure 3.2. Data collection

Step One: Document Analysis

Documents provide valuable information to help understand the central phenomena and are a good source for text data (Creswell, 2008). They not only provide information about the organisation and key figures but also provide important corroboration of information received from informants through interviews and observations (Hammersley & Atkinson, 2007). This process provides an important approach for triangulating data and establishing aspects of validity and reliability of the data (Creswell, 2008; Patton, 2002). Documents collected for analysis included public and private documents including:

Public Documents (coded D.A.1)

- National Curriculum policy documents
- Supreme Court Ruling
- State Curriculum documents
- Books and other resources from the institution's library

Private Documents (coded D.A.2)

- The syllabus used by the institution
- Teaching modules
- Annual reports
- Minutes of staff meetings
- Assessment reports – past examination papers (Appendix 1)

These were obtained from the Internet, the institution's library and from the Principal who agreed to provide the same. Following the initial immersion step, the second phase of data collection was conducted which involved semi-structured interviews with all the teacher educators.

(In the data chapters that follow, all document data sets have been coded as D.A.1 for the Public Documents and D.A.2 the code for the Private Documents.)

Step Two: Semi-Structured Interviews

Interviews are important data generation tools that provide insight into participants' thoughts, perceptions, feelings and accounts (Denzin, 2001). They permit participants to describe detailed personal information. The interviewer also has the advantage of guiding the interviewee using specific questions to elicit information of interest (Creswell, 2008). These semi-structured interviews (Appendix 2) included open-ended questions that allowed participants to share their knowledge while at the same time allowing the researcher to guide the interview so that the 'focus' is maintained. Lofland (2006, p. 105) describes such 'guided conversations' as encouraging interviewees to 'speak freely in their own terms about a set of concerns you (interviewer) bring to the interaction, plus whatever else they might introduce'.

All the teacher educators (n=11) at this institution were interviewed. The outline for interviews was derived from the literature review and theoretical framework. The interview protocol was not tightly structured but acted more as 'a list of things to be sure to ask about when talking to the person being interviewed' (Lofland et al., 2006, p. 105). Fresh copies of the interview protocol were used for each interview with some space for taking notes – key sentences, names, etc. Participants were requested to complete an interview face-sheet (Appendix 3), which sought simple details about their names, educational background, subjects taught, and languages spoken.

Data was logged very carefully. Both a digital voice recorder and a video recorder were used during the interviews. (This provided a backup in case one of the two devices fails.) Shorthand notes were taken during the interview. Interviews were also reviewed immediately after each session using a post-interview sheet (Appendix 4).

Patton (2002, p. 383) considers the period immediately following an interview as 'critical to the rigor and validity of qualitative inquiry. This is a time for guaranteeing the data'. Tapes were checked to make sure there had been no malfunction. Also interview notes were checked for certainty and lack of ambiguity. This provided an opportunity to double check with the interviewee about any unclear or critical aspect of the interview. The post interview comment sheet enabled the researcher to write observations, comments and reflections on the interview while the experience was still 'fresh in the mind'.

Interview transcripts were forwarded to participants for their feedback with requests to make modifications if necessary. This helped increase the accurateness of the transcripts, engender trust and confidence in the researcher and provide the informants with a sense of contribution (Cutter-Mackenzie, 2009).

All data from these are data coded with the pseudonym of the Teacher Educator being interviewed and an associated number. For example every reference to the interviews with Anjalie will be followed by the associated Interview number, which in the case if Anjalie is 1.

Step Three: Participant Observation and Researcher Journal

Participant observation refers to the process in which an investigator established and sustains a many-sided and situationally appropriate relationship with a human association in its natural setting for the purpose of developing a social scientific understanding of that association. (Lofland et al., 2006, p. 17)

Direct participation in, and observation of, the phenomenon of interest is arguably the best research method (Patton, 2002). There are limitations on how much one can learn from what people say. Therefore observing participants complements the interview process and helps understand what they do in practice. According to Patton (2002) direct observation has several advantages:

- It helps better understand and capture the contexts within which people interact.
- Allows the researcher to be open, discovery-oriented and shed prior conceptualisations.
- Provide the researcher with opportunities to see things that might have even escaped the participants involved.
- It provides the researcher with the opportunity to learn things that people might not be willing to discuss in an interview.

The aim then is to look and listen and better understand the context within which the participant interacts. In the deeper immersion phase of data collection, the researcher observed participants in their classrooms. Careful notes were recorded on the Observation Notes sheets (Appendix 5). Field notes were maintained from the very beginning and all through the three data collection phases, which included recorded thoughts, mental notes, key events, personal impressions and feelings, and observations and many 'corridor conversations'.

All data from these sources have been coded as PO (participant observer) or RJ (research journal). and numbered appropriately, For example., R.J. or P.O.

Data Collection Problems and Issues

There were some typical questions posed by the teacher educators such as: "So what kind of survey do you want me to fill out?" "Why do you want to ask me all these things?" "Can I take the interview protocol home and just answer your questions instead of talking about it?" and, "Why do you want to record everything that I am saying?" These teacher educators were curious that I was only there to talk to them. I had to spend considerable time talking to them and explaining my project. Gaining their trust was an important step and only when I was able to cross that barrier were they willing to share their work with me.

Poornima [Interview 4] told me that she could not believe that someone was, 'here to just talk to her' and ask her about her opinions and what she considered important. This according to Anjalie [Interview 1] was the first time in his 28-year career that someone had asked him for his opinion and his thoughts. Being from the same region (my parents had migrated from nearby towns to Bombay) helped in terms of some familiarity with the local language.

Ethical and cultural considerations also demanded extra sensitivity. Interviews were conducted in a separate room within the library, which provided privacy with little interruptions. This was necessary, as people would just 'drop in' to see what I was doing and ask if they could watch me working. This was generally done out of curiosity and courtesy and wanting to say 'Hello' but it was important to be able to garner the privacy needed without appearing to be rude. The separate room however was an old, dusty storeroom that had not been used in years, which made it physically demanding to be in the room for too long.

Data Analysis

The semi-structured interview protocol set the basis for a thematic analysis of the data. Data was coded and analysed using NVIVO software. It was coded into five themes – each theme was organised into tree nodes and free nodes.

Extensive notes while transcribing the data and also while coding helped in the data analysis process in terms of interpretation and elaboration where necessary.

The themes that emerged from the analysis of the data are outlined (below) and briefly described in order to facilitate understanding of the coding process, which underlies the emergence of the five themes.

Before elaborating on the five themes it is important to revisit the aims of this study which were to understand the:

1. ways in which EE is understood, negotiated, determined and implemented by teacher educators in this institution in India.
2. organisational culture of teacher education in India and its role in implementing EE in the context of the culture of teacher education; and,
3. characteristics – the qualities, issues and problems – that enable and/or constrain the development and implementation of EE in teacher education.

In order to fulfil these aims, as described earlier, data was collected in three different stages and comprised documents, interviews and observations. The data threw up five themes that helped to respond to the above mentioned aims.

Theme 1: Teacher education and the role of EE. This theme was devoted to the teacher educators' descriptions of their life journeys, their educational background, their own expertise and areas of specialisation and experiences with EE. How these teacher educators reached this stage/phase in their careers, their induction into the profession, their views on EE and its place in their practice is captured in this theme.

Theme 2: Personal connection. Cultural understandings and traditions are exceptionally important in the context of India because of its rich and diverse traditions with regard to the environment. As elucidated in the literature review the environmental ethos and views of 'every living being as one' are ingrained in the religious and spiritual ethos of most Indians. These teacher educators' background and life experiences were influential in how they viewed the environment and EE in particular. This theme showed how these teacher educators' beliefs were influenced by their upbringing and childhood experiences.

This theme also drew attention to a Utopian vision of the environment, which saw an escape to a pristine environment – like their native villages –as a means to counter the hopelessness they felt towards the environment in which they currently lived. Despite the onslaught of modernisation participants were well entrenched in traditional religious practices like *'in front of our house we have a plant – Tulsi and we do 'pooja' (worship) around it' (Nammy, Interview 3)* and *'we worship some of the trees as God's – God lives in some of these trees' (Medha, Interview 2).* Within this theme also came a compulsion to provide scientific reasoning that validated their practices beyond being mere 'blind faith' and being done for the sake of the environment.

Theme 3: Understanding, perceptions, feeling and attitudes. These teacher educators' understanding of what the environment meant to them and their feelings towards the environment is explored in this theme. Their concerns and feelings often of hopelessness about the state of the environment both nationally and in their own surrounding community were clear. Concerns ranged from large-scale issues about environmental problems due to overpopulation, industrialization, and globalisation to smaller scale issues like keeping their immediate surroundings clean. It is essential to understand the influence these personal feeling, beliefs, traditions, and culture have in shaping their eco-identities. It was clear from their responses that their own beliefs and cultural practices were not necessarily connected to their eco-identities, which were heavily technocentric, and pro-development even if that meant compromising the environment. For example despite espousing the virtues of Indian ethos and philosophies about the environment most of these teacher educators strongly recommended Sustainable Development and advances in Science and Technology as an answer to all environmental problems.

Theme 4: Implementation of EE. This theme emerged through the Teacher Educators' experiences with the implementation of EE, which were characterised by perceptible issues including: resource; curriculum; assessment techniques; incentive; and, encouragement to go beyond that, which is prescribed. Their views about EE in India and how they considered it was being implemented were quite diverse yet converged on one main point – more needed to be done, for example, *'We thought there would be a big movement, like a big change or a big transformation, there would be reformation in the education system, but it hasn't taken place' (Blue, Interview 10).* The policy practice gap was perceptible in this theme with clear indicators of how and why the implementation of EE was limited.

Theme 5: Curriculum/policy at an institutional level. These teacher educators' understanding, knowledge and investment in the recent policy changes was central to their implementation of the policies at their institution. This theme captured data about their perceptions of these policy changes with particular reference to the recent National Curriculum Framework and the National Curriculum for Teacher Educators, which had both been revised in response to the Supreme Court mandate. The debate on the plausibility of implementing these curriculum changes was a sub-topic within this theme. Numerous reasons were raised during interviews around enabling factors and hurdles for change in this theme particularly with regard to the support provided to and by the institution.

Overall the five themes emerged as the data was being analysed with a few sub themes that lie within these themes and will be addressed in the next chapter. According to Wolcott (Wolcott, 2008, p. 5) often 'the promise of ethnography is compromised by its ambition'. Despite the clear ambitions of this study, every effort has been made to present the participants' perspectives and their voice through the presentation of the data. In Mckenzie's (2005, p. 404) words 'given the pervasiveness of the researcher in the research process' it has also been important to minimize as much as possible any sense of bias or over-interpretation of participants' lived experiences. Voices that I have heard, issues that I highlighted and words that I have used in some way clearly reflect my own positions and understandings. However, as cited earlier there can be no ethnography without the ethnographer (Bohannan, 1995), hopefully, these personal touches add to the richness of the study rather than diminish its authenticity. Despite the inherent difficulties of 'being up close and personal' with the participants, the study is structured and written in ways that offer an honest attempt to explain the situation in accord with that which was clearly present from the participants' perspective.

NOTE

[1] Beliefs are seen here as personal constructs – understandings, premises and propositions that are felt as true by Teacher Educators (Richardson, 1996).

SECTION 2

UNFOLDING THE PERSONAL STORIES:
ABOUT SELF

TEACHER EDUCATORS – PERSONAL CONNECTIONS, BACKGROUND, CULTURE, KNOWLEDGE AND BELIEFS

If the nation's classrooms are to be filled with teachers who can teach ambitious skills to all learners, the solution must lie in large part with strong, universal teacher education. (Darling-Hammond, 2006, p. 5)

INTRODUCTION

The above quote is the premise on which Linda Darling-Hammond bases her book 'Creating Powerful Teacher Education.' In expecting all schools in India to implement EE across all grades in India, governmental policy makers have placed a huge onus on India's teachers and thereby teacher educators. In order to usher in the policy reforms, there is a need to understand the quality of teacher education and teacher educators – those who are largely expected to implement these policies.

Teacher educators' understandings of EE and its implementation in their everyday practices were subject to numerous influences and considerations. In this chapter I present and discuss the data and its analysis. The data had been thematically analysed as part of the research process that developed while working with the participating teacher educators in this project. The analysis led to the emergence of the five themes in the data – laid out at the end of Chapter 4, which are now presented in detail in this chapter. There are places where the data merges and overlaps so that it can be part of two themes at the same time. I have attempted to stay true to this by mentioning the overlaps while being cautious of not being repetitive. In order to bring greater coherence and for easy of reading the themes have been amalgamated into the next two chapters. The themes are organised in such a way that teacher educators discuss matters about themselves in the beginning slowly moving towards broader issues of curriculum, policy and implementation.

Environmental education occurs in schools not so much as a result of curriculum mandate or government policy as the personal commitment of teachers who turn their personal theories into practical professional actions in their classrooms, schools, and communities. (Hart, 2003, p. xiii)

Teacher educators have been considered as 'linchpins' of all educational reforms (Cochran-Smith, p. 5). In India too, teacher educators are mainly responsible for preparing educated and competent teachers. In bringing about sweeping reforms in environmental education policies, teacher educators in India too have by default become 'linchpins.' Cochran-Smith insists that before considering professional development it is crucial to define their identities as teacher educators.

Teacher educators' identities are 'embedded in cultural and political national contexts' and are therefore shaped by 'their personal motivation and initiative as well as by the possibilities and impossibilities of the context of teacher education and the wider context of education' (Swennen, Jones, & Volman, 2011, p. 142). Therefore, it stands to reason that any attempt to define teacher educators' identities should take into account to these different contexts. Tanner (1980) proposed that there was a need for educators to understand the kind of experiences that motivated responsible environmental behaviour. He argued that this would add to educators' ability to foster the development of an active and informed citizenry. In Chapter 3 the role of beliefs, experiences and knowledge in shaping teacher educators' environmental identities was clearly established. This current theme builds on those underpinnings through the data in an attempt to better understand the personal experiences, beliefs, knowledge and cultural influences that have helped to shape the environmental identities of teacher educators involved in this study.

Childhood and Early Experiences in Natural Environments

> I don't know if because I have taught that I have developed interest [in the environment] or before starting teaching perhaps that interest might be there in me. (Bhargava, Interview 9)

Louise Chawla (1999) in a study of significant life experiences' translation into effective environmental action established the importance of formative life experiences amongst environmentally conscious people. Such people attributed 'extended times spent outdoors in natural areas, often in childhood; parents or other family members, teachers or classes; involvement in environmental organisations; books; and the loss or degradation of a valued place' (p. 15) as the main reason for their environmental interests or actions. Informal outdoor experiences and experiences of natural areas in particular ranked as the number one reason.

The Teacher Education College involved in this study is located in a small semi-urban town in India. Although it started out as a small town, today it is a fast growing medium sized city in India with a population of over one million. All the teacher educators involved in this study grew up in and around the town where the teacher's college is situated. When asked about their experiences in natural and outdoor environments all of them recalled 'nice' childhood memories.

Some of these memories were part of playing outside in the nearby green areas.

> Picking up mangoes and water lilies and one small [couldn't tell the English name] nice flower and making lotus chains and wearing them, playing with

mud. Then there were elephant palm trees; we used to hide in them. So I had nice experiences playing outside. Nobody used to bother if you are dirty…we have eaten so many weeds and wild fruits. (*Kala, Interview 11*)

During my examinations I used to read on the trees. There is a small forest near my house, there is a big mango tree, I climbed that to study. Not only me but all my friends also come there to study. And we also used to conduct games there – nature games. (*Chidambar, Interview 7*)

Other memories were associated with spending time outdoors when visiting family living in greener areas. One teacher educator in particular (Axmi) was almost lost in the experience for a few moments when recalling her childhood memories. She recalled sadness when the place was sold by her uncles and mentioned how even today she made sure she visited the place even though their family had moved out. She attributed these childhood experiences to her current interest in the environment in line with Chawla's (1999) findings.

During vacations I would go to my grandmother's place. It's a village, very beautiful, calm, quite, free from pollution. They had nearly 25 acres of land, fields, forests, big lake, during rainy season the water would fill and flow through – overflow like a waterfall… it was beautiful… I think maybe that provoked me gave me an interest in the environment and such things. (*Axmi, Interview 5*)

Poornima evoked similar memories about her village:

It is a very rare village I can say. It is an island and on all four sides there is a river, the island is in the middle of that river. There are no connections like bridges, nothing is there. If we have to purchase even a matchbox we have to get to the next bank by making use of a small boat … (smiles) … only 7 houses are there … (laughs) … it is truly natural. But it is nice if we go on one Saturday and come back the next day … Staying there itself is very difficult. (*Poornima, Interview 4*)

Interestingly while she too got lost for a few moments while recalling the memories (R.J.) she was emphatically clear that she would not be able to live that life forever. Her children do not like the place at all as there is no television and electricity on the island and do not intend to settle there.

Many of the teacher educators came from agricultural families. They showed strong connections with nature and their childhood experiences were in relation to their work on their farms.

I lived in a village for many years. My maternal uncle's family is an agrarian family. So I know about harvesting and all those traditional things. (*Anjalie, Interview 1*)

Basically we are farmers, my father is a farmer and so am I. My brother does the farming and I stay in the quarters here. But when I go home, even today also I work on the farm. (*Chidambar, Interview 7*)

While teacher educators recalled experiences with natural environments as a matter of play or work only one of them recalled these as special efforts made by family members to expose their children to nature.

My mummy used to take us for trekking and I have done my rock climbing. (*Blue, Interview 10*)

Otherwise most of these experiences were a part of growing up and were not planned family events. Special family activities like camping, outdoor trips or picnics were not mentioned as part of their childhood experiences. When specifically asked if they went out with the family on nature trips one of the teacher educators commented

Yeah we used to go here only to nearby places like the beach, temples. Not exactly parks. Because here in this area you find less number of parks. (*Leena, Interview 8*)

Two of the teacher educators however did mention their family members as having an influence on them.

My wife comes from a village … and has been brought up completely in the middle of nature – on a plantation. At home we have a small and beautiful garden … She is an expert and because of her influence of late I have started loving nature and I have interest in watching birds. (*Anjalie, Interview 1*)

Teachers were also seen as providing inspiration and acting as role models. They added to the understanding that teacher educators carried:

So we had practical knowledge. And for lectures also we had a very good lecturer. He is also a researcher and so he knew the importance of nature. He knew a lot and whatever research he did he would bring and expose it to us. (*Kala, Interview 11*)

Experiences with the natural environment also laid the foundation for teacher educators' future 'teaching' about the environment.

Basically we belong to agricultural family. And when I was a boy, when I was a student at the degree level … and even afterwards also- we used to do a lot of work at home pertaining to agriculture. So we cannot be separated from the field, from the soil [from earth]. So for example in Geography – soil, soil types – and I used to enjoy teaching that because we have seen it. (*Bhargava, Interview 9*)

Volunteering in environmental clubs or groups also was seen as an important part of early experiences.

> When I was in college I was in the Eco club, we did a lot of work. We used to go to the ashrams, when the rain was coming we went and saw all small insects. We had done a study on ants – ants are very important and why we should not kill them. (*Blue, Interview 10*)

There was also indignation at the loss of favourite childhood places.

> Our house was in the middle of the coconut garden, about one – one and half acre area... [we played] cricket and kabaddi. And that time the environment was very nice; it was not very much polluted like today. (*Arya, Interview 6*)

Anger at the loss of species and general quality of the environment was also strongly expressed by another teacher educator who had this story to share. He expressed despair at the state of the environment:

> We speak so much about conservation but frogs are disappearing. When I used to go to college I used to see so many frogs around but now it is very difficult to find one. You hear them all around especially when it rains ... in my house there were frogs, I don't know what species but they were burnt orange in colour. Nearly 50–60 members lived in my house permanently, they stayed under the cot and at night they all line up and they go out. Everyone goes out even a small baby frog wont be there. In the morning when you open the door again they will be standing outside in a queue. They don't do any problem except sit under utensils which are not being used, under the cot and if you go near them they will pass out urine because they get scared ... but now even such frogs are not there, their population has gone down, people have killed them because not everyone like having frogs in their homes. Even in my own house my aunty [uncle's wife who came in later when the uncle got married] captured around 200 frogs and put them in a gunny bag and threw them in small water channel. But those frogs are not water living, they are land living and maybe they died. Bow frogs are rare. These experiences make me think that unless we decide to change nothing can be done. And one person, an ordinary person doesn't have a voice, that also I know. (*Kala, Interview 11*)

As the data (above) highlights, all teacher educators seemed to have had numerous direct experiences with nature mostly as part of their childhood play experiences or as part working on the fields. The above experiences are in line with Chawla's (1999) findings about the sources of commitment to environmental protection amongst environmentalists. It does seem reasonable to suggest that these earlier experiences served a role in shaping their current views and concerns for the environment and the future. This point is developed further in the next section.

Experiences that Influenced Beliefs about the Environment

The aim in asking teacher educators to recall particular significant experiences was to further jog their memories and extend the conversation to experiences that have had maximum impact on their beliefs. Interestingly most teacher educators focused on mainly negative experiences and concerns about the environment.

> Things are changing very fast and it is unfortunate to say that it is negative. I have told you previously just 20–25 years back when we were children it was very nice here but it is horrible today. Sometimes I feel very bad and I don't know what is going to happen in the future. (*Arya, Interview 6*)

One teacher educator narrated the pain of having favourite trees cut down.

> When we were small we used to live in a house it was surrounded by many trees and a large compound. Then later it was divided and each and everyone we have our own part. And while building the house we need to cut the trees. And we had so many mango trees in our house but now what we find – we don't have any mango trees. In those places [where the trees stood] we have houses, my uncle's house, my aunt's house, parent's house and my house. (*Leena, Interview 8*)

Another talked about the growing use of plastics, which was destroying the natural environment.

> … in metros and even small cities [names some cities] everywhere you can see plastics. It is very bad and I get irritated whenever I see plastics. So in our area, in my coconut garden I used to pick up daily … And whenever you see a stream or a river then you see plenty of plastics in it. It is really irritating and we feel that even though people are educated they are not behaving properly. They don't know how to dispose of the waste … they throw it on others properties or the public property – especially streams, rivers and lakes. (*Arya, Interview 6*)

In my first meeting with Arya I introduced myself and told him that I work in the field of environmental education. His first reaction was to take me outside into the corridor. From here we could see an open ground strewn with plastic bottles, glasses and plates. He told me that this was the venue for the local municipal elections over the previous weekend and 'this is how the place was left once the elections were done" (R.J.1.) His quote (above) then takes this notion further and shows how strongly he felt about the use of plastics in his area.

Awareness about the environment due to exposure to pollution was also seen as particularly significant.

> I have read articles – herbivores die because of consuming plastics. And when I go to big cities and I see pollution there – when you go out you can just wipe your face with tissue and see the black grime deposited on your face.

I think that has also influenced me and has provoked me to think about the environmental issues. (*Axmi, Interview 5*)

Experiences in villages were held as closer to the natural environment and Nammy in particular feared for the future of cities.

Village is the place where you have fresh air and pure water… in the coming years I have a strong feeling that in metropolitan cities and towns it may be very difficult to get fresh air and water, villages are the only place. If you go to a big city like [name], if you travel for a distance and then wipe your face, your hand will be black. It is highly polluted. (*Nammy, Interview 3*)

Kala, continued to find the loss of species (like the Bow frogs as quoted in the earlier section) as an important long-term experience. Encounters with increasing shortages of natural resources were also seen as significant experiences.

At home … we face acute shortage of water during summer season and of late people are talking about water harvesting that is collection rainwater because most of it is wasted in this part of the country, so the aim is to collect water and use it in the future. At home we have done this [provides details]… because of that the water table has improved … there is lots of improvement. (*Anjalie, Interview 1*)

Only one teacher educator mentioned positive experiences in the natural environment as significant enough to influence beliefs.

In our area – we have got 12 acres of land in our village…there were many forest areas… behind our house; there is a big Nagabana (house of cobra) even today with tall trees. And religious beliefs are that we should not cut the trees from that – it will affect the Naga, it is considered sacred … sometimes snakes are also found in that … but I used to enter into that quite often, especially during the times of examination. Because it is a very nice place, no disturbance, tall trees, good shade, good breeze and no disturbance … I was influenced by that - the birds, their songs, the trees. Even when we were small we sued to climb up and play different games inside that protected area. We were not afraid of the snakes. (*Bhargava, Interview 9*)

Eminent personalities, books and/or movies appeared to influence some of the teacher educators.

A great environmentalist [name] is from my village. He is a well-known scholar all over the world … I read so many environmental books written by him. And also a movie by Suresh Hablikar called 'Manne' which is about the earth and the environment. (*Chidambar, Interview 7*)

Studies about memory (Neisser, 1988) have shown the effectiveness of unrestrained recall – i.e., situation in which participants provide an account of their past lives at their own pace. As the data (above) suggests, delving into participants' significant life experiences offers a window into their environmental consciousness.

Personal Action: Involvement in Environmental Groups or Activities

While these teacher educators recounted their childhood memories in natural environments and discussed important experiences that influenced their beliefs, they also highlighted their concerns for the state of the environment (this will be discussed in detail in Chapter 8). Studies have indicated that intended behaviours are not necessarily an effective indication of actual behaviours (Granton, Sinclair, & Punell, 2004). Thinking, feeling and speaking congenially about the environment is of little value if not followed by action. In this section of the chapter, how these teacher educators' environmental concern translated into action is examined.

Only one amongst these teacher educator was currently directly involved in an environmental group as part of her other job as a schoolteacher.

> … Yes, I am a member [of Eco club]. One year I was also the coordinator. They hold so many activities like enactment, which should be based on any scenery or based on the environment; then drawing, debates and also identifying medicinal plants. Even our students have won prizes. (*Medha, Interview 2*)

Others had been indirectly involved in some environmental activities in the past. One of them was a member of a group that conducted some environmental activities in the villages as part of its agenda.

> For a few years [3–4] I was in the Rotary club … There I got a bit of opportunity of associating with the local people … we had to go to the people, contact them … (*Nammy, Interview 3*)

Another had been a member of the local scouts and was involved in environmental education as part of this group.

> I was a Scout Master at the school level in addition to my regular teaching. I used to take students also for observing nature, nature studies, hiking … Nature Study Hike. So I used to ask them several questions – what are the trees that you see where we have stopped? Prepare a list or if you don't know you ask the local people. (*Bhargava, Interview 9*)

Still another teacher educator talked about environmental problems during other public speaking occasions, which he did as part of a second job.

> I do [works as] Master of ceremonies for public functions and when I do that I give a message that you have to be very careful about the environment, we are losing everything now. (*Blue, Interview 10*)

The main reason these teacher educators gave for their lack of involvement was a lack of time. There was also a fear of the amount of commitment needed although there seemed to be at the same time a resolve to do something in the future.

I really wanted to join [an environmental organisation] but sometimes what happens is that we know our lacunae's, our weaknesses etc., if you involve yourself you have to give a lot of time and dedication and you have to commit yourself. But I cannot do much ... but one day I will join, that is my intention, I will do something. (*Kala, Interview 11*)

Distinct bifurcation of responsibilities was also a reason why teacher educators were not involved in the 'nature club' (the environmental group) operating within in the college. The Environmental Education specialist was seen as being in-charge of the club and other teacher educators had their own clubs to take care of.

No it is only for them [names the teacher and students]. I am having [names a different club] [to run]. (*Kala, Interview 11*)

Another teacher educator who was involved in environmental activities because of being part of the Scouts mentioned the lack of 'scope' or opportunities to continue his involvement.

There are some experts in this area [environment] who involve themselves in many projects at the National level but at the local level activities comparatively are very less. There should have been many clubs. The eco-clubs are at the institutional level [not at a community level]. (*Bhargava, Interview 9*)

As this data (above) shows, there was a lack of major involvement by any of the teacher educators in any environmental activities – although that outcome was as a consequence of various reasons. The next section looks at one of the possible reasons for teacher educators' lack of involvement in environmental education and related activities.

Knowledge about Environment and Environmental Education

Teachers' knowledge of the content is said to affect both what they teach and how they teach it. They are more likely to emphasise areas that they are more knowledgeable about and avoid areas where their content knowledge is limited (Grossman, 1995). As was seen earlier in this chapter these teacher educators predominantly relied on traditional forms of teaching in their practices. These methods included such things as the teacher as the 'receptacle' of knowledge to be transmitted to the students. In the following section I asked these teacher educators to assess their 'formal' knowledge of the environment and environmental education. In order to do this, I asked them to rate themselves on a scale of 1–10 on their knowledge about the environment and environmental education. Except for one of the teacher educators, they all rated their knowledge about the environment at 5 or above. They felt that although they held sufficient knowledge they were still learning and had a long way to go.

> I would be in the middle, because I have many things yet to learn about the environment and education, recent things that are happening. (*Kala, Interview 11*)

Five of the teacher educators rated their knowledge about Environmental Education at or below 5. They felt that although they had some knowledge about Environmental Education it was not sufficient. They mainly relied on books and periodicals to remain aware of major environmental issues in India and abroad.

Knowledge of environmental concepts and the knowledge about Environmental Education will help boost teacher educators' confidence in implementing EE. There is need to open up avenues for enhancing teacher educators' learning experiences.

Belief and Commitment to Teach Environmental Education

> What teachers believe, and what teachers do in the classroom ultimately shapes the kind of learning experiences that young people get. (Hart, 2003, p. 18)

The next aspect of this exploration of the participants' views was to determine whether or not they held a special belief or commitment to teach environmental education in an attempt to see if they had any explicit links between their views and their perceived role as an environmental educator.

All the teacher educators felt that there was a need for a special belief and conviction in order to be able to teach environmental education. They felt that only if an individual had that belief, only if he/she loved the environment and nature, could they teach it in their classrooms as teachers or teacher educators.

> Basically a person must love nature otherwise he cannot teach Environmental Education. So that belief he must possess. (*Poornima, Interview 4*)

The right attitude was also seen as necessary.

> Yes, attitude is of course needed because if you love nature then you can teach it. (*Leena, Interview 8*)

A strong commitment and clear 'idea' about the issues was also seen as vital.

> Really he should have commitment otherwise the person who is teaching the subject is preaching the subject, if he doesn't have commitment there is no point you see – it has to come from his heart. (*Arya, Interview 6*)

> A strong commitment is needed to teach Environmental Education. And another thing is that teachers sometimes go by their weakness. That should not

be there, the teacher should have a clear-cut idea regarding the issues. (*Nammy, Interview 3*)

Education alone was considered insufficient for environmental consciousness; there required a more deep-seated reasoning.

It has nothing to do with your graduation [education], nothing to do with your educational background. What we call 'Tulitha' – it means it has to come from your heart, that I want to do something about the environment- that has to be there. (*Blue, Interview 10*)

Teaching about the environment as a subject entailed not just a commitment but also a love and devotion to the subject.

I personally believe that you should have a commitment ... first you must love the subject and then you must have the commitment, then only you will have the fervour to teach otherwise it is just transmission of information. Because only if the teacher is interested in Environmental Education or creating environmental consciousness he teaches sincerely and tries to organise a number of activities ... otherwise if is just confined to classroom teaching. (*Anjalie, Interview 1*)

Teaching not preaching was emphasised, which meant that there was a need to model the environmental philosophies being prophesied – some found that to be problematic.

Simply for the sake of Environmental Education, because everybody is telling that teacher will also be telling something about the environment. If he doesn't keep the environment well, if he is not following the rule and regulations then what is the use? (*Arya, Interview 6*)

Yes because we see so many things [issues] about the environment but practically it is difficult to teach all that. When I was teaching environmental education I was facing this problem. I would say if you use vehicles it causes pollution but personally I would come to college in a vehicle. We say plastics should not be used but sometimes I have to use it – so that way it became a bit contradictory. (*Axmi, Interview 5)*

Technical knowledge about the environment or Environmental Education could not, according to Axmi, compensate for a lack of personal commitment.

Ok, we can give the knowledge [to the students] but practically again there are contradictions if we don't have that commitment. (*Axmi, Interview 5)*

The 'environment' was seen by one teacher educator as situated in 'nature' or outdoors, consequently people who were not fit physically were deemed unfit to 'do' Environmental Education no matter. This quote goes on the exemplify the misconceptions and demarcation of EE that exists.

And you have to be physically fit to do that [Environmental Education]. If you are a sick person and you cannot trek, you cannot go outside and find out what is happening there, then again you cannot do it. (*Blue, Interview 10*)

All the teacher educators then felt strongly about the need for a particular belief and commitment to teach Environmental Education, as exemplified by Medha.

One who doesn't have it [belief/commitment] cannot teach it. (*Medha, Interview 2*)

The Influence of Personal Beliefs and Culture

Teacher actions … have a historical embeddedness in personal experiences as well as sociocultural practices in which the deeper values are implicated … Teachers actions occurs within a historical as well as sociocultural context and only the growing consciousness of both may enable them to overcome some of their determinants and understand the personal as well as the wider social practices by which teachers intentions are made intelligible. (Hart, 2003, p. 4)

In this section of the chapter, the cultural influences on teacher educators' views and teaching specifically of environmental education are examined in detail. The literature review (Chapter 2) elaborated on the cultural diversity of India. Even within regions and subregions there is a range of diverse cultures and traditions to be found. India is also still a very spiritual nation with spiritual and religious practices deeply embedded in daily practices. It is a land of thousands of cultures defined by the land, its geography, its plants and languages; superseding narrow sectarian divisions of fundamentalist practices (Shiva, 2005). This is also seen at this particular teachers college where classes in the morning start with morning prayers. All the student teachers stand and say their prayers led by the teacher educator; they then greet their teacher before they sit for the class. Every period when the next teacher educator comes in, the students stand and greet the teacher and sit only once the teacher has asked them to do so (P.O.). These practices stem from the deep-seated beliefs about learning as sacred and teachers as revered and respected facilitators of learning. These age-old customs seem to be rapidly changing with 'modernisation', which has been ushered in by the liberalisation policies adopted from 1990 onwards. Teacher educators (all of whom were above 30 years of age) would have grown up in more traditional times and would likely be holding on to some of these older values. How teacher educators are woven into the social fabric of Indian society and how this influences their views and teaching of the environment is explored in this next section.

A major influence on these Teacher educators was their family

Yes, it is my family background, hereditary background that has shaped me. (*Blue, Interview 10*)

Mainly because in my family – my immediate family – my mother, father and siblings have a positive attitude about the environment, like we should not waste anything, that concern is there... and that has influenced me. (*Kala, Interview 11*)

Because we spend so much time with our family, we are bound to be influenced by our family. (*Kala, Interview 11*)

These teacher educators pointed out numerous family traditions and rituals they practiced which they also saw as environmental practices. These practices seemed have the biggest influence on them. Festivals, many of which are based on nature, are very popular in India. These revolve around celebrating seasons, animals or trees and although are celebrated for religious reasons carry a strong environmental message with it.

We celebrated a lot of festivals about nature, which made me love the environment. It influenced my habits, my nature, and dress manner, code of ethics. (*Chidambar, Interview 7*)

We have harvesting season [festival] – people coming ... new harvest is brought into the house and a 'pooja' [ritual] is performed, we have a feeling that we have wealth in the form of paddy grains... sometimes I feel that ours was a culture which gave preference to all things along with humans nature is also worshipped. Because we believe that this is the one, which is giving us bread and butter, so we have to respect nature. (*Anjalie, Interview 1*)

Worship of nature and natural elements as a source of life is a part of the cultural ethos of India. These teacher educators talked about its significance in their lives.

Because in our culture we pray to plants, we take fire, air, rain as God, so it has influenced me I would say. (*Axmi, Interview 5*)

We are glued to nature, Hindu religion is part of nature. For example Bhu pooja [worship of earth] and Nag pooja [worship of cobra snake] ... In front of our house we have a plant – Tulsi [Holy Basil]. We do pooja [ritual of praying] around it. (*Nammy, Interview 3*)

Our beliefs and faith has definitely enhanced our knowledge about the environment, even a kind of awareness and love and respect towards nature has been increased due to our own beliefs. For example, the nature worshipping belief ... that is because of the Vedic culture... centuries have passed but we are still following those principles in our society, they are the contributions of our Hindu society... even worshipping the river, worshipping the Gods who are responsible for the nature, for the rainfall, wind etc. – they are all the things that represent the effect that our Hindu culture and belief has upon the environment ... they have shaped my beliefs. (*Poornima, Interview 4*)

These beliefs were also seen as very important in saving the environment.

> We say God's live in those plants and we should not cut them down. In a way it is a belief [superstition] but in another way it can help in protecting and saving the environment. (*Axmi, Interview 5*)

Many of these beliefs are in fact practices acquired as a part of the daily rituals, which these teacher educators said they adopted without questioning as children. However, as adults they questioned these rituals and have figured out the 'scientific' reasoning behind them.

> Since childhood, in the morning as soon as I get up, we will take bath and go round [worship ritual] the Tulsi [Holy basil] plant, we have to water it. Even now everyday in the morning I do it before I come. First we used to do it mechanically ... afterwards we started to ask ... of course we worship trees as God's. God's live in some trees. Maybe the elders have given that idea because we should not cut the trees – that may be their intention but we were following it blindly. Later we come to know that trees give us a lot of Oxygen, preserve our atmosphere and the environment. (*Medha, Interview 2*)

The scriptures, especially the Vedas and Upanishads,[1] seemed to shape many of their beliefs.

> ...even in the Vedas and all – there is a strong connection to the environment. For example we see God in everything, we see God in animals, in plants and even in a stone. That means Hindu culture has always respected the environment. If you read the mythology of India, it covers all environmental issues we see today. (*Nammy, Interview 3*)

> ... the scriptures the Vedas, Upanishads, they speak highly of nature and they always say that nature is to be protected. According to the scriptures even a plant, flower or tree is God, it should be protected and it should not be hurt. (*Anjalie, Interview 1*)

However while teacher educators described specific scriptures, it was also felt that culture was not religion specific.

> It may not be religion, because culture means the way we are living and growing, so in that area there may be Hindu's, Muslim's, Christian's – anyone will be there. So society in which we are living – that influence will be there. (*Kala, Interview 11*)

Teacher educators like Bhargava saw themselves as an integral and inseparable from their cultural traditions.

> yes definitely, these are actually inseparable, it is very difficult for us to separate it ... definitely my culture has influenced me. (*Bhargava, Interview 9*)

It is evident that a range of beliefs influences teacher educators' environmental practices. To a large extent these beliefs are embedded in the customs and traditions of Indian society. These are beliefs they have been born into and are nurtured by their familial traditions. Teacher educators also reflected upon the secular nature of their environmental beliefs. If environmental education in India has to gain ground it would do well to work with these inherent practices. Plevyak (2001, p. 36) maintained, 'Successful implementation of Environmental Education includes teacher preparation and emphasis on attitudes.' Highlighting the environmental philosophies and attitudes associated with the Indian tradition will help further the cause of Environmental Education in India.

Loughran (2010, p. 214) states that,

> It is important to remind ourselves who we are and how we operate so that we can critically appraise our work.

It is clear from the data that these teacher educators held special childhood memories of experiencing the natural environment. Most of these experiences were part of their 'play' as children and not recollections of 'created' experiences. Excepting one, none of the other teacher educators described any deliberately planned experiences like family outings or camps. Their exposure to nature was often part of their upbringing and work. This included memories built while living/visiting villages where they had first hand experiences with nature. For those teacher educators who hailed from agrarian families – working on the farm was their closest experience with the natural environment. They felt that this experience had a major influence in shaping their relationship with the environment. However, when asked to recount particular experiences that influenced their beliefs about the environment they did not fall back on their childhood memories – instead they discussed their concerns about current environmental issues like the rampant use of plastics and increased pollution.

As established earlier in the chapter these teacher educators continued to rely on traditional methods of teaching. An important aspect of that practice is that formal knowledge is seen as vital and teachers as 'holders' of that knowledge. When asked to assess their own knowledge of the environment and environmental education most teacher educators rated themselves around 5 on a scale of 10 on their knowledge about the environment and still less on environmental education. Interestingly they commented on their need and willingness to learn more. This is in no way attempting to say that if teachers had more knowledge they would be better teachers or teacher educators or that they would then go on to solve all of the problems associated with environmental education. That would be a very simplistic approach. Instead this study is attempting to point out one of the many aspects of Environmental Education – the competency or lack thereof of teacher educators to teach Environmental Education which can also be attributed to their lack of content knowledge. While policy changes mandate and demand that teacher educators revolutionise their practices, the simple exaltation to change is clearly not sufficient.

While teacher educators were greatly concerned about current environmental issues (to be further discussed in the next Chapter) they were not currently involved in any major environmental activities or groups. The main reason for it was the lack of time as they saw this as a major commitment. A lack of opportunity for participation at both the college and community level was also seen as a major hindrance. There was a 'Nature Club' in the college, which was considered the main avenue for environmental activities (R. J.). However, time and syllabus constraints had severely hampered the Club's activities. The other teacher educators were not part of this club as they all had different 'clubs' and responsibilities. Another reason could be the fact that the Nature club was mainly seen as a 'cleaning' club with major activities including the 'cleaning' of the aquarium, the 'cleaning' of the college precincts and the 'maintenance' of the potted plants (*Blue, Interview 10 & Leena, Interview 8*). A dilemma faced by these teacher educators was also their lack of confidence that an individual can make a difference.

> These experiences make me think that unless we decide to change nothing can be done. And one person, an ordinary person doesn't have a voice, that also I know. (*Kala, Interview 11*)

All the teacher educators in this study deemed that a special commitment was needed to be able to teach environmental education. They were of the opinion that only environmental education needs to be taught 'from the heart' and there is need for a distinctive conviction to be able to do that. This reiterates Hart's (2003) findings that successful environmental educators have a particular fervour that motivates them to articulate these beliefs in their practice.

Beliefs held by teachers influences their practice and learning from professional education and teaching. Feiman-Nemser (2008, p. 698) contended that, 'without an opportunity to examine critically their existing beliefs in light of new possibilities and understandings, teachers may ignore or distort new ideas and practices.' Teacher educators' environmental beliefs are heavily influenced by the culture in which they are situated. They are embedded in their religion, traditions, rituals and practices. This is not surprising given the history of India and the nature of Indian society, which has to a large part been rooted in environmental philosophies. Indian society has learned 'the lessons of diversity from nature itself, as Indian civilisation is based on a cultural identity shaped by nature's diversity' (Shiva, 2005, p. 21).

India from within has always been named for the earth and its physical features namely its rivers, mountains, and ecosystems. Hindu – although now being used as a religious identity – was an earth identity and not a religious identity. As a geographical identity it encompassed all the other religions. India's cultural distinction stems from the idea that life in the forest is the highest form of cultural evolution. This notion has perpetuated a civilisation that is in the most fundamental sense harmonious with nature. This harmony 'extends to India's unique concentration of spirituality, rather than a unified religion' (Shiva, 2005, p. 22).

These teacher educators reflected this identity to a large part by discussing the influence of their culture and 'religion' on their beliefs and hence their views about the environment. These beliefs were rooted in their practices of worshipping nature – for example the rituals around the Tulsi (Holy Basil). They sought (and in a sense tried to justify or find meaning) to find a scientific rationale for their beliefs and practices.

Loughran (2011, p. 284) asserts that, 'it is by learning through reflection that teaching about teaching can be informed and that teacher education itself can be seen as moving beyond a technical-rational or training approach to teacher education.' For these teacher educators, the interviews in this research project offered them a serious starting point for reflecting on their beliefs and other influences that shaped their identities and practices and, therefore, could arguably help enrich their ongoing environmental education experiences.

NOTE

[1]   Vedas and Upanishads are ancient texts which are the source of Hinduism and heavily influence Indian culture.

UNDERSTANDINGS ABOUT THE ENVIRONMENT AND TEACHER EDUCATORS' ECOLOGICAL IDENTITIES

Clearly teachers are people who bring themselves into the classroom and the formation of their identities involves an interplay between external and internal forces. (Rodgers & Scott, 2008, p. 732)

INTRODUCTION

Orr (1992) espoused the rise of an ecologically literate and ecologically competent citizenry who understand global issues, but who also know how to live well in their places. According to Orr, 'unless we learn how to manage problems of global security, sustainability anywhere for any length of time will be moot' (p. 2). Education has been seen as having a major role to play in helping develop an ecologically literate and competent citizenry. If that is accepted as being the case, then it is imperative to study teachers' and teacher educators' understanding of the environment, their ecological philosophies and identities and also their attitudes towards the environment. In so doing, the results should shed light on how teacher educators interpret and make sense of their environmental experiences and how this influences their practice. This theme attempts to examine these critical issues. It elaborates on teacher educators' understanding of the term 'environment' and their 'feelings' about the environment as also garners their opinion about global, local and national environmental issues. This final section explores participating teacher educators' environmental or eco-identities. Data is drawn from interviews (see Chapter 4) in which participating teacher educators responded to statements about their environmental philosophies (see Appendix 2).

Understanding and Defining the Term 'Environment'

Part of the problem [in the field of environmental education] may lie in definitions. (Smyth, 2008, p. 2)

Often there is an ambiguity in defining or understanding the term 'environment' (Smyth, 2008). It is reasonable to suggest that an individual's definition of the environment or what they understand by the term environment can shed light on their ecological viewpoints. People often define the environment as green, as something that is out there (often somewhere far away) which needs to be experienced. It is then something that is 'secondary to what it surrounds, and less important, even although we depend on it totally, every moment of our lives, and continually change it just by living' (Smyth, 2008, p. 2).

For many of the teacher educators' understandings of the environment were mainly limited to their immediate surroundings.

> Environment is something, which we live in; anything that is in my surrounding where I live becomes my environment. (*Kala, Interview 11*)

> Everything, what I can see if I just look around is the environment. (*Bhargava, Interview 9*)

> It is nothing but the surrounding, the atmosphere or the area where we live which will influence our day-to-day activities. (*Medha, Interview 2*)

Throughout the interviews, teacher educators often used the term 'environment' as a synonym for the word 'nature'. They did not provide a more sophisticated or a more rounded view of the environment despite the cultural richness that they carry as seen earlier.

> When I hear the term environment I think that the picture that comes to me is a very clean beautiful green nature filled with greenery, fresh air, and large number of animals. (*Axmi, Interview 5*)

> Environment means the surroundings in which we are living. For example it included all the plants, animals, the weather, water, air – everything in the surroundings, the place in which we are living in. (*Nammy, Interview 3*)

> According to me environment is an all-comprehensive broader term ... [which includes] the association between nature and man. (*Anjalie, Interview 1*)

Some though carried different connotations pertaining to their definitions. For example:

> ... it includes all the plants, animals, weather, water, air – everything in the surroundings, the place in which we are living in. It also involved human environment if there is one such word – which means the people with whom we are interacting. Human environment is also very important aspect of environment. (*Nammy, Interview 3*)

> When I say environment it is political, cultural, geographical, ecological, economical, social – all put together form the environment. (*Anjalie, Interview 1*)

> What I feel is that it [the environment] is not manmade, it is natural. And environment according to me is really a big house; if you are adjusting with the environment you will be very comfortable. (*Blue, Interview 10*)

Overall then these teacher educators primarily saw the environment as their immediate local surroundings with some extending this definition to include other elements – particularly those of direct human influence. They however did not yet mention anything about the interconnectedness of the different systems or the complex links that exist. These teacher educators' understanding of the term was then on a basic or elementary level.

Feelings about the Environment

Feelings and concepts according to Thomashow (1996) are intricately related. He argues that memories and life experiences are dynamically related to the profound intellectual concepts of environmentalism and serve to validate them. Feelings about the environment are based on these memories and experiences and can be seen as the breeding ground for environmental activism. This section of the chapter probes the teacher educators' feelings about the environment.

The predominant feeling amongst the teacher educators was one of concern about the state of the environment as is exemplified by the following quote.

TE: Definitely problems are there in the environment, day by day it is increasing, the pollution have been increased in various forms in different ways. Day by day it [the environment] is getting polluted.

Researcher: How does that make you feel?

TE: Worried. (*Poornima, Interview 4*)

TE: Sometimes I feel very bad and I don't know what is going to happen in the future. (*Arya, Interview 6*)

Overall, the interviews illustrated that these teacher educators felt anxious about the current state of affairs.

And nowadays this environment is corrupted. Every environment whether it is the natural environment, the political or the educational environment has been corrupted. (*Leena, Interview 8*)

In the view of the interviewees, this corruption extended to the way things were being handled by concerned authorities.

Yeah environmental problems today are many ... many companies are coming to India and they are luring people by giving them money. They catch hold of government officials and they break the rules with muscle power and the common man is put to a lot of hardship today and unfortunately the common man is not able to create an organisation, unit and fight, that is the problem everywhere. (*Anjalie, Interview 1*)

There was a sense of ownership about the state of the environment. Teacher educators felt that they had a part to play in the deterioration of the environment. Some of them felt that it was easier to preach than to practice environmentally friendly practices [Axmi, Interview 5]; others felt that environmentally friendly practices were a tougher option to choose [Nammy, Interview 3]. One of the teacher educators for example felt that every natural calamity was in some way caused by human action and could be used as an opportunity to increase awareness.

> What I feel is that what is happening in and around me is because of our doing. So whenever we get any natural hazards or anything for example I feel it is good because at least from that we learn a lesson. That is what I feel... I don't blame the environmental hazards when it happens, when we get harmed, maybe it is negative thinking. I don't feel the way I think is wrong, because what we have done, we are getting repaid for that from nature. With the environment I feel if you don't conserve we will only have to face it and we can't say it is somebody else's fault. (*Kala, Interview 11*)

One of the main contributing factors towards the rapidly deteriorating environmental conditions was seen as increasing self-centredness. Teacher educators felt that current lifestyles that encourage spending, the over commercialisation of society and increased consumerism had created a life style that did not promote care and concern towards others.

> Unfortunately we have not understood the significance of the environment, many a times we disturb the environment, we destroy the environment and we come in the way of others also who are protecting the environment. That is what I feel ... most people are selfish, they want to get everything from the environment, they get maximum from the environment but they give back the least to the environment because they are selfish. (*Bhargava, Interview 9*)

It also meant that every individual was concerned only about his/her well being without a thought to others. When thinking of ourselves it is difficult to think of our neighbours – human or otherwise or of the environment – as is demonstrated by Nammy's response.

> And sometimes what happens is that people are selfish I feel. There is very less awareness about the environment about keeping the surroundings neat and clean. We clean our house and throw the rubbish somewhere else. (*Nammy, Interview 3*)

Teacher educators also perceived a lack of 'voice' for the average citizen as another major hurdle in environmental action.

> They [the average citizens] don't have a voice, hardly one or two rise up to fight ... [goes on to describe a current local issue] ... but there is a ray of hope in Medha Patkar and Arundhati Roy who take up the issue and fight. (*Anjalie, Interview 1*)

Some of them then tried to find a place, an area where they could retreat to in order to experience their 'pristine' or 'unsullied' environment; where they could get away – to the 'perfect' environment.

TE: I see now it is totally different from what concept I have related to the environment.

R: How does this make you feel?

TE: I feel ... sad in a way. But sometimes when I am free I try to go to places where I can find those places where I can find good, beautiful nature and clean environment. (*Axmi, Interview 5*)

These teacher educators felt the need to prioritise environmental awareness in order to improve the standard of living. This is a technocentric approach towards the environment, where the environment needs to be preserved and taken care of so that it better serves humans. The environment then is not valued for its own sake but more so that it can better provide for us. Here it is seen as a resource that would make life 'easy' and that is where its importance lies.

It [the environment] is very important and it should be given top priority, only when there is food environment life will be safe, life will be easy. (*Bhargava, Interview 9*)

Education was seen as the primary avenue for raising this awareness. Teacher educators directly and indirectly attributed education (or a lack of it) as the main factor in increasing environmental consciousness. Teacher educators felt that education improved understanding about environmental issues, which in turn led to more environmentally friendly practices.

My opinion is that students should be educated from the primary level to take care of the environment. This is most important ... students can be trained properly to maintain the cleanliness in the environment especially encouraging them to grow trees. That is most important. Proper education should be given and environmental education should be made as one of the subjects [compulsory] from the primary level. (*Medha, Interview 2*)

Today there is a lack of concern about the environment in my pupils ... our education contribution is less. (*Chidambar, Interview 7*)

In this area we don't say that [environmental degradation is high] because here literacy is good, education is good, they [people] won't destroy the environment even if it is not possible for them to preserve it or improve it – they won't destroy it. (*Bhargava, Interview 9*)

Education was promoted not only as a means of raising awareness but also as a means of rising above the current highly commercialised lifestyles. These teacher educators felt there was a need for EE to move beyond mere lip service.

> But today there is a lack of concern about the environment in my pupils, they are more commercialised, easy going life, use and throw culture. Only commercial, material benefits, out education contribution is less – we only use platform language; we will talk about environment all the time but basically in his house he is never interested in that matter. (*Chidambar, Interview 7*)

While discussing their feelings two of the teacher educators expressed strong sentiments in support of sustainable development.

> We have to improve the standard of living of the people for which what is required – economic development. So when there is higher rate of growth there will be higher standard of living ... somewhere we need to strike a balance between development and ecology. So for the development sake we must not sacrifice the environment. So the challenge of the hour is protecting the environment without sacrificing growth, which is the concept of Sustainable Development. (*Nammy, Interview 3*)

> There must be balance between modernisation and protection of the environment. Alternative resources must be tapped; alternative measures must be taken without causing much harm to the public. These industries should come up ... this is Sustainable Development. (*Anjalie, Interview 1*)

Overall then, these teacher educators' feelings illustrated a sense of concern while also being seen as an avenue to raise awareness and curb environmental degradation. They also seemed to pin their hopes on the concept of sustainable development (which is discussed further in the last section of this chapter).

State of the Local, National and Global Environment

> If today is a typical day on planet earth, we will lose 116 square miles of rain forest, or about an acre a second. We will lose another 72 square miles to encroaching deserts, the results of human mismanagement and overpopulation. We will lose 40–250 species; and no one knows whether the number is 40 or 250. Today the human population will increase by 250,000. And today we will add 2,700 tons of chlorofluorocarbons and 15 tons of carbon dioxide to the atmosphere. Tonight the earth will be a little hotter, its waters more acidic, and the fabric of life more threadbare. (Orr, 2004, p. 7)

Environmental problems both on a global and national level are rising steeply (as discussed in detail in the literature review in Chapter 2). This section of the chapter explores teacher educators' feelings about the state of the environment in their immediate surroundings, in India and the world. The purpose of this section of the chapter is to understand that which participants considered important environmental issues and what affected them personally.

All of the teacher educators described the profound affect that a recent issue had on them. The teacher education institute where this study was conducted is situated in a small town. It lies on the main highway connecting two important and larger cities. Earlier a single lane highway linked these two cities – which had been operational for a long time. However, with the growing population and increased traffic flows it was now inadequate. Recently a new wider highway had been constructed to replace the old one. To construct this new highway hundreds of trees lining both sides of the road had to be cut down (R.J.). These were fully grown old trees, which according to one of the teacher educators were nearly a century old.

> … my father used to tell that these trees were planted more than 100 years ago, when he was small he has seen them. (*Medha, Interview 2*)

There was a strong sense of loss amongst the teacher educators when these trees were cut down in particular because there was no effort made to replace them.

> Like our city here is growing, they are cutting so many trees in the name of making roads. Of course that is also important but no importance is being given to planting them again. (*Axmi, Interview 5*)

> We believe even today that we have to protect the environment, if we cut trees we have to grow them and again it is not simple planting, we have to look after it – that is important. (*Bhargava, Interview 9*)

Cutting of these trees was seen to have had a direct and almost immediate effect on the climate of the area.

> Now all the trees are cut and because of that within one year we can see the rise in temperature. At night the temperature is more that 30–40 degrees, we have never had this experience before … everyone even my neighbours tell – it is not my only my opinion, that all this because all the trees are cut and because of that the temperature is more this year. (*Medha, Interview 2*)

> In another one-year's time the temperature in this part of the country will be very high because of the felling of the trees. Already we are experiencing; if you go from [X] to [Y] in the hot summer you will experience the blister of the summer. Earlier it was not the case because of the trees on both sides of the road, so life here will be unbearable shortly … this summer was the highest temperature ever in 2010. (*Anjalie, Interview 1*)

The felling of all these trees seemed to have impacted all the teacher educators. They felt it was a very significant event that had recently unfolded and that affected them, their family and their friends. Yet while all talked about how the tree cutting made them sad, they also lamented the absence of any opposition or struggle. Most importantly teacher educators felt that there were not enough protests or resistance to these actions. However none of them looked internally to the kind of protests or actions they could have taken. As teacher educators and leaders of the community they could have initiated some of these protests, however they did not seem to have felt empowered enough to do this. They seemed to be looking for leadership from outside as illustrated by Anjalie's [Interview 1] comment on the need for more Medha Patkar and Arundhati Roy's or Axmi's [Interview 5] comments on the need for more governmental bodies and NGO's.

> Nearly 300 trees were felled ... there was not a single protest from the general public, maybe through newspapers, through general forums or maybe by way of agitation, not even a single thing happened [here] which is supposed to be highly educated and literate districts in India. So I am afraid – what is the impact of these things. (*Anjalie, Interview 1*)

This goes back to the feeling that an individual or average citizen does not have the power or the voice to change. This was expressed by Anjalie and also by Kala who felt:

> Unless we decide to change nothing can be done. And one person, an ordinary person doesn't have a voice. (*Kala, Interview 11*)

Environmental problems have been rising rapidly in India and on a global scale as has been established in the literature review in Chapter 2. This small town does not seem to have remained unaffected by these global changes. These teacher educators felt that their town was far more polluted and far less green due to the rapid industrialisation, increase in population and heightened development in recent times. (This place is now one of India's leading educational towns and also has a large number of industries around it, which has led to rampant deforestation and pollution.)

> Now it has become all man-made [artificial] ... I say it was a beautiful forest before, not just forest we had hills, valleys. (*Blue, Interview 10*)

> At that time this place is just like a forest. (*Chidambar, Interview 7*)

They recounted some environmental issues in their immediate surroundings. Blue for example talked about a place nearby where:

> You find 100–200 acres of land with bamboo trees- everything has died [because of the construction of a dam nearby which has cut off the water supply]. These bamboos cannot be planted, it is natural – everything, you can travel just 2 hours from here and see – everything is dead. (*Blue, Interview 10*)

There seemed to have been many environmental issues that directly affect the quality of these teacher educators lives. The nearby river was heavily polluted and choking with garbage (particularly plastic). There were streets with overflowing garbage bins and vehicular pollution was rampant, Arya expressed sadness at this increasing pollution of nearby places.

> The lakes, the rivers, even the streets – if you just look at the roadside. Even in the K [nearby river] formerly it has pure water flowing through it but now it is all dirty and waste water. It ultimately joins the sea but is now giving very bad smell. 20–25 years back it was having very good clean water. Even the people throw plastics and other waste materials in that river. (*Arya, Interview 6*)

Health and sanitation were seen as important aspects of the environmental issues. Lack of an ability to keep the surroundings clean was then a pressing problem. It was also seen as a problem at the grassroots level which could be solved with some basic intervention. Even simple solutions like not spitting on the streets and disposing of garbage carefully would bring about big changes according to these teacher educators. In Kala's words:

> So basically I am saying that we have to do it [keep our surroundings clean] on our own. I am not saying that we have to pick up paper on the road but I normally try not to contribute by adding to it. But what I feel very angry about is that people don't look if somebody is there behind you or not, they just spit out. (*Kala, Interview 11*)

One of the examples provided by Medha sheds further light on this.

> Of course here sometimes you can see, when there is a big crowd like big celebration is being held then you can see people throwing plastic and paper pieces here and there on the road. That day I saw a procession was going in front of my house and one lady supplied juice to all the people who were participating in the procession. They all drank the juice and just threw all the containers on the road. It was there till 2 days. It is all because people are not aware; they are just polluting the surroundings. (*Medha, Interview 2*)

So while the crowds enjoyed the cold drink there was no concern about disposing of the garbage in a proper manner. In the same light, while the organiser provided the drinks, he/she did not make any arrangements to encourage the crowds to properly dispose of the containers. It is changes at this basic level that are urgently needed to bring about an attitudinal rethinking amongst the general citizens in India. Education is then a big source of hope to help bring about these changes. The following example provided by Nammy reports similar feelings of frustration with people's inability to maintain cleanliness.

> Yeah … there is very less awareness about the environment, about keeping our surroundings neat and clean. And sometimes what happens is that people are more selfish I feel. We clean our house and throw the rubbish somewhere else … I have near my gate people who just throw packets of rubbish and go. They

have their eatables and stuff and just litter the packets. The awareness is not there that we have to throw it in a dustbin and it has to be disposed of. There are special places where it can be disposed, the roadside is not the place but people simply throw and go; the habit formation. (*Nammy, Interview 3*)

Nammy sees a need to bring about a change in the habits that have been formed amongst people. Education and a realisation of how small habit changes could help the environment could help make a difference. The use of plastics is one such habit. In my personal experience in India people often understand that plastics are harmful to the environment but use them more as a habit. If provided with alternatives and strict regulations, the habit of using plastics could easily be reversed. Axmi expressed the rampant use of plastics and other non-biodegradable substances as a serious concern to the local environment and called for strict governmental action.

I feel that the people are not very environmentally conscious and even the government, the municipality do not take much care about the environmental aspects. Restrictions on the use of plastic or waste management of biodegradable and non-biodegradable matter are not there. (*Axmi, Interview 5*)

A specific trend towards modernisation and increased development was also identified as a possible reason for environmental problems on not just a local but also national and global scale. This again meant a disconnection with traditional practices.

This year was especially hot because of the concretisation work and everywhere people want glamour, nobody wants their legs to be in the mud, everybody wants concrete, tiles and granites, marble. Nobody wants a dirty place – they call dirty place. Mud is not a dirty thing according to me. (*Blue, Interview 10*)

This adoption of modernisation often came at the cost of more eco-friendly options. The environmentally friendly options were not necessarily more expensive to adopt but were less in line with the modern outlook as is exemplified by the following comment.

Gobar gas [fuel made using cow dung which is easily available to farmers in India who still use cows/bulls] if you came from an agrarian family is better but now people have gone for electricity, instead of electric geysers people now have gas geysers, although that is also more expensive. (*Anjalie, Interview 1*)

How or what gives shape to these 'modern' outlooks is difficult to determine but post colonial influences can be attributed to play a significant role. These influences and needs for a modernised life seem to hold much more ground in large urban areas. Teacher educators felt that the environmental problems were more rampant in larger cities.

Recently I had to go to X [a major metro in India]. Nearly 15–20 years back also I had visited X many times. But this time I identified lots of differences in connection with the environment. In those days there were trees everywhere, wherever we used to go we used to observe so many trees, but that is not the case anymore. Because of the developmental activities also sometimes the environment has to be neglected ... our city is still a growing city, in this locality we cannot identify so many differences [changes]. But whenever we go to the main roads, the centres of the cities definitely we see that a number of trees have been cut off. (*Poornima, Interview 4*)

In our district [locality] there is a little bit of concern but in other metropolitan cities like Delhi, Calcutta, and Bangalore – these are highly polluted areas. (*Chidambar, Interview 7*)

Here it [environmental degradation] is also there but compared to other districts [in the state] we are far better, we are little more aware. (*Nammy, Interview 2*)

Some of the teacher educators, like Arya, felt that often there was greater emphasis on publicity rather than actual effort in undertaking environmental action. This means that while often there is concern expressed it does not translate into any kind of initiative or deeds. An earlier example seen was the lack of protest against the felling of hundreds of trees despite this being cited as a major cause of concern by all the teacher educators. Arya sees this emphasis in mere talking rather than on real action as concerning.

We are not giving much attention or importance to the environment even though everybody is preaching but nobody is practising. That is the problem in the media, even the newspapers, television, even the resource persons. Of course the preaching is also necessary to give publicity but still things are not happening well. (*Arya, Interview 6*)

These teacher educators felt that education was the key ingredient that caused this difference as has been discussed in the earlier section. They expressed hope in education for alleviating environmental problems. This placed huge onus on education and educators and focused more on learning 'about' the environment in order to take care of its problems. There is also the clear danger of building ecophobia. According to Sobel (1995) this presents a clear danger of making young people distant and disconnected with the environment. Teaching children about the horrors of what could happen to the environment does not motivate them to save it. Sobel (1995) also advocates a living relationship to flourish with the environment before future generations are asked to work towards rescuing it. Teacher educators expectation of education as the saving tool and children as the 'saviours' of the environment can then be highly misplaced.

In this area we don't say that [the environmental situation is very bad] because here literacy is good, education is good, they [people] wont destroy it. (*Bhargava, Interview 9*)

93

> In some places like [the one we live in] good care is taken towards education in primary and other education. But in most of the places in North India in the remote areas no proper importance is given for education, for educating the children. (*Medha, Interview 2*)

The general consensus then was that while there were many environmental concerns in their immediate surroundings, teacher educators felt that the situation was much better when compared to most other parts of India. However, they were concerned that the situation was rapidly changing and there was an urgent need to work towards stemming this deterioration. Education they felt had given them the edge over other places and they placed hopes in education to increase public awareness about the environmental situation.

Teacher Educators' Ecological Identities

The next section of the chapter explores participants' ecological identities. Hart (2003, p. 156) contends that understanding teachers (and thereby teacher educators') EE practices should be based on 'knowledge of them as people, knowledge of their working lives and their thinking about children, about the purposes of education, and about the future. In light of the above statement understanding teacher educators ecological identities is vital in understanding their environmental practices given that 'people take action, or formulate their personality based on their ecological worldview' (Thomashow, 1996, p. 4). Teacher educators personality, their values, actions and their sense of self helps construe their eco identities, their life experiences shape them and their connections to the earth form the basis of these identities (Thomashow, 1996). As explained in Chapter 3, understanding teacher educators' ecological identities will help interpret their actions and their motivations, the factors that enable or constraint them from implementing EE. Each person's path to ecological identity will be different and reflective of his or her 'cognitive, intuitive and affective perceptions of ecological relationships' (Thomashow, 1996, p. 5).

Ecological identities can range from the technocentric or anthropocentric views to ecocentric views. 'Human centeredness' is the central ideology of a technocentric approach. It encompasses views such as technological optimism – where technology and research are expected to help 'manage' all unintended negative consequences. Another technocentric view is 'atomism' where nature is seen as a separate entity made of several building blocks. Anthropocentrism sees humans as of sole value and meaning in the world, and all nonhuman nature is there for no purpose but to serve mankind (Eckersley, 1992, p. 51). On the other hand ecology-centred perspectives influence the eco-centric views. Ecocentrism recognises 'the interrelatedness of all phenomena together with its prima facie orientation of inclusiveness of all beings' and 'is far more protective of the Earth's life-support system than an anthropocentric perspective' (Eckersley, 1992, p. 52).

An ecocentric perspective values the environment for its own sake not for satisfying any current or future human needs (Cutter-Mackenzie, 2009).

Thomashow (1996, p. xiii) refers to ecological identities as 'how people perceive themselves in reference to nature, as living and breathing beings connected to the rhythms of the earth, the biogeochemical cycles, the grand and complex diversity of ecological systems.' Ecological identities as conceptualised by Zavestoski (2003, p. 299) are 'that part of the self that allow individuals to anticipate the reaction of the environment to their behaviour.' These ecological identities that individuals carry eventually lead to how they perceive and then implement EE. Reflecting on one's own commitment and views about environmentalism provides an opportunity for introspection.

As detailed in questionnaire (See Appendix 2), participants responded to a series of statements and the diversity of views helped to bring out their perspectives. The statements were used as an organisational and presentation framework designed to help better understand the nature of their responses and what that might mean for their identities. A quick review of the four statements presented to teacher educators:

- Statement 1: The environment is a resource to be used by human beings
- Statement 2: Economic growth should and must continue, even if it results in damage to the environment
- Statement 3: The environment should be protected, even if it results in a reduction in economic growth
- Statement 4: The environment should be preserved and protected no matter what the cost

With the exception of one participant, all of the other teacher educators agreed that the environment was a resource to be used. These responses are indicative of a more anthropocentric view where the environment is considered to be a resource to be used. Overtly this could be considered a tilt towards ecocentric views as it does consider the preserving the environment and living in harmony with nature. However the view that the environment is a resource does fall within the precincts of a technocentric view whereby the only reason one has to preserve the environment is so that future generations can use it. This approach reeks of self-centeredness and human superiority over every other thing. It is important to understand what drives these teacher educators to consider judicious use of the environment.

Again with the exception of one, all the teacher educators also felt that economic growth has to continue, as it is the only way to alleviate poverty. All of them showed a clear understanding that often, economic growth does come at a cost to the environment and that it is a tough balance to maintain.

The following quotes exemplify this stance

I disagree with it … [takes a long pause] … our environment is very important not economic growth (*Chidambar, Interview 7*)

95

No economic growth should not damage the environment, it [the economy] should grow but without disturbing the environment. (*Medha, Interview 2*)

Economic growth can continue but not by compromising the environment. (*Kala, Interview 11*)

It should be balance – both economic growth as well as environmental aspects … I think some ways and means can be thought about through which at least some damage can be reduced. (*Axmi, Interview 5*)

Interestingly, participants did concede that economic growth is not always possible without causing environmental disturbances.

There should not [be] much harm to the environment; of course little bit [of] harm will be there but not much. (*Poornima, Interview 4*)

The above responses indicate that while most teacher educators agreed that the environment was a resource they do not advocate rampant use of this resource to foster economic development. This is interesting in a country like India, which has been galloping forward in terms of economic development and is currently the second fastest growing economy in the world. On the one hand teacher educators seem to have a need to be a part of this growing economy, they see the economic development as a means to raise the standard of living for a billion Indians, as an avenue to overcome poverty. On the other hand they realise that this kind of unplanned, explosive growth is teamed with profound environmental changes. Placing their faith in scientific and technological breakthroughs to overcome these problems, investing money in coming up with these breakthroughs all seemed to be a rather simplistic approach to the future.

As indicated by their response to statement 3 the teacher educators would not vouch for protection of the environment over economic growth. None of them agreed with the fourth statement that sought protection of environment at all costs.

This clearly highlights, the ecological identities that these teacher educators portray appears to be based largely on technocentric or anthropocentric viewpoints. They all believe that the environment is a resource that needs to be used; albeit judiciously. This judicious use stems from the need to preserve the environment for as long as is possible so that future generations can continue to benefit from it. All of these teacher educators endorsed the idea of sustainable development, which according to them meant that while economic development continues to progress, environmental problems are also minimised.

Overall this chapter illustrates that these teacher educators had a very broad and all-encompassing understanding of the environment. This understanding was heavily influenced by their everyday lives, their family heritage and cultural backgrounds. They saw their immediate surroundings as their environment but their views also included the larger national and global scenario. For many of them the term environment was synonymous with nature, the natural or the outdoor environment.

However, some also saw their homes, neighbourhoods and places they lived in as their environment. This was especially true when discussing the need for health and sanitation and the importance of keeping their 'environment' clean.

These teacher educators were concerned and worried about the state of the environment. This was evident in them feeling anxious and helpless in bringing about any change. They felt that as ordinary citizens they lacked the voice and power to bring about any radical changes.

Interestingly, they were of the view that while they were teaching about environmentally friendly practices they were not necessarily able to follow these practices themselves – for example using plastics and driving to work rather than walking or using public transport. This made them feel at odds with their own teaching – they felt that they were preaching rather than teaching environmentally friendly practices they were, as Whitehead (1993) explained it, they were Living Contradictions. These teacher educators felt that a lack of prioritisation and poor education abetted a lack of environmental consciousness and over commercialised lifestyles added to the problem.

Heightened environmental problems, particularly in their immediate surroundings, were a major cause of concern. These teacher educators were particularly distressed about the felling of hundreds of trees for the reconstruction of a major highway. While they supported the modernisation efforts they felt that often a lot of harm was done in the process. They also saw a lack of hygiene and cleanliness as a major environmental concern. Actions like improper garbage disposal – especially of plastic bags, littering, spitting – added to the environmental problems in not only their area but all over India. While they felt that environmental problems had been on the rise in their surroundings these were far worse in larger metropolitan cities. They felt they had been shielded to some extent but that development was quickly catching up. Overall these teacher educators felt that the situation was fast changing and education was the key to creating environmental awareness.

Teacher educators' ecological identities were generally tilted towards being technocentric or anthropocentric. Most of the teacher educators held the view that development was necessary and could not be slowed down. Economic progress was seen as the way to lift India and Indians out of poverty. There was however general consensus that economic development does not have to come at the cost of the environment. These teacher educators felt that the environmental resources needed to be better-managed and developmental projects better planned to minimise environmental damage. The environment was widely seen as a resource to be used (and in a few cases shared) by all. None of these teacher educators appeared to carry ecocentric views – taking care of the environment for its own sake.

The Brundtland Report (World Commission on Environment and Development, 1987, p. 43) defined Sustainable Development (as outlined in Chapter 2 there is no uniformly accepted definition of the term Sustainable Development, this is the most widely used one) as 'development that meets the needs of the present without compromising the ability of future generations to meet their needs'. There was also 'technological optimism' in the ability of science and technology to help find solutions for all environmental problems. Most of these teacher educators, while concerned about the environment, were not keen on relegating human economic progress to a lower priority for the sake of the environment. There were constant calls to plan better, to look for scientific solutions, to upgrade technology so that economic development continue unhindered. (This goes against the grain of Indian culture, values and traditions as discussed in Chapter 6. Old traditions and cultures in India tend to have a more ecocentric approach whereby the nonhuman world is not seen as the background or means to fulfil human need (Eckersley, 1992). So while these teacher educators claimed a strong influence of their cultures on their belief systems it does not seem to have influenced their ecological identities.)

There seemed to be a lack of sophistication in teacher educators' understanding of the environment. Their understandings were limited to their immediate surroundings and immediate problems. There was a lack of far-sightedness when expressing their views and issues about the environment. So while they discussed with a lot of vigour the felling of trees, the dumping of garbage and the littering of streets, they failed to dwell on larger issues like rapid deforestation, loss of biodiversity and global warming.

Viewing EE merely as a means to stem environmental problems is a narrow approach, which can often dissuade students from relating to the environment (Sobel, 1996). A more holistic view of EE is the need of the hour. Instilling love for the environment and a vision of valuing the environment for its own sake will go a long way in creating a sense of ownership. This kind of approach would however require teacher educators to make a shift from thinking about the environment as a mere problem that needs fixing. Falling back on the environmentally sensitive cultural and traditional practices of India (which teacher educators highlighted in Chapter 6) would be a more rewarding approach to EE.

Teacher educators are held a high level of respect in the Indian culture. As highlighted in the literature review in Chapter 2, teacher educators are considered to be "guru's gurus" and are revered not only by their students but by society as a whole. Given this position teacher educators are in an ideal position to take up leadership roles in their communities. Instead of looking for other governmental, non-governmental and private bodies and individuals to provide this leadership, teacher educators could look to themselves to take responsibility, lead their students and communities in raising environmental consciousness. In that way they might lead a path to the future.

Just as Gonzalez-Gaudiano (2008) found, so too in this Indian teacher education context, it appears that of the three factors used to represent Sustainable Development namely economy, society and environment, the data in this chapter suggests that it is the economy that ultimately and overwhelmingly prevails. That creates quite a dilemma for teacher educators who might identify as being environmental educators.

SECTION 3

UNFOLDING THE PROFESSIONAL STORIES:
ABOUT EXTERNAL FACTORS/IMPACTS/BEARINGS

TEACHER EDUCATION AND ENVIRONMENTAL EDUCATION

It is evident from the earlier chapter that aspects of the participants' personal beliefs, their understandings, their identities are key influences of these on how teacher educators and how they determined, understood, negotiated and implemented EE. However for environmental education to be taken seriously the external professional stories are equally crucial. This chapter elaborates on these – external influences on teacher educators' professional personas including the organisational culture, curriculum, policy initiatives and the support systems in place to augment implementation of EE.

Education is of fundamental importance when aiming to create an environmentally educated citizenry (as outlined in detail through the literature review in Chapter 3). Including EE in pre-service teacher education programs has, in the past, proven to be challenging (Plevyak et al., 2001). Teachers have been hailed as 'unsung heroes' and are being looked upon as the hope for creating more sustainable societies (McKeown, 2002). The role Teacher Educators in building quality in teaching about teaching has also been well established. Their lasting influence on teachers' knowledge, their readiness to teach, their professional progression and lasting influence on their students' achievements has been well documented (Cochran-Smith, 2004). Teacher Education as a profession is believed to have four major partners (Shagrir, 2011, p. 56), namely: 'the student teachers, the body of knowledge, the teacher education institutions and the teacher educators'. The following chapters consider how these partners work together at the particular teacher education college, which was the site for this study.

Teaching in India typically relies heavily on the traditional model of 'chalk and talk' (Batra, 2005). Traditionally teacher educators are seen as experts who present knowledge to students who learn and reproduce that knowledge (mainly by rote memorisation) – especially during exams. Like teacher educators elsewhere in the world, those in India are mainly former classroom teachers who become teacher educators with little formal training and with very little ongoing professional support (in accord with that described by Berry, 2004).

In this chapter I begin by exploring the journey that the participants took in becoming teacher educators and their interests in choosing this profession. I also investigate their preparedness to teach EE. In order to do this I probe these teacher educators' education and examine the kind of educational support they received in their teaching of EE as part of their pre-service or in-service training. Teacher education in

EE has been identified as an area of concern in EE over the years (Disinger & Howe, 1990; McKeown-Ice, 2000; Powers, 2004). In fact McKeown-Ice (2000) identified teacher training in EE as the "weakest point" in EE. Therefore an examination of teacher educators' views about how pre-service teachers in their institution are being prepared to teach EE (and sustainability) and understand their perspectives clearly emerges as an issue important to this research project.

The aim of this chapter is to establish teacher educators' views of EE in relation to their perspectives on how EE and sustainability is prioritised in their curriculum and pedagogy. To do so, I investigate how teacher educators have kept pace with the changing times and the range of teaching strategies being used by them. I also examine how these teacher educators have been involved in teaching EE either directly or indirectly or through extra curricular activities.

TEACHING AS A PROFESSIONAL 'CHOICE'

I didn't have any dreams of becoming a teacher (*Anjalie, Interview 1*)

Except for one of the teacher educators, all of the others described themselves as having stumbled upon teaching or taken it up when they were presented with the opportunity rather than teaching being their first choice for a profession – as illustrated by the indicative quotes below:

There is a government college where I studied. There was a need for a teacher there. The managing member there was also my lecturer. He asked me why I couldn't join the school as a teacher. He said you are anyway sitting at home. So I thought I will do it while I am at home. (*Poornima, Interview 4*)

Actually I can say that it is more by chance than by choice. Because I had an ambition to do MSc Microbiology but the day I had a call for the interview my mother had to undergo an operation. I didn't have any option so I came here. (*Kala, Interview, 11*)

Actually I was a national sportsperson – I represented India … I lost my leg while I was doing the long jump, my leg was broken at the joints … my father then said never mind, you have to finish your BEd and you can help some children. So that's why this was my choice. (*Blue, Interview 10*)

I had applied for MA Economics. But at that time the university had just begun and there were no hostel facilities there. I had to stay somewhere and then come again to college. It was very expensive and economically it was not possible. So I dropped the idea of doing post-graduation and joined B Ed. (*Nammy, Interview 3*)

Because of my diploma in Kannada and B Sc, the headmaster sent a word to me to come and join [a school]. I worked there for nine months. Then I started evincing an interest in teaching … that made me join this college and that's how I became a teacher. (*Anjalie, Interview 1*)

There was a vacant post here and at that time the former principal asked me to come and work for a short period "until you get a better job." (*Arya, Interview 6*)

Given that this was not a profession of their choice it is not surprising then that most of the participants did not have much training for their roles as new teachers and teacher educators. Most of the participants' learning was reported to have happened as part of their jobs once they started teaching. They commented on how they fell in love with the profession once they started teaching.

Once I became a teacher I realised that there is a teacher in me. (*Anjalie, Interview 1*)

Indian traditions hold teachers in very high esteem. Teachers are respected and considered worthy of worship as they are seen as the propagators of wisdom. While teachers still command a high degree of respect, fewer bright and talented individuals enter the profession as a matter of choice. Johnson and Kardos (2008) list many reasons why globally teaching as a profession does not appear to attract a highly skilled and steadfast cohort. Chief among them are, 'more comfortable and supportive workplaces elsewhere, higher pay and status and greater opportunities for advancement and decreased commitment' (p. 447). In India similar constraints of poor salaries, stressful work conditions and lack of job security are noted as some of the prime reasons why teaching as a profession does not attract the best talents. Three of the teacher educators at the institution (where this research was conducted) were hired through the governmental body – the Universities Grants Commission (UGC). These three commanded much higher pay in comparison to the other 8 who were paid approximately Rupees 15,000 per month (RJ1). This salary is much less than what university graduates with a Masters degree would draw in another profession. These teachers worked in conditions and with class sizes that many teachers in other 'developed' countries would find confronting:

Today is my first observation … I have an observation notes sheet and some of the things that I have to look for. But then I feel like I already know the answer when I step in. With 100 students to one teacher- what is the scope for innovation? (*R.J.*)

There was little access to resources and even basic comforts. Classrooms had two fans each to deal with the sweltering heat outside and there was a fan above the podium used by teachers, which was broken and not working. Temperatures and odour inside the class create quite an uncomfortable environment.

It is exceptionally hot today. I had to stand on the podium where the lecturer stands and that fan is not working. So it is very uncomfortable for the teacher to teach – Dr Anjalie is sweating profusely and has a handkerchief in his left hand, which he constantly uses to wipe himself. I can tell that he is physically uncomfortable – just as I was when I had to talk earlier. (*P.O.*)

Students are seated in rows facing the teacher as shown in Figure 6.1 with the teacher on a podium. 4–5 students sit together on one wooden bench with barely enough elbowroom to write. Teachers have ready access to a chalkboard and an overhead projector. While there are no computers or access to Internet for either students or teachers, there is provision for using PowerPoint presentations but this has to be specially arranged and is reserved only for some occasions (R.J.). Even access to basic amenities like photocopiers was tightly controlled.

Teacher educators were clearly overworked and over burdened. All had to teach in both the morning and afternoon sessions. The morning sessions were devoted to core subjects and so had approximately 100 students in the class. The afternoon sessions were on the Area of Specialisations or optional units – with classes more manageable at approximately 20–30 students. Apart from carrying out the regular marking and preparation for teaching, teacher educators were also responsible for other extra-curricular activities and clubs in the college. This left them with very little time for other scholarly work. Their access to information and the latest articles was also limited. This was partly due to the fact that they did not have access to the

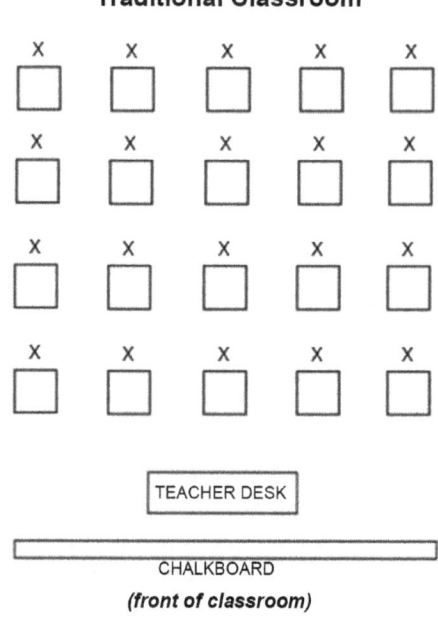

Figure 6.1. Classroom layout

Internet and also that the library was not very well stocked. Many of the teacher educators were also admittedly not particularly "computer savvy" – some did not have their own email address.

It has been noted in the literature that the ability to attract the 'best talent' to the profession of teaching is a challenge that exists across the globe (Johnson & Kardos, 2008). It is of little surprise then that the data on the small scale in this study is indicative of that trend with only one teacher educator having taken up teaching as a first choice. Poor pay and working conditions have contributed to a shortage in teachers in India as recently highlighted by the report of the National Knowledge Commission (NCFTE, 2010). However, despite the prevailing situation and workplace conditions, many of the participating teacher educators stated that they had developed a love for their line of work once they took it up.

> I worked for one year as an untrained teacher … after my post graduation –in that time my father died- so I am blank (free) for one year … At that time I found teaching to be interesting and I became a teacher. I then decided to do my B Ed. (*Chidambar, Interview 7*)

An overall synopsis points to the fact that while all the teacher educators were highly educated (well credentialed), they lacked education, exposure and training to teach EE. None of them had received any support to teach EE. Although they saw the need for EE, they seemed to lack the education to integrate the field into their teaching practice. There was a noticeably heavy reliance on the traditional methods of teaching. This was seen in most of the classes I attended as an observer and is exemplified in the following example.

> This class is about the usefulness of 'Supplementary Readers' in schools. Today's lesson is a story called 'Bhima and the Blessed' from the 'Mahabharata'. In this story Draupadi wants a particular flower called the 'Saughandika' and Bhima goes into the forest to look for it, in 'quest' of the flower. This is a beautiful story and there were so many opportunities to draw/discuss environmental themes, issues and beliefs here. In contrast the teacher went on with the usual class. Teacher dwelled heavily on the meaning, part of speech and spelling of the word 'quest' and its pronunciation. Asks a student to stand and read the notes from the earlier class. Then dictated more notes on the uses of a supplementary reader, why and how it can be used. This lesson was only in the lecture format – the teacher missed out on the essence of the story. (*P.O.*)

Except for one class, all the classes I observed followed the abovementioned traditional format, i.e., students seated on benches facing the teacher; the teacher using chalkboard or sometimes an Overhead Projector and talking. Often he/she dictated notes, which the students carefully wrote down then used in cramming for the exams (R.J.).

Darling-Hammond (2006) identified three major challenges that needed to be addressed when new teachers were learning to teach: new teachers needing to understand teaching in ways that are quite different from their own experiences as students; encouraging new teachers to not only think but also act like teachers; and, to understand and respond to the many dilemmas that multifaceted classrooms throw up on a regular basis. Traditional lecture methods of teaching (elaborated further in the next section) new teachers could be seen as seriously falling short in addressing these three important challenges.

In response to this situation, these teacher educators were of the view that they were 'forced to follow this format' as they were hampered by the constraints of the syllabus, a rigid curriculum and an examination oriented assessment approach, which left very little time and scope to deviate from the set tasks.

> I don't focus on environmental education, because we will be more concerned
> on how to finish the syllabus, that is a necessity. (*Kala, Interview 11*)

These teacher educators were unified in the sentiment that EE had an important part to play in teacher education. An obvious conundrum then is that as India is currently going through intense changes and has ambitious plans for economic growth in the future it is troubling that teacher education appears out of step with the changing social and economic agendas of Indian society in relation to the nature of the environmental issues that accompany such rapid changes.

ENVIRONMENTAL EDUCATION AND ITS IMPLEMENTATION

The history of education reform is that another reform always emerges to replace that most recent reform. There are many reasons for that continuous cycle, such as promises made by political leaders, trends that move across the nation or world, new demands in the marketplace for workers with updated skills, unwise decisions about the most recent reform, ineffective implementation of reform, or a change of president, governor, superintendent, principal, or interest group agenda, among other reasons. Perhaps educational improvement should be continuous, but it should also be realistic, practical, sensible, directed towards genuine problems, and shaped in part, perhaps in large part, by the people who are most responsible for causing improved learning to happen in classrooms – teachers. (Babbage, 2008, p. 89)

In the current context of educational reform in India new laws, policies and regulations are fast becoming the norm. India has churned out three major policy documents in the past few years namely the National Curriculum Framework in 2005 and 2010 and the National Curriculum Framework for Teacher Education in 2010. Law, policies, regulations and systems can help, but these could prove to be superficial if not coupled with direct action by teachers and teacher educators themselves. Although systems, structure, organisation charts, laws, policies and regulations are important, the main goal of education (students' learning) depends largely on what teachers and students do in the classrooms (Babbage, 2008). Concentrating on structural reform without providing impetus to practical reforms is a seriously flawed approach. Improvement efforts in education rely heavily on teachers and teacher educators' as they are ultimately responsible for that which happens in classrooms.

The amount of effort teacher educators exert in implementing new policies depends on many factors – a big factor is how much they were involved in the policy making process. 'People support what they help create' (Babbage, 2008, p. xi) and so drawing teachers and teacher educators into the policy making process is an important step towards effective implementation.

According to Plevyak et al. (2001) including EE in pre service teacher education programs is a challenging task. Numerous courses in general and professional education are thrust upon teacher education institutions by the federal and state governments, leaving little room for speciality areas such as EE. As the previous chapters attest, this has certainly been the case in the particular teacher education institution in which this study has been conducted.

As detailed in Chapter 5, EE is offered as an Area of Specialisation, taken up by a handful of students. Environmental education is only taught as a small component of a core subject under the sub topic 'Problems of Education in India.' For EE to be effective, it could well be argued that it needs to be a part of the teachers and teacher educators' ethos.

Orr (1992) contends that most educators regard the environment as a problem that can be fixed using technologically advanced remedies. "Solutions" to environmental problems then stem from the top of society with governmental and organisational "intellectuals" passing them down to "passive citizenry" in the form of laws, policies, and technologies. The aim is to create a sustainable technocratic society. He postulates that this takes away 'the need to create an ecologically literate and ecologically competent public, so EE is most often regarded as an extra in the curriculum, not as a core requirement or as an aspect pervading the entire educational process.'

Earlier chapters have pointed towards a more technocentric and anthropocentric view amongst the teacher educators that participated in this research. This chapter analyses these teacher educators' views about EE, the policies particularly the changes since the Supreme Court mandate and implementation of the new policies (detailed in Chapter 2). The chapter considers the issues, dilemmas and struggles that teacher educators experience while implementing new policies. The chapter therefore attempts to determine how these teacher educators negotiate the teaching of EE in their classrooms and how they prepare future teachers to teach about the environment in light of the prevailing policy development and implementation conditions.

TEACHER EDUCATORS' VIEWS ABOUT EE

I believe that environmental education will change attitudes in the future generations. (*Kala, Interview 11*)

This section explores teacher educators' views about EE. While the perceived importance teacher educators see in education in terms of raising environmental awareness is clear it needs to be followed with further elaboration on this position by considering that which these teacher educators think about EE, the goals of EE, their perceptions of the current 'state of play' and the areas of concern and/or in need of further improvement.

Few attempts have been made to understand teacher educators' views – their subjective realities – in EE. Certainly, no such effort has been made in India to date. In fact, as described in the methodology chapter (Chapter 4) these teacher educators were quite surprised to have a researcher interested in their thoughts, their views and their feelings about EE. When asked about their views about EE in India all felt that while there were improvements being made in the field, there was need for a lot more to be done. These teacher educators felt that there was a need for greater emphasis on EE.

> EVS [Environmental Science] is still there but in the lower classes ... it should be taught at least on the primary level from 1 to 7th standard. (*Medha, Interview 2*)

> At the primary level we are giving more importance to environmental education – because at this level science is taught as EVS [Environmental Science] – till higher primary... its all EVS. Then it will get deviated into Physics, Chemistry and Biology in the secondary level. But even then the importance is only given to environmental education till high school level. Of course environmental education is considered as a part of Biology and not environmental education as a separate subjects – it is only considered as a minor part of biology. (*Leena, Interview 8*)

At the teacher education level, EE was being taught as an optional paper namely as an Area of Specialisation in this particular institution. This meant it was accessible only to students who opted for it. Apart from being an Area of Specialisation, it was also being taught as a small component of one of the core subjects – it was taught as one of the 'Problems' of Education in India (D.A. 2).

> It is there in the B. Ed [Bachelor's of Education] curriculum... there is one unit – Problems of Indian Education, under that they include several problems; one of the problems in this is environmental education. Population education, environmental education – there are many such problems discussed so all the students are supposed to learn that. (*Bhargava, Interview 9*)

This approach reiterates Orr's (1992) claim that the environment is often seen as a 'problem' that needs to be solved. Teacher educators saw the environment as an integral part of education.

> Without environment we cannot even think of education. It is a part of education right now but the way we are implementing it maybe there are differences. (*Nammy, Interview 3*)

Teacher educators felt that all their students needed to be exposed to environmental problems and think of solutions to these problems.

> They are going to teach students [in schools] you see, so for them before they teach they should know about the environment, how to teach it, how to control it and all such things. They should have some basic idea regarding environmental education and the environment, otherwise they cannot teach it. If they are not conscious about the environment then we cannot expect them to teach the subject. (*Arya, Interview 6*)

They saw the importance of integrating EE into the entire curriculum. However, they also felt that it could only be understood in terms of due importance when taught as a separate subject. As Poornima implies (below) she is forced to teach EE due to the fact that it is not available to all students as a separate subject.

> It will be better if it is viewed as a separate course, separate period, separate classroom – then automatically there will be an increase in the seriousness towards environmental education. If we teach it in an integrated approach there won't be any seriousness. But when I have got no other way, which is why I am trying to integrate it. As a teacher educator I cannot teach environmental education separately that's why we have to integrate it. (*Poornima, Interview 4*)

One reason for this view could be linked to the lack of training teacher educators receive [highlighted in later sections of this chapter]. A case in point is the lack of integration of EE even in units such as physical education; which could well be viewed as a unit that presents interesting opportunities. Teacher educators did not appear to look for these opportunities or to actively utilise them. Their call for EE to be taught by separately trained, competent teacher educators could then be seen as a means of circumventing their existing view of the problem. Chidambar [below] termed this as an 'easy going nature' and called for a separate curriculum [and thereby separate teachers].

> In Indian circumstances there should be environmental core courses [in the curriculum] but that is not happening. It should be a separate subject. There is an integrated approach but most teachers are of an easy going nature – they never bother about that, they don't have interest in that matter. So it must be a separate curriculum, which will be much better. (*Chidambar, Interview 7*)

Calls for making EE a separate subject were strengthened by Leena who suggested that no matter what the stream or field of education, EE should be taught as a core and compulsory unit.

> … at the B Ed level it should be made a compulsory subject. Because all are becoming teachers, any teacher whether in humanities, humanitarian subject teachers [or science teachers] they have to have a concern about the environment. So at the B Ed level it should be a compulsory paper – that is my opinion. (*Leena, Interview 8*)

Leena went on to describe the reason that a decision against making EE compulsory in teacher education had been implemented. This particular teacher educator described the debate that occurred at one of the training sessions that she had attended.

> At the B Ed level it is optional… last year we had a discussion about whether it should be compulsory paper at the teacher education level – I mean D Ed, B Ed and TCH. So majority of the opinion was that it should not be a compulsory

paper, because when we compel the students they won't study, because when we compel there will be negligence and rebellion nature will be there. So that was the opinion. ... so environmental education should be an optional paper, because when we infuse everything, the students develop aversion. (*Leena, Interview 8*)

The above argument, or reasons, for not including EE is clearly based on a particular logic that could well be argued is imbued in the culture of the Indian education system. Like many issues in Indian education, EE appears to suffer from the view that the solution is mainly dependent on another subject being added to the curriculum, thus carrying with it the notion that some more notes could then be memorised and some more questions answered during exams. This presents a very traditional and narrow approach towards education. If EE is to be introduced in the abovementioned traditional manner there could be an overdose and possible create aversion to the subject. However if done in a holistic manner – although it may not guarantee that student teachers will teach it once they graduate – it at least increases their disposition to do so.

While teacher educators called for EE to be compulsorily taught to all students irrespective of their academic background, there was no consensus on whether it should be a separate subject or integrated in the curriculum. NCTE (National Council for Teacher Education, 2009) does call for integrating EE in the teacher education curriculum (D.A.1). One of the reasons for a demand to teach it as a special subject was that specialist teachers who were adequately trained to do so would then teach it. These teacher educators seemed to lack the confidence to teach EE and were unable to maximise the opportunities to integrate it in their curriculum.

Teacher educators therefore complained about the over reliance on textbooks and provision of theoretical knowledge to students. They felt that every effort made towards implementation of EE simply fell back on a heavy reliance on inclusion in the textbooks.

We do 'give' environmental education in India; again what is happening is that we are giving more and more theory to the students at all levels I am seeing. Theory-wise we are very strong and perhaps we believe that if we give theory everything will become alright, but to protect the environment practical aspects are more important than the theory and I believe more in practical aspects rather than the theory. I don't say theory is not important; I feel that theory should be put into practice. This is truer in the case of environment. (*Bhargava, Interview 9*)

Teaching according to these teacher educators was restricted to following the textbooks. As pointed out in Chapter 7, giving examples while lecturing was the popular mode of integrating EE.

Nowadays it has become a fashion, everything is included in the textbooks. (*Blue, Interview 10*)

These teacher educators were unhappy with this approach of integrating everything into the curriculum as it made it very insipid and uninteresting. According to them it contributed to making the teaching of EE too technical and boring adding to their frustration. They also felt that EE could be relegated to being a mere trend, which would fade with time. Adding a few chapters to the already overburdened textbooks was one of the 'aspiring level' solutions that Orr (1992) mentions.

> But I am not really happy with the way in which environmental education and environmental consciousness is implemented because there is overdose of environmental component in all the text [in a number of subjects] … so every now and then teachers have to teach these things and students also get bored because same kind of lessons are introduced, there is not much charm – for example a dry essay is introduced instead of stories and poems… either we have no enthusiasm or we are over enthusiastic. (*Anjalie, Interview 1*)

This heavy reliance on the textbooks was triggered by the rigid curriculum that these teacher educators felt they had to follow [this will be discussed in detail in the following sections]. Another major problem according was the almost total reliance on centralised examinations as tools of assessment.

> So it is only a subject for the sake of the study and to pass the examination. So they are only reading, memorising, get marks. So there is no transfer of learning as such, that is the main bane of Indian system of education according to me. (*Anjalie, Interview 1*)

> It's our nature to do commercial work and students only look at examinations and do employment related work. (*Chidambar, Interview 7*)

This over emphasis on examinations appears to have led to a perceived shift in the purpose of education from learning to a means of 'getting a ticket' (finishing a degree) in order to find employment, thus diminishing the value of learning.

> If you simply give theory they [students] are very good, they will write all the answers and will secure 100% marks but they may not do anything in their regular life to protect the environment. That is the saddest thing. (*Bhargava, Interview 9*).

Bhargava's view is in full accord with that which Orr (1992) described as the pitfalls of education – 'the missing joy in education' – and reducing it to a mere set of memorisations and examinations. Kala discussed the need to explore alternate avenues to education. According to this teacher educator, there was a need to look within one's self and to take initiative for one's own learning.

> I have also talked about self-learning, we should not solely rely on others for environmental education or on formal education, the change should come from within or through exposure to other activities or non-formal education… because whatever education we get – it is ultimately we who do it. Because

you may teach me anything but I am the person who acts on it, so if I don't change my viewpoint whatever education you give me goes to waste. (*Kala, Interview 11*)

The obvious question then is how does one motivate individuals to take charge of their own learning if they do not feel enough interest or passion for the issues? Presenting EE as a problem with solutions to be found and relying on traditional rote memorisation methods does not appear sufficient to create the enthusiasm needed to drive an individual towards self-learning.

The inability to teach outdoors was another frustration for these teacher educators.

... in rather giving them theory [theoretical knowledge] take them – at least once a month to the environment and make them understand the impact – we are spoiling the environment, then if you connect with theory that will be beautiful. (*Blue, Interview 10*)

Sadly, confining EE to the classroom and the overreliance on textbooks appeared to create a sense of apathy towards the subject.

Yeah not imbibing [textbook knowledge] and we have not been teaching effectively, we may not be giving them practical approach taking them to a spot and making them understand these things. (*Anjalie, Interview 1*)

They will just get mark and pass, so [their attitude is] why should we learn. That attitude is there. (*Kala, Interview 11*)

This apathy was attributed to a lack of exposure to nature. Teacher educators like Anjalie illustrated how developing a love and passion for nature was a necessary aspect of EE. From his perspective, taking students outdoors to experience nature fostered such passion. Therefore, lack of exposure to nature appeared to create a disconnection between the environment and an individual. Louv (2010) described this as a 'nature deficit disorder' where individuals' exposure to nature had been severely restricted by the change in lifestyles.

And more of activities, nature walks for example or going to a pond and understanding what is happening to the pond, or taking students to a forest area and making children go watch the birds, plants, flowers, bees etc ... yeah they must be able to love nature. Today you see in the cities there is not much love for nature. Only people coming from rural backgrounds, agrarian families, they still have love for nature. (*Nammy, Interview 3*)

The distancing or disconnection of how the world works and the curriculum is framed seems increasingly evident in these participants' views. Orr (1994) decries education that revolves around memorisation, boring lessons and activities not in sync with students lived experiences and restricted to indoors, an overemphasis on grades. This kind of passive learning damages the sense of wonder, which is inherent to quality education. He calls for overhauling the substance and process of education. This change could well be needed if India is to counter the effects of its rush for economic liberalisation.

Overall then, these teacher educators elucidated a clear confidence in education as a means of bringing about attitudinal change, but were of the view that while some effort was being made in implementing EE in schools, a lack of effort in tertiary education (particularly in teacher education) was evident.

TEACHER EDUCATORS' PREPAREDNESS TO TEACH EE

The institution being studied has a reputation as being amongst the best teacher education institutions in the area and is also well known across the country. The Teacher educators it hires are very highly qualified (as indicated by Table 7.1). Table 7.1 was compiled using the Interview Facesheet data that the teacher educators

Table 7.1. Summary of personal data of teacher educators

Teacher Educator	Education/Degree	Subject	Experience as school teacher (Total years)	Experience as teacher educator (Total years)
Anjalie	B.Sc., M.A., M.Ed., PhD	Educational Psychology	5 years	28 years
Medha	B.Sc., M.A., M.Ed.	Mathematics	21 years	1 year
Nammy	M.A., M.Ed.	Educational Technology	25	9 years
Poornima	M.A. (History), M.Ed., M.Phil	History	3 months	10 years
Axmi	M.Sc., M.Ed., M. Phil.	Biology	Nil	10 years
Arya	B.Sc., B.Ed., M. Lib Science	Librarian	Nil	33 years
Chidambar	M.A. (Kannada), M.Ed., N.E.T. (UGC test)	Kannada	1 year (as untrained teacher)	10 years
Leena	B.Sc., B. Ed., M.A., M. Ed.	Environmental Education	Nil	9 years
Bhargava	M.A., M.Ed., M.Phil.	History	8 years	17 years
Blue	B.Com, M. A. (Sociology), PhD	Physical Education	8 months	23 years
Kala	B.Sc, M.A., M.Ed., PGDELT (English language teaching)	English	2	8

provided as a lead up to the interviews. All teacher educators (except one) had double postgraduate degrees, one each in a subject area and in education. The Principal was seen as a very supportive individual who valued education highly and encouraged staff towards further education.

While the teacher educators were undoubtedly very highly educated it was interesting to see how well they were educated to teach/integrate EE in their practices. The National Policy on Education drafted in 1986 pointed out the role of teachers and teacher educators in creating environmentally consciousness amongst all people – particularly children (CEE, 2010). This aim was furthered by India's peak teacher education body The National Council of Teacher Education (2005), through its new curriculum – 'Environmental Education Curriculum Framework for Teachers and Teacher Educators'.

> Unless environmental education becomes compulsory and integral component
> of education and teacher education, its message cannot be conveyed to all.
> (NCTE, 2005, p. 5) (D.A. 1)

This has been followed up by recent recommendations to integrate education about the current environmental crisis into the teacher education curriculum through the National Curriculum Framework for Teacher Educators (NCFTE)

> In the present ecological crisis, promoted by extremely commercialised and
> competitive lifestyles, teachers and children need to be educated to change
> their consumption patterns and the way they look at natural resources. For this,
> teachers need to be equipped to understand these issues and incorporate them
> in their teaching. The new teacher education curriculum framework will need
> to integrate these perspectives in its formulation. (NCFTE, 2010, pp. 13–14)
> (D.A. 1)

Considering the above policy documents, I now shed light on teacher educators' preparedness to take up these suggestions made by these prominent governmental policy making bodies. As indicated in Table 7.1, all the teacher educators were postgraduates with a Masters degree in Education; while two had doctoral degrees. All had studied through the mode of distance education for all their postgraduate degrees. However, the teacher educators were not necessarily teaching subjects within their areas of specialisation. For example while Kala's major in her postgraduate studies was English, she was also teaching psychology.

Interestingly none of the teacher educators had received any training in the teaching of EE as part of their pre-service or in-service teacher education. Their only exposure to this area was through the rather infrequent sessions held in the college for their student teachers.

> At the college level also [as part of their own education] we have not undergone
> any training as such related to environmental education. We organise some
> talks for our students maybe through eco clubs or environmental education

camps ... They give talks about various aspects of the environment ... so through that along with students even the faculty members get exposure to environmental education. (*Axmi, Interview 5*)

Even the EE specialist had not received any training to teach EE other than a one day workshop conducted a couple of years ago. Her undergraduate degree was in Science and she had post graduate degrees in both Arts and Education. EE was not a part of her education for any of these degrees. She felt that she was not adequately prepared to teach the subject.

Environmental Science [as a subject to teach] was given to me. Not by choice, I used to teach population education; environmental education was taught by someone else. It was given to me. (*Leena, Interview 8*)

As this data suggests, in contrast to that which the policy documents (e.g., 1986 National Education Policy, and the 2005 and 2010 recommendations by the National Council of Teacher Education – DA 1) propose, there appears to be little real impact on practice.

Also few of the participating teacher educators had prior experience as teachers in a classroom. 7 out of the 11 teacher educators were alumni of the same college; they completed both their Bachelors and Masters degrees at the same college and then joined as teacher educators with very little experience as classroom teachers.

I did M Ed straight after B Ed ... All 3 of us were together for both B Ed and M Ed. Here almost all our staff are past students including our Principal. (*Chidambar, Interview 7*)

Teacher educators maintained that a lot of their learning was acquired 'on the job'. They were of the view that they had learnt the required 'skills' over the years while working as teacher educators'. This is reiterated by the following comment

I came into teaching – it was by chance but after coming here I have excelled in it. (*Kala, Interview 11*)

It can also be inferred that teacher educators rely on their own experiences as students to teach. This can, in part, be linked to that which has been described as the influence of the impact of the 'apprenticeship of observation' problem (Lortie, 1975). As a consequence, it can mean that for some teacher educators, the apprenticeship of observation can be translated into a view that a few strategies, skills and some technical routines are all that is needed to be good teachers (i.e., following on from that which they observed as student teachers). One outcome of this situation is that the notion of learning as a mechanical 'transfer' of information, or transmissive teaching (as observed in the teacher educators' practices) is more likely to become an entrenched aspect of practice. Most notably present is the perception that the ability to talk is envisaged as a major strength:

I like talking – even at the school level and college level … facing the audience is not a problem. Perhaps that was one of the important reasons for joining this profession. (*Bhargava, Interview 9*)

A prevailing perception as a consequence of this situation then is that there was a lack of expectation for any special orientation or initiation in order to become a teacher educator – apart from a basic academic degree. More so, there was even less expectation or requirement for any induction into teaching EE. This was compounded by limited access to information resulting in a lack of awareness of major policy reforms taking place in India, or indeed, globally. Shagrir (2011, p. 57) drew attention to the fact that 'Teacher educators are the ones who impart to their students knowledge, tools and teaching skills on the one hand, and perceptions and values on the other'. It stands to reason then that without adequate preparation teacher educators' ability to teach about teaching can be severely hampered.

PERSONAL EXPERIENCES IN IMPLEMENTING EE

Every effort to improve education relies on effective implementation in classrooms. The teacher is the person, more than anyone else, who impacts what happens or does not happen in classrooms. (Babbage, 2008, p. xi)

The aim of this section of the chapter is to explore these teacher educators' experiences in teaching in EE. The underlying theme was to understand what teachers do in the classroom – how, when or if they teach EE; and to investigate how they work within the curriculum and syllabus strictures. The aim being to better understand how these teacher educators negotiate and implement EE.

Interestingly, these teacher educators once again criticised the lack of opportunities to teach students in the outdoors. They felt that student teachers were only being provided with theoretical knowledge without providing any practical inputs.

Everywhere education is given intramural – within four walls. Within the walls in the sense it has not to be in the concrete walls, you have to take them [students] outside and give them a personalised experience, take them for a walk. I send them – go for a walk and see and come what trees are there. (*Blue, Interview 10*)

While Blue's enthusiasm for outdoor education is admirable her vision about EE seems to be very narrow (as similarly noted earlier in Chapter 7). This was further exemplified when asked how she worked around these limitations:

Yes, I ask them to bring the leaves and no doubt the person who brings the most leaves will get a prize. (*Blue, Interview 10*)

Another teacher educator recalled her experiences as a teacher and working outdoors with school children. She felt those were memorable moments for her students and brought more meaning to her teaching.

> I used to take them outside and tell them to do what you want but find what a particular insect is doing etc, small things – small kids 1st and 2nd grade – but they used to enjoy, they never wanted to sit in the class afterwards, they never used to listen to me, they used to run outside, even today they remember me for that. Not the theory I taught but this – the practical. (*Kala, Interview 11*)

When asked about how she took her teaching of EE outdoors, now Kala immediately reacted in the negative. She felt that her teaching was strictly categorised and since she taught non-Science subjects she had no opportunity to take it outdoors. She mainly concentrated on the methods of teaching and only gave examples during her lectures for illustration:

> No way ... it [her teaching] is completely separated and compartmentalised ... We are concentrating [names her subjects] the methods and examples. (*Kala, Interview 11*)

One of the main reasons for not being able to work on projects that would involve working outdoors was the duration of the course and once again the rigidity of the curriculum was noted. Teacher educators felt that there was no flexibility offered by the program and therefore limited their ability to try out different things.

> More freedom should be given to conduct the activities. Of course I cannot say that because the duration [of the course] is less. If the duration was more we can, because when it becomes 2 years [length of the program] we can take the students outside the college. And we can give little projects. Because there is proper time to complete it, sufficient time can be given to the students to complete it. (*Leena, Interview 8*)

In addition to the length of the program, another reason cited for not being able to move beyond the classroom walls was the lack of time and the structure of the program.

> No, no, no [when asked if they ever work on projects where they take students out]. The duration is very less, we have to give more importance to other activities and other subjects ... it is a 50 minute period and it is in the middle of the day and not at the end ... also [the duration of the course] within 9-10 months they have to complete B Ed. (*Leena, Interview 8*)

Many teacher educators cited the duration of the course as a major impediment. Officially the course ran for a year but because of the number of holidays and breaks the actual contact time was reduced to 9 or 10 months. This according to the teacher educators seriously impacted the quality of the program. Teacher educators struggled to finish most of the allotted work in a 50-minute class period. They complained of this lack of time and an ensuing race to finish the syllabus leaving them with no time to plan or provide any other activities or innovative teaching strategies. If teacher educators did not follow the curriculum their students would not fare well in the examinations, which would probably lower their and their institutions reputation. The prevailing view was that there was inadequate time for them to do justice to the units that they were teaching.

> We have 15 days vacation and 1½ months of teaching practice [practicum]. We have to complete the whole course, the duration is very less. Now they [concerned authorities] are thinking about a 2-year course maybe in the coming years. Then we can think about taking certain projects, if we have time. (*Leena, Interview 8*)

> … at least more than 10 months [duration of the course] is required. At least 1 or 1½ years. (*Kala, Interview 11*)

These teacher educators also felt that they had very little scope of integrating EE in their daily teaching practices mainly because of the highly compartmentalised approach towards teacher education. Each had a fixed syllabus to follow.

> It [the syllabus] is very rigid – it is rigid in the sense that we have to cover the syllabus. (*Axmi, Interview 5*)

An interesting assessment issue arose in considering the curriculum. At the end of the course students were expected to appear for a centralised examination – the questions for this exam being based on the syllabus. If the syllabus was not completely covered there could be questions in the paper, which the students could not answer. This would result in lower marks for the students who would then lay blame on the teacher educators. It also led to an over reliance on textbooks as they were centrally prescribed. Teaching strategies were mainly limited to lecturing which took away the joy of education often making it dull and boring. Given this scenario it is natural that any additional units would mean some more rote learning and memorisation and a few more exams to write – causing students and teaching to see EE as a burden. Teacher educators encapsulated these sentiments when they said that their students did not have the right attitude and approach:

> They themselves [the students] do not have the feelings, they just put up a show to get the marks/points, but you believe me that afterwards they just go back to their own ways. (*Chidambar, Interview 7*)

There was also a view that EE was mainly seen as a part of Science. This perspective appeared to limit interviewees' ability to holistically integrate EE in their daily teaching.

> Wherever there are references we teach – for example Science there is a lot of scope, especially in biology. (*Nammy, Interview 3*)

No, not much [teaching environmental education] but there are some science teachers who are interested in these things and in turn they guide their students who take up environmental projects and do it. (*Anjalie, Interview 1*)

This attitude was prevalent amongst students too – which could be why it attracted mainly Science students. Science is traditionally seen in India as a tough subject and students from an Arts and Humanities background tend to stay away from it. They often felt that Science, and so EE, were too hard for them to handle.

Yeah because for environmental education usually only Science students come. Science students will be having some background information about the environment, but very few would come from humanities background, they all find it very difficult to understand these concepts related to environment. Anyhow they learn it in their high schools but when they come to PU [Grades 11 & 12] – they are totally out of it. So they find it a bit difficult but the science students would enjoy and understand things better ... they may have forgotten what they have learnt in high schools as students and once they are in PU they are in a totally different field so maybe they have not thought of all these aspects. So they find it difficult to understand. (*Axmi, Interview 5*)

This situation appeared to similarly impact professional development or 'training' of the teacher educators'. When asked if they had received any training Kala responded:

Right now, there is no scope. Because usually when they call for such programs, they call for science teachers, only teachers who are handling science, not language or any other subject. In the circular [about the professional development session] it was mentioned that the Science teacher educator should be sent. It was not for us ... what I feel is that why only Science because environment is related to all of us and all the teacher educators, all the citizens in the county should know something about the environment. (*Kala, Interview 11*)

(The lack of support and professional development for teacher educators to be able to implement EE will be discussed in detail in the final section of this chapter.)

As is evident in this section, while teacher educators expressed strong views about the need for EE in teacher education programs, they had very little experience of actually incorporating it in their daily teaching practice They blamed the rigid curriculum which they felt offered them few opportunities to move away from what had been prescribed. The length of the program they were teaching was considered very short – which again left them with few opportunities to delve into innovative teaching strategies. This was also the reason suggested for working strictly indoors – they never ventured outside. A major hurdle was the rather superficial approach teacher educators seemed to carry about EE in large and the role of outdoor education. Teacher educators' expectation of an outdoor program seemed to be limited to exposing students to nature rather than experiencing it or involving local communities within that experience.

STUDENT TEACHERS' PREPAREDNESS TO TEACH EE

Before presenting the participating teacher educators' views about how EE is taught, I offer a brief review of the policies regarding EE (a fully detailed review is included in Chapter 9). Major policy documents in India have focused on the importance of pre-service teacher education and the role teacher educators play in developing quality education. The National Curriculum Framework for Teacher Education for stresses:

> Initial teacher education especially, has a major part to play in the making of a teacher. It marks the initiation of the novice entrant to the calling and as such has tremendous potential to imbue the would-be teacher with the aspirations, knowledge base, repertoire of pedagogic capacities and humane attitudes. (NCFTE, 2010, p. 12) (D.A. 1)

While highlighting the importance of pre-service teacher education, the National Council for Teacher Education also sees this along with in service education as an area of major concern:

> The training of teachers is a major area of concern at present as both pre-service and in-service training of schoolteachers are extremely inadequate and poorly managed in most states. Pre-service training needs to be improved and differently regulated both in public and private institutions, while systems for in-service training requires expansion and major reform that allow for greater flexibility. (NCFTE, 2010, p. 16) (D.A. 1)

The National Curriculum Framework (2010), drafted in response to the Supreme Court action, mandated EE across all grades in all schools in India. The question then was: "How are teachers being educated to implement this policy at this particular institution?"

Reviewing the Handbook for B Ed Students – the key policy document drafted by the institution – refers to how EE is included in the curriculum. The handbook is followed very strictly by the teacher educators and so describes in detail the policy of the institution. As part of its specific 'Objectives of the B Ed Course' the Handbook mentions the main intent of the degree:

> The Bachelor of Education Degree course is mainly designed to prepare effectively secondary school teachers to work in schools of State X. The course essentially aims at helping student teachers become aware of certain new content, develop certain competencies and understand his/her multiple role in the present context. (A Handbook for B Ed Students, p. 8) (D.A. 2)

The document lists several objectives that the course attempts to develop in a student teacher. For example understanding of the essential foundations and basic principles of education; the systems, practices and problems of education in the country; and, the nature and problems of secondary school children are listed as important objectives. Developing competency over subjects and also over the planning and execution of lessons are also prominent objectives. While there is no direct mention of the environment or EE there is one objective which could be considered to cover EE.

Developing competencies and values related to physical fitness, social skills, community/group living. (A Handbook for B Ed. Students, p. 8) (D.A. 2)

The syllabus consists of nine units. The final unit among these is called 'Problems of Indian Education'. This is where EE is listed – as a part of the nine problems facing the Indian Education system:

• Equalisation of Educational Opportunities
• Vocationalisation of Education
• Population Education
• Distance Education and Non-formal education
• National and Emotional Integration
• International Understanding
• Education of the disadvantaged (SC/ST, Women, Rural)
• Environmental Education
• Education for the future

The EE specialist teacher educator mentioned that as part of this sub unit, providing the definition of what the environment means, providing a brief synopsis of the methods and technologies of teaching EE and eco-friendly lifestyles was important to do (R.J.).

This unit is part of the core subjects and is available to all student teachers as a compulsory component. The entire unit has 15 allotted instructional hours, which means that a total of 1.4 hours in an entire year is allocated to teach all the above. There is strong research based evidence that 'teachers' subject matter knowledge and knowledge of teaching and learning actually appear to interact in determining teacher effectiveness' (Darling-Hammond, 2006, p. 31). Therefore, as the above suggests, there is hardly enough time to even skim the surface of this content, let alone to delve deeply into the subject.

EE is also available to student teachers as an optional Area of Specialisation. It is taught as a separate subject with 40 hours of allocated instructional time and is an extensive subject. This seems to be the trend in this region in this particular part of India (Chidambar, Interview 7). (Discussion on this issue is offered in detail in Chapter 9.)

There were mixed reactions when the teacher educators were asked if they thought their pre-service teachers were being adequately prepared to teach EE. Some thought that while it was 'only a subject as an Area of Specialisation' that they do in fact try to integrate it into their subjects.

I think that to the general extent all of them try for example to integrate the concepts of environmental education. In all subjects both the core subjects and optional subjects, they try. (*Poornima, Interview 4*)

While others thought that people were like 'frogs in a well' and did not try to venture beyond their prescribed syllabus. Still others thought that the content knowledge provided was inadequate.

They (the students) may answer on a peripheral level but if you go deep into the subject they fail to answer. Depth in the subject, mastery over the content is not there. (*Bhargava, Interview 9*)

As seen above, there was therefore clearly a lack of consensus amongst teacher educators regarding the scope and implementation of EE in its educational programs.

STUDENT TEACHERS' EXPERIENCES IN IMPLEMENTING EE

Towards the natural world' education today 'emphasizes theories, not values; abstraction rather than consciousness; neat answers instead of questions; and technical efficiency over conscience... Education is no guarantee of decency, prudence or wisdom. (Orr, 1994, p. 8)

This section of the chapter explores participant teacher educators' view of their student teachers' experiences in implementing EE. While this section aims to find out how their student teachers implement EE it also attempts to understand their general teaching experience and how students are supported during their practicum.

At this teacher education institution the practicum was held at the end of the teaching period. Teacher educators were not able to provide much detail about their students' experiences while teaching. One of the reasons could be that they had little one on one contact with their students after the teaching practice sessions. However, the perception was that their student teachers integrated EE in their teaching only when prompted to do so and they were not sure if it was further implemented when they became teachers.

During teaching practice they do it because we tell them and we give them feedback like that only, so they will do it but after becoming teachers I didn't observe them so I cannot say ... no they did not give me feedback of that type. (*Poornima, Interview 4*)

If we give suggestions they accept it but on their own they will not do anything. They are not serious about these things – they won't come and seriously discuss these things with us, if we on our own say this can be done and this things also – they listen to us. (*Bhargava, Interview 9*)

This lack of initiative was attributed to a heavy reliance on the prescribed textbooks. Students often tended to just go to their classrooms and read from the textbooks with little attempt to deviate from the set lessons.

> Rarely rarely [teach about the environment] – here and there sometimes without giving any example of their own environment [local environment and local issues], the lesson will be over, because they stick to the content given in the textbooks, they don't try to correlate the content with other things, to correlate one should have a wide perspective which they don't have. They think that teaching means what is given there, presenting it to the learners- that is all and their job is over. (*Bhargava, Interview 9*)

There was a lack of depth in their teaching, which is why even when provided with opportunities to teach about the environment they were not able to utilise them appropriately.

> They can [integrate environmental education] when they go to the schools whenever they get such lessons which is based on environmental science like … such lessons when they teach they can really highlight and teach about the current happenings and compare it. But – I told you in the beginning – many of them just read [the textbook] and complete – some of them do it. (*Kala, Interview 11*)

> Even amongst the students there is less deep thinking, they don't come to us, they don't approach us. (*Bhargava, Interview 9*)

Since the textbooks are published centrally teachers tend to be unable to integrate local knowledge and/or communities in their teaching. Environmental education therefore was seen as being distanced from the daily contexts of the student and teacher lives. This according to another teacher educator was the reason for the lack of depth in teaching. Another reason cited for the lack of initiative in teaching EE was the use of lecturing as the chief teaching strategy.

> They teach only using lecture method [So they just read a lesson in front of the class] … they think that it is a burden. (*Chidambar, Interview 7*)

One of the teacher educators felt that students indulged in 'platform language', which means that while they talked highly about the need for EE in their classrooms they did not really put it to practice.

> Platform language – like they will say that our environment is getting spoiled or that I am very sad and very sorry to see this – we should protect our environment – they speak like this, but in their personal life they are never interested in that matter. (*Chidambar, Interview 7*)

Another teacher educator believed that students were genuinely concerned and understood the importance of education in creating awareness.

> Students understand and sometimes they come to me and say that 'this is really required sir and we now understand the significance of protection of nature'. (*Anjalie, Interview 1*)

Finally, how student teachers approached EE tends to be linked to their own individual position. If they had the motivation from their earlier life experiences they would implement EE no matter what the hurdles.

> It all depends upon the individual, the teacher. There are teachers who come from agrarian background who take it up sincerely because they work at home and come to school. (*Anjalie, Interview 1*)

Motivated students often worked on environmental activities in their free time. EE was often seen as an extra, which had to be done by working in free periods. So only students who were keen on the topics indulged in it without complaint.

> Of course for them [student teachers] some difficulties will be there, like to administer the activities they have to take free periods. What we do is we are giving them one period. So they will have only one period per say, so they have to find free period to conduct these activities. So that was one problem. (*Leena, Interview 8*)

This motivation was not limited to the student teachers alone. One of the teacher educators felt that it also depended on the quality of EE they received during their teacher education course. Inspirational teacher educators provided the encouragement for student teachers to take their interests forward.

> Of course most of the students are interested but provided on how we motivate them. (*Medha, Interview 2*)

Teacher educators expressed concern about the commercialisation of teaching which, as stated in earlier sections, was seen to dilute the quality of education that students sought and received. This was why EE – which was seen as extra work – was considered to be a burden. Once again, passing examinations with the highest marks in order to secure good well paying jobs was an issue raised.

> They think it is a burden … it's our nature, commercial work and students only look at examinations and employment related work … they only come here because they want a good job and once they are settled in life all they are concerned about is the monthly salary. (*Chidambar, Interview 7*)

This attitude meant that even when EE was made a compulsory subject students were not very keen. This is an interesting outcome because it challenges these teacher educators' earlier claims that one of the biggest hurdles against EE was that it was not a core subject. Including EE as a prerequisite requirement in pre-service teacher education does not guarantee that student teachers will implement it in their classrooms (Plevyak et al., 2001). Chidambar felt that even when it was a core subject student interest was low. However, he was not able to provide any concrete reasons as to why that might be the case.

> For the past 3 years it is a core subject at the degree level. But students are not interested, they never attend the class, they do proxy attendance and study for the exam – they buy one guide, rote memorise it and write it. This is what happens. (*Chidambar, Interview 7*)

Overall then student teachers appeared to have very limited experience of teaching EE. According to their teacher educators they seemed to carry a narrow outlook. They felt that their students relied too heavily on the prescribed textbooks and lectures as a teaching strategy. This lack of sophistication stemmed in my understanding out of a lack in sophistication of their own understanding of EE. This also meant that student teachers did not involve the local communities and local knowledge in their teaching. The topics they taught could then be distant and far removed from their local contexts. There is an urgent need to further explore these student teachers experiences when they step into their own classrooms. Teacher educators however felt that it depended to a large extent on individual student teachers and their motivation. Teacher educators felt that the increased commercialisation in education had lowered the standards, which probably hampered student quality and motivation. This according to some teacher educators meant that their students were only keen on the end product – the degree that would lead them to a job – rather than the educational journey.

SUPREME COURT MANDATE AND ITS IMPLEMENTATION

> We thought there will be a big movement, like a big transformation, there will be reformation in the education system – but it hasn't taken place. (*Blue, Interview 10*)

India's top judicial body – the Supreme Court of India –mandated the compulsory inclusion of EE in all schools and undergraduate degree programs in India in 1991 and followed it up with a stronger mandate in 2003 (as described in Chapter 2, Supreme Court of India, 2003) (D.A. 1). This mandate ordered the main curriculum drafting body of India – the National Council for Educational Research and Training (National Commission for Education Research and Technology, 2005) to draw-up a new curriculum incorporating EE. The mandate also triggered a number of policy reforms including the new syllabus for teacher education drafted by the National Council for Teacher Education in 2005 (National Council of Teacher Educators, 2005) (D.A. 1) and more recently in 2009 (National Council for Teacher Education, 2009).

This section of the chapter explores these teacher educators' views about this significant development in the EE field in India and how the mandate is being implemented. All of the teacher educators were of the view that the mandate was timely and necessary.

That [the judgement] is nice actually, at least that is the legislative act through which one can try to incorporate environmental education in the school curriculum. It is a good idea. (*Poornima, Interview 4*)

It is good. I am also happy in recent years courts are becoming active, they are understanding the problems very seriously and they also understand that some of the government's are helpless and there is an apathy on part of the government officers and politicians. So they are taking up the activist's role and passing some serious judgements, which is good for the country and for the betterment of the society. Earlier that was not the case. (*Anjalie, Interview 1*)

Some teacher educators saw it as an indication of society's failure to take action against environmental degradation.

If the Supreme Court has given the judgement means that we have failed, it shows our failure in educating the citizens or people about environment. (*Blue, Interview 10*)

The mandate was also seen as a reflection of the government's apathy towards taking any steps toward improving EE.

Yes, the court is also aware of such things you see because when the government is not taking any decisions or steps such are the circumstances that the Supreme Court should interfere and guide the government. (*Arya, Interview 6*)

There was also a view that the mandate was a little late. Bhargava in particular felt that this stern action should have come a long time ago before the situation had worsened to the current level.

What the Supreme Court has said is 100% correct. Actually it is too late – not 2004, it should have been done long back. (*Bhargava, Interview 9*)

As the Supreme Court is comprised of 'learned judges' there was an expectation that any mandate from them would be better accepted by the general public not only because of the power it carried but also because it was seen as coming from educated sources.

Because the Supreme Court judges- they may not be educationists, but before pronouncing any judgement they study all documents and they observe and examine issues in a holistic way and then they come out with the judgement. It has to be accepted. (*Anjalie, Interview 1*)

Policies can often be reduced to staying on paper unless backed up by strong support for its implementation. This is especially true when the policies have been framed elsewhere with no inputs sought or provided by the teachers and teacher educators who are expected to implement them. Loughran (2010) calls this the top-down approach where policies framed elsewhere are expected to be implemented in classrooms. As a consequence, these teacher educators were not confident about how the judgement would be implemented; something they saw as a crucial issue.

Researcher: So when you heard about the mandate – what was the first thing that came to your mind?

Leena: you know – its good!

Researcher: that was the first thing? And then the second thing?

Leena: Implementation here is very difficult… the thinking is good but implementation, whether it is implemented or not – that is the question. (*Leena, Interview 8*)

Other teacher educators expressed similar concern about how the policy would be implemented. Their main worry was about how the different bodies would work together and coordinate things, also how seriously the mandate would be taken. Most organisations and even governmental bodies neglected the first mandate in 1991 and teacher educators were concerned that this latest mandate would also be relegated to being a policy 'merely on paper'.

Again in our country Supreme Court has said and it is right but what the people do, how do they react to it is more important than the statement made by the Supreme Court, what the people do, how do the different State governments work at various levels, what do they do to conserve, are they serious about the statement – that is more important. (*Bhargava, Interview 9*)

When asked if the policy changes were being implemented some of the teacher educators voiced serious doubts. They were unsure if changes were deep and entrenched in the system or merely superficial. Arya had noticed that there had been some changes made to the school textbooks.

To some extent it is being implemented but I don't know the result. But it is there right from primary level – we are giving some idea and concept regarding environment to our children. I have seen the textbooks and in that it is there. (*Arya, Interview 6*)

Anjalie was able to describe in detail the 'implementation conundrum' especially when it came to agreement between all state and governmental authorities.

No, because most states are yet to implement National Curriculum Framework 2005, now the curriculum is being prepared and slowly it is being implemented. In think the CBSE and ICSE [central education boards] have made an attempt to implement this for 2 years now. But the state governments are yet to implement it. (*Anjalie, Interview 1*)

Another problem was the fact that it was hard to trace how the mandate was being implemented.

> What happens you know – most of the judgements are passed but they are not implemented properly. A judge cannot come and examine how it has been implemented, unless there is some objection from some quarter, once again you have to file an objection in the court if it is not being implemented. (*Anjalie, Interview 1*)

> That is very good [the mandate] but accountability is a problem. (*Chidambar, Interview 7*)

Although these teacher educators were not sure of the changes in the curriculum (apart from in some textbooks) they did feel that the mandate had prompted changes in the co-curricular activities. One of the major new initiatives implemented was the setting up of eco-clubs all over India (R. J.). Eco-clubs are small groups run in schools, which organise nature related activities for school students. These are generally run as after-school programs and are often provided with some support and funding from the government, non-governmental organisations and in some cases even private organisations.

> Exactly under curricular aspects I don't know [about the changes] but under co-curricular aspects almost all schools have eco-clubs. So through these clubs they organise a number of activities throughout the academic year. So in that way they are trying to develop awareness amongst the pupils regarding environmental education. (*Axmi, Interview 5*)

> Yes of course [there have been changes]. Only after that [Supreme Court mandate] we started the eco-clubs, before that there were no eco-clubs in the schools. In all the schools the department of education has said- they sent a circular that every school should have an eco club and different activities, which can be held in those schools are also listed. (*Medha, Interview 2*)

There was also a view that the Supreme Court mandate was necessary and could provide impetus to the cause of EE in India. However, there was a lot that needed to be invested in order for the policy changes to be properly implemented. Not surprisingly, as other studies have also found, successful implementation of EE to a large extent depends on teacher preparation and emphasis on teacher attitudes (Plevyak et al., 2001), as the following concluded:

> … [Taking action] for the sake of implementation and sincerely implementing is another thing. In India all core directions and rules and regulations of the government are implemented half-heartedly, so it will not fetch results. Environmental education is to be introduced, the headmaster [principal] has asked me to tech the subject, so I am teaching – that's all. (*Anjalie, Interview 1*)

Interest – teacher's interest is very less, for them it is a burden. Most of my degree colleagues [teacher educators] tell me that it is a very artificial work. They are never interested in that matter. (*Chidambar, Interview 7*)

Overall teacher educators felt positively about the federal courts directives mandating EE in all schools and colleges in India. They felt that is was a good and necessary decision (some felt it was needed much earlier) and had triggered a number of policy reforms. Since the ruling came from learned judges teacher educators felt that it drives home the seriousness of environmental issues. It also now provides a platform for EE to be pursued more earnestly.

The general concern however was about how this ruling and the policy changes are being implemented. Teacher educators saw policy implementation as a major hurdle – they did not know how it was going to work. While it was easy to draft policies teacher educators felt that monitoring how it is being implemented was a tough task for the state. There was a lack of accountability, which could translate to a lack of answerability. The different government bodies needed to work in tandem and share responsibilities especially when it came to drafting the policies and providing support. There is a need for a uniform centralised push towards ensuring policy implementation. Policy reforms seem to have ignored 'knowledge and skill base that would be required of teachers if they were to teach effectively' and of teacher educators if they have to transform conditions in schools that influence what teachers do (Darling-Hammond et al., 2005, p. 453). This could be a serious reason for the failure of successful implementation of EE. Overall all these teacher educators viewed the mandate as a positive step and felt that if implemented in all its seriousness it could bring about major reforms in EE in India.

I don't think it is happening [implementation] exactly but it is a ruling, which should be implemented because if we go on corrupting the environment at this rate I don't think life can exist on earth. So we have to develop awareness in our younger generation so that to some extent they will be able to preserve and conserve the environment for their future generations. (*Axmi, Interview 5*)

ORGANISATIONAL AND INSTITUTIONAL SUPPORT

In an important study with over four hundred and fifty institutions in the United States, McKeown-Ice (2000) found that most of the colleges and universities involved in her study had not institutionalised their commitment to EE in the ways that they had with other subjects like reading, science and special education. She suggested that this was one of the reasons why EE was failing to have a stronger impact. While policies are set by central and state bodies implementing them is often left to individuals and their respective institutions. Earlier research has pointed to three factors that are important to successful EE: teaching conditions; teacher competencies; and, teaching practices (May, 2000). This section of the chapter explores the teaching conditions and the kind of support the university and the institution provided to individual teacher educators.

UNIVERSITY AND INSTITUTIONAL SUPPORT

Teacher education institutions hold the key to equipping teachers to address sustainability in their classrooms and thus shape the future of communities and nations around the world. (McKeown Ice & Hopkins, 2002, p. 252)

Interviewees outlined some of the changes that had taken place at their particular institution but were unsure as to whether or not these changes were due to the recent policy changes.

Yes – by celebrating environmental days for increasing awareness amongst the student teachers, highlighting the concepts of environmental education, conducting workshops – all of these things have been conducted in our college. That may be due to the influence of the Supreme Court ruling, I am not sure but since all these things have happened now I am associating it and I think it maybe because of that ruling. (*Poornima, Interview 4*)

These teacher educators felt that they had access to whatever materials they needed to teach EE. However, that view was in stark contrast to the fact that most only had access to a very poorly stocked library with very few books on the environment and EE; books that were out-dated, of a poor standard and none on environmental theory and practice. Further to this, neither the teacher educators nor their students had easy access to the Internet, thus severely restricting their access to local and international literature and latest developments in the field. As explained in the earlier sections, these teacher educators were also severely constrained by time and logistics. Interestingly, despite the situation, when queried about the level of support they received from their institution, all expressed satisfaction.

Leena: The syllabus comes from the university and the materials are provided here in our library. And based on that we have our own strategy.

Researcher: You have access to materials and resources? If you need can you get them from outside also?

Leena: Yeah, I can … at the institutional level we are getting enough support but not at the governmental level (*Leena, Interview 8*).

From college [institution] we are getting the support – any new books or journals relating to environment – such books come to our library and also our students get an opportunity to read about new aspects related to environment. Other than that we have not got any help from uni or anywhere else. (*Axmi, Interview 5*)

Poornima was of the view that as teacher educators they did not have any expectations and so were satisfied with what they had, while Medha felt that support would be given when and if asked for.

> Ultimately our students should get the idea, which is our intention. With that intention only we teach, so we don't expect support or any initiatives from others. ... we have basically not asked for any support. (*Poornima, Interview 4*)

> Medha: Of course if we implement it we will get the support. If we seek any kind of support from the higher authorities of course they will give it.

> Researcher: have you received any such support?

> Medha: no so far I have not. I am new to this institution. (*Medha, Interview 2*)

There was a view that the institution was not providing adequate support but only because they were not dealing with the EE. They felt that it was beyond the purviews of their subject and still others felt that they would not receive any support even if they asked for it. This is exemplified by the following comments.

> ... We have our own niche; I was sent for [training related to my work] ... so that way since we handle each subject, it is like you are concerned with it [so you get supported] because everyone cannot attend. (*Kala, Interview 11*)

> No, because that is not the nature of my work. I am not teaching environmental education, I am only integrating the subject, that's all. So I cannot ask for support and they will not give it to me. (*Poornima, Interview 4*)

Somewhat paradoxically, these teacher educators also claimed that they were self motivated and hence did not expect support from anyone:

> That [teaching environmental education] is due to my own wish and I will do it. (*Poornima, Interview 4*)

While teacher educators stated to be self-motivated and implemented EE in their teaching on their own initiative, classroom observations and other parts of their interviews did not reflect his. As described earlier (Chapter 5), apart from providing a few examples while lecturing, an in depth, serious approach seemed to be missing. The biggest problem that teacher educators focused on was the out-dated curriculum. As mentioned earlier they were expected to strictly follow the curriculum. However, the curriculum (it is used in the form of modules at this institution – D.A. 2) had not changed in more than 12 years, which meant that it did not incorporate any recent developments. As even a superficial glance at the literature illustrates, the field of EE continues to grow rapidly. It has seen numerous changes in this past decade with no impact on these teacher educators' curriculum.

They have prepared the curriculum long back, it has become old now… it was formed in 1998 … and it has not been revised. (*Bhargava, Interview 9*)

Kala: Till now our curriculum has not changed yet, we are following the previous curriculum only.

Researcher: Do you remember in which year the previous curriculum was written?

Kala: year… because when I joined the same curriculum I am following – so almost 10 years. (*Kala, Interview 11*)

The curriculum was constructed by centralised boards of education either at the state or central level. These teacher educators were not involved in the process of writing the curriculum and had no input with regard to that which was – or was not – included.

The syllabus is not prepared by the institution, that is prepared by the experts working in various schools of education, board of studies etc. whatever is prepared is accepted. (*Anjalie, Interview 1*)

Instead of feeling involved in the educational process these teacher educators felt neglected. The university, according to Bhargava, was somewhat apathetic towards their work in EE.

University does not intervene; it does not ask what special activities have been organised in environmental education. Whether we are organising any practical work and all such things it does not ask. (*Bhargava, Interview 9*)

Overall, the general impression that interviewees created was that although the were of the view that they had a supportive environment at their institution, the reality was that they were not consulted while creating curriculums nor were they required to provide any expert opinions as practitioners to any policy-making bodies and had little control of what was done, how or why with regard to the overall direction and application of policy to their work.

SUPPORT FROM GOVERNMENT/NON-GOVERNMENT BODIES

All of the teacher educators were candid about their perceived lack of support from outside agencies. Each of them stated the need for more support for themselves as individuals and their institution if they were to implement EE. They complained of virtually no support from government bodies.

Sometimes we get some support but may not be from [government bodies] like UGC. (*Anjalie, Interview 1*)

Non-governmental bodies or NGO's did provide them and their institution with some support but it was described as being at a very basic level – and there was need for a lot more. Most of the time these NGO's provided funds to organise some programs for the students. Organisations like the CEE (Centre for Environmental Education) and WWF (World Wildlife Fund) had organised a couple of programs related to the environment. As Arya explained:

> Of course some voluntary organisations come and conduct 1–2 day workshops for our students and they give some materials, that's all. But apart from that there is not much significant development in this regard from the government or from other agencies (*Arya, Interview 6*)

Apart from this the only support these teacher educators received was from a local environmentalist who volunteered his time and energies to the institution [Anjalie, Interview 1]. He was a teacher educator in one of the local colleges and was often cited by some of these teacher educators as their inspiration. This person, on his own initiative, was working towards helping this institution and would often assist them in gaining funds to organise programs.

Overall then, Teacher educators received limited support from their institution, university, from the government and from non-governmental agencies. They were unsure of the kind of support they needed too. So while in reality they did not receive any support, teacher educators did not really ask for much either. Since their work was highly compartmentalised they worked within their own 'niches' and did not see the need for any support. Similarly since they felt that EE was beyond the purviews of their subject still others felt that they would not receive any support even if they asked for it. Teacher Educators claimed to be self-motivated and did implement EE in their teaching on their own initiative. However as described in earlier chapters (mainly Chapter 5), apart from providing a few examples while lecturing, an in depth, serious approach seemed to be missing.

In general these teacher educators were of the view that there was a need for more support from governmental and non-governmental bodies in order for them to be better able to implement EE in their practice.

PREPARATION IN TEACHING EE

> The development of new knowledge is a central tenet of academic life and when that knowledge directly impacts practice, then in teaching about teaching, that is surely a powerful and significant outcome. (Loughran, 2011, p. 289)

The opportunities presented to teacher educators to develop their skills and to bring themselves abreast of the latest developments is of crucial importance in helping to develop new knowledge in accord Loughran's suggestion (above). In taking up this issue, this section of the chapter is designed to examine the nature of the education these teacher educators received in preparing them to teach EE. These teacher educators were probed about their exposure to EE both as part of their pre-service and in-service teacher education.

As became quickly apparent, none of them had received any formal training to teach EE. The main reason put forward for this was the fact that EE was compartmentalised in science education and so only science educators were provided with 'training' opportunities.

Right now, there is no scope. Because usually when they call for such programs, they call for science teachers, only teachers who are handling science, not language or any other subject. (*Kala, Interview 11*)

I am not a science educator and everybody feels that a [subject] educator should only teach that subject. (*Blue, Interview 10*)

These teacher educators did not agree with this compartmentalisation. They felt that there was a need for all of them to receive quality education so that they could better teach EE.

In the circular [about the training sessions] it is mentioned that the Science teacher educator should be sent. It was not for us ... so sometimes what we do is we compartmentalise these things – this is a science teacher, this is a humanities teacher – but a topic like environment is meant for all because we are influenced by the environment and we influence the environment. (*Bhargava, Interview 9*)

Many carried a sense of discrimination with regard to further training and were of the view that their need for education was more than fair to expect because it had not been part of their undergraduate or postgraduate studies.

I think others [non-science teacher educators] should also be given a chance because she is into environmental education. She [the current specialist] is into environmental education naturally she will learn more about it. Others who are not into environmental education will not be knowing more about it because they will be concentrating on their own field, so for others also such training should be given, so that they can incorporate the aspects of environmental education in their teaching also. (*Axmi, Interview 5*)

This 'discrimination and compartmentalization' was seen as a major reason as to why EE was not being practiced in teaching institutions. Teacher educators like Axmi were keen on integrating EE into their daily teaching practices but felt inadequately trained to do so; her education had not prepared her to do so and so she lacked confidence.

Maybe again they [teacher educators] are not getting enough training, people teaching other subjects – they do not know many concepts related to environment and how to incorporate them in their subject – like in an integrated manner. (*Axmi, Interview 5*)

EE was not part of their undergraduate or postgraduate studies. This despite the fact that all the teacher educators had a Masters degree and many had also completed an MPhil and two of them had a PhD. Even recent postgraduate degrees did not have a unit or topic on the environment or EE. Medha, who had recently completed her Masters degree, pointed out this gap in her education while Anjalie highlighted the presence of 'untrained' educators.

> In some cases in some colleges there may be a person from humanities teaching environmental education without the background of ecology and all that, he or she is supposed to teach that [environmental education]. Maybe sometimes the individual is put through hardship, not understanding the subject very well, not studying properly and basically not evincing interest in the subject, that also happens. (*Anjalie, Interview 1*)

Given the lack of exposure to EE as a part of their formal education, these teacher educators relied on non-formal education to fill the gap. However, even their exposure to non-formal education and in-service education was seriously limited. They had attended a few environmental programs that had been organised in the college mainly for their student teachers.

> But one thing is there, though we are not trained as such, a lot of programs are organised here in the college and lot of people come and discuss here about environment, about culture and other things. So all faculty members may be present. They do attend the programs and they get a lot of information about these things. (*Anjalie, Interview 1*)

They also drew attention to the fact that they often learnt the concepts on the job (i.e., while teaching):

> So for example when teaching say rain harvesting even I did not know much but actually I learnt while teaching. (*Nammy, Interview 3*)

These teacher educators' view was that there was a need for an overhaul in their education system, and that EE should be a compulsory part of not only undergraduate but also all postgraduate teacher education courses.

> Of course it should be changed and as I said at every level of education one topic, one compulsory topic on environmental education. It maybe a specialisation, it need not be a main topic we can have it as a specialisation too. At least one small subject should be introduced at every level of education. (*Medha, Interview 2*)

SUMMARY

Teacher educators train new teachers, provide professional development for practicing teachers, consult with local schools, and provide expert opinion to regional and national ministries of education. Teacher educators write and teach not only pre-service teacher-education curriculum, but also contribute to committees that create teacher-education standards and officially mandated curriculum for primary and secondary education. They also write textbooks and sit on advisory committees from local to national levels. Because of this broad influence in curriculum design, implementation, and policy setting, faculty members of teacher-education institution can bring about far-reaching educational reform – even beyond training the teachers in the world. (UNESCO, 2005b, p. 3)

Teacher educators have been hailed as the ushers of change and are considered to be agents of reform (Darling-Hammond, 2006, 2008). According to McKeown (2005, p. 2) – by working with the administrations and faculties of teacher education institutions, governments can bring about 'systematic, economically effective changes'.

Empowering teacher educators will help empower the field of EE. This chapter's aim was to explore how the teacher educators who participated in this study viewed EE and how they felt empowered to teach it in the classroom. In doing so the chapter investigated their views about EE; how they (and their students) carried it out in their classrooms; what they thought of a major reform opportunity like the Supreme Court's ruling mandating EE in all schools and undergraduate colleges; and the support and education they received to usher in major policy reforms.

Teacher educators felt that although recent policy reforms had sparked off some changes in the field of EE it was not enough. They felt that there was a lot more to be done in order for EE to make in roads into every school and classroom in India. One of the challenges facing the field was the fact that EE was seen as mainly a Science field restricting access to learning and professional development in EE for students and teacher educators from a non-Science background. More importantly having a mainly scientific outlook took away the human and social aspects of EE with little or no emphasis on politics, social equity and justice that are crucial to the field. This helped to propagate (as has been established in earlier chapters) a technocentric and anthropocentric view towards the environment where the environment is seen as a problem that needs to be fixed often relying on scientific and technical solutions.

Teacher educators called for EE to be compulsorily taught to all student teachers irrespective of their academic background either as a separate subject or integrated into the rest of curriculum. These teacher educators seemed to lack the confidence to teach EE as a separate subject and were also unsure of their ability to maximise the opportunities for integration in their curriculum.

These teacher educators complained of a very rigid curriculum that had to be strictly adhered to. The culture of centralised examinations triggered a race to complete the syllabus and an overreliance on textbooks. Teaching strategies were mainly limited to lecturing which took away the joy of education; often making it dull and boring. Given this scenario it is natural that any additional units would be perceived as more rote learning and memorisation, and a few more exams to write – causing students and teachers to see EE as a burden. Education was entirely limited to the classrooms, which once again meant that students were not provided with opportunities to develop the sense of wonder and passion for the natural environment. Orr (1992, p. 89) described this situation as one of the major difficulties with enhancing ecological literacy. According to him, 'ecological literacy is becoming more difficult not because there are fewer books about nature but because there is less opportunity for direct experiences of it'.

Teacher educators complained of the lack of depth in their student teachers' outlooks and experiences with EE and their lack of motivation. The Federal Court's directives mandating EE in all schools and colleges in India was seen as a step in the right direction. While it had sparked off a number of policies, teacher educators were concerned about implementation, especially due to a lack of consistency, training, monitoring and accountability. Though the changes had initiated reforms in the central curriculum and sparked the setting up of eco-clubs, it had not particularly affected their work. A major challenge for them was the curriculum, which had not kept pace with the reforms and had remained unchanged for over a decade.

These teacher educators received limited support from their institution, the government or non-governmental agencies. They had minimal access to the latest research and developments in the field, and no professional development to augment their own learning and teaching. Their work was strictly categorised into subjects and they rarely sought or received any support towards integration of EE in their teaching. Apart from some basic support from two central NGOs (CEE & WWF) they had not received any help. CEE was the only organisation that had worked with these teacher educators (in fact only one specifically) in the area of teacher education. The others merely organised programmes for student teachers to familiarise themselves with some of the environmental issues.

These teacher educators' education lacked any serious preparation to teach EE. They had not received any training or professional developmental to help increase their skills and practices to implement EE in their teaching. This lack of training/ education was a serious inhibitor to helping them integrate EE in their teaching.

Categorising EE as a science subject reserved for teachers and students of science seriously hampered their exposure to EE if they came from a non-science background. This diluted their preparedness to teach EE. Shortcomings in their education prevented them from having a more holistic view of EE. The lack of EE in higher education was also reflected in the tertiary education system in India with none of the teacher educators receiving any form of EE during their postgraduate education.

In general, teacher education (as per this study) does not seem to have kept pace with changing times. These teacher educators received no education or training to teacher EE. They worked under stringent work conditions to complete a rather inflexible curriculum. Their teaching clearly reflected their own experiences as students and classroom teachers. There appears to be an urgent need for a shift from the existing situation to one whereby 'teaching [is] informed by knowledge of practice that goes beyond recounting of one's own school teaching experiences or being limited to the passing on of tips and tricks about teaching; it is moving beyond a view of teaching solely as doing' (Loughran, 2011, p. 284).

Teaching is far more complex when meaningful learning is the goal. Delivering or transmitting information is far easier than purposefully developing learners' engagement with content. In the environment that these teacher educators work, expecting them to (or hoping they will) bring about reforms without the necessary support is a fallacy.

CURRICULUM AND POLICY

Realities and Possibilities

The best curriculum serves as a bridge between the inner and outer worlds, between play and work, between dreams and reality. The best educational system will shape adults who both love the earth and are smart and competent. (Sobel, 2008, p. 154)

Reform efforts that have ignored the preparation of teachers have been doomed to fail, as they have assumed change could be achieved without attention to the knowledge, skills, and dispositions of the primary change agents without whom little transformation is possible. (Darling-Hammond et al., 2005, p. 442)

This chapter builds on the previous one in that it discusses curriculum and policy reform in detail. It draws upon the changes (or lack thereof) in the curriculum and teaching strategies to reflect the policies and reforms initiated in EE. The chapter goes on to discuss the role of the institution in guiding teacher educators toward implementation of EE. In particular, this chapter highlights the teacher educators' elaborations of the barriers and hurdles that they face in successfully implementing policy changes. They discuss ways in which they try to work around these barriers. Lastly the participating teacher educators elaborate on the kinds of support that they need and that would enable them to implement EE in their practice.

HOW EE IS PRIORITISED IN THE CURRICULUM AND PEDAGOGY

You are not given the opportunity to learn new things here. (*Blue, Interview 10)*

When asked about their own practices and how EE was prioritised in their teaching – curriculum and pedagogy – all teacher educators had mixed reactions. These teacher educators felt they could not give much importance to EE as it was not a part of their prescribed syllabus.

I don't think that much of importance is given – except when environmental education is taught as an area of specialisation. In the syllabus there are no aspects or concepts that are related to the environment ... nothing is specified in the syllabus. (*Axmi, Interview 5)*

While all participants agreed that it needed to be part of their everyday teaching practices they were unsure of the scope that the syllabus provided them to do this. Some felt severely hampered by the syllabus:

> In the B Ed syllabus it [environmental education] is not there. Maybe when we are teaching we give examples, we can tell them as teachers but directly if you go through the syllabus it is not there ... but if you come to myself or my subject – no its not there. (*Kala, Interview 11*)

Others did not find the syllabus all that constraining.

> Yes, it [environmental education] is there, weightage is there, in the curriculum it is not clearly shown but it is there and we have to identify, for example in the correlation between history and geography – definitely there we have to highlight the importance of the environment ... so in integration we teach, but not in isolation. (*Poornima, Interview 4*)

These teacher educators also felt that the integration of EE was subject dependent; while some subjects provided the opportunities others did not.

> We are not teaching environment as a separate subject as such. For example I am teaching X and where there is scope I will give reference. Basically it depends on the subject. (*Nammy, Interview 3*)

Some teacher educators did make an attempt to integrate EE in their classes.

> And even though it is not there in B Ed syllabus – they (student teachers) go to teach grades 8, 9 and 10. These grades have environmental science as one of the unit. So I bring such topics for discussion like pollution, global warming. (*Axmi, Interview 5*)

In general, while the teacher educators view EE as important they felt limited by the strict restrictions imposed by the rigid syllabus.

INFLUENCE OF RECENT POLICY CHANGES ON PERSONAL PRACTICE

Reform in education is a constant in these ever changing times. Court orders, government decisions and directives from educational boards drive reforms. However, in order to be successful, educational reforms need to be matched with classroom realities. Such realities include how teacher educators view reform, how they are engaged in the process and their sense of desire or motivation to carry out the reforms in their own classrooms. Unless matched by active implementation in the classroom, any effort to genuinely develop change through the reform process will be diminished. And as Cochran-Smith (2003) has noted, viewing teacher educators as 'superheroes' who effortlessly usher in reform is erroneous.

This section explores how these teacher educators internalised the reforms and the effects of the policy changes on their practices. It explores if and how they implemented change in their classrooms. It aims to understand these teacher educators' struggle to find purpose while being immersed in the 'sometimes schizophrenic rush to meet both curriculum standards and pupils' needs' (Hart, 2003, p. 1).

During interviews, these teacher educators briefly mentioned their struggles with the curriculum, which created opportunities to enquire further into their views about changes in policy and curriculum. They unanimously expressed their frustration about the curriculum, which according to them, had not kept pace with times. It had remained unchanged in over a decade and they were hoping for change in the immediate future. They were of the view that the curriculum did not provide them with much flexibility, especially because of the emphasis on maximising students' achievements in the final, centralised exams, which set the standards of the institution. As Blue stressed, this was the main reason for the strict adherence to the syllabus.

> Yes very strictly [follows the syllabus], because ultimately we have to evaluate and evaluation is from the syllabus. (*Blue, Interview 10*)

> No, no [when asked if any changes have been made], because we are following whatever syllabus is given so within that what we can do – we do. (*Kala, Interview 11*)

The federal court orders (Supreme Court of India, 2003), the National Curriculum Framework (National Commission for Education Research and Technology, 2005), the reforms in teacher education ushered in by the NCTE (2005) as well as NCTE (2009) had not, according to these teacher educators, triggered major reforms in their own practice or the practice of schools in which they were involved.

> I have not observed any such cases according to that Supreme Court intervention and even how it was earlier – similarly it is being continued. How environmental education was taught to students before 2004/05 is so the similar pattern is being continued. (*Poornima, Interview 4*)

> One Nature Club is there in our institution … nothing has been ordered, no special thing has been done, and whatever was there earlier we are following the same things. We did not stop it - that's all. (*Bhargava, Interview 9)*

Poornima went on to say that while the National Curriculum Framework (2005) had triggered some changes in her subject, these changes had not yet been implemented, as his own syllabus had not changed.

> In connection with the National Curriculum Framework – there in connection with the [subject] curriculum – few changes have been made. A few things have been affected but we have not implemented that 'til now. (*Poornima, Interview 4*)

Bhargava thought that one of the reasons for this could be the lack of awareness about the new policy and its details. This is because while there were random discussions held about the new policies there was a lack of coherence in the approach. While the National Curriculum Framework (2005) called for and provided plenty of opportunities for integrating EE, teachers and teacher educators were not geared up to practically implement these in their own practice.

> The National Curriculum Framework has come into work in 2005 but again most of the people are not aware of it. And only here and there some discussion has taken place but I am sure all the teachers are not aware of it. And in that it is clearly given how to teach [integrate] different subjects. (*Bhargava, Interview 6*)

Strong relationships between teacher educators and teachers are crucial to any good teacher preparation program (Darling-Hammond, 2006), but in this case, there were no clear and apparent links visible between these teacher educators and the local schoolteachers. Further to this – or in support of this view as hinted earlier in the study – these teacher educators had limited information about their student teachers' experiences in teaching EE during their practicum; suggesting a lack of strong communication and rapport with the schools in which the students were practising. For example, for one of the courses, student teachers started their exams straight after their teaching practice and never met their teacher educators afterwards.

> Nammy: No, they never come on their own [to discuss their teaching experiences]. If we ask they will tell …
>
> Researcher: so after their teaching practice do they ever come back [to relate their experiences].
>
> Nammy: No. What happens is that after the workshop they go for teaching practices and after that they will have terminal examinations and their course will be over. So they are not coming back and having an interaction. (*Nammy, Interview 3*)

There appears to be a lack of consistency between the changes made in the school curriculum and the changes in the teacher education system so new teachers are not so likely to be kept abreast of the current reforms.

> Yes [the curriculum] is almost 10 years old, which is a sorry state of affairs. I discussed this with the university people then, because whatever new changes are taking place at the secondary school level they are not very well reflected in the teacher education syllabus. We are also not allowed to drastically change it [syllabus] because once the regulation is framed, here and there minor changes are allowed only. (*Chidambar, Interview 7*)

An important point to note is that all these teacher educators expressed a deep willingness to learn. They were keen on implementing new policies and were willing to keep pace with the reforms. However, they were not ready to take the initiative themselves unless told to do so, they needed to be pushed or directed to act as leaders of educational reform; a curious situation.

Like they have not come down to us, if it comes down to us then it can have its effect. They say policy has been reconstructed, National Curriculum Framework 2005 is there but it has to come to implementation. If it is implemented and they say yes you have to teach about environment, or in an integrated approach teach about the environment – naturally I will do it. (*Axmi, Interview 5*)

As the data demonstrates, these teacher educators felt that they needed the push to be able to take action but they certainly didn't feel responsible to anyone to take on the issues for themselves.

When people are there to ask us – why you have not done this, why this is not done and all – then every person will be serious about it. But if nobody is very serious about the matter [in asking the teacher educators], then things will just go on. (*Bhargava, Interview 9*)

According to Bhargava a major factor in implementing EE is the personal initiative and motivation of individuals. Laws and acts, he suggested, were of little consequence unless an individual takes it upon himself to make the necessary changes.

What I personally feel is that even before that [the Supreme Court mandate] we were doing that, see to do something for the Supreme Court order or directive is not important. I was doing something about this even before the order and even after it also but what I am doing has nothing to do with that [the mandate]. Actually if one wants to do something good for society he need not wait for an order from the Supreme Court, even without the order he can do and he need not do anything even after the order is issued ... it has to come from the heart. (*Bhargava, Interview 9*)

Medha echoed similar sentiments as she stressed individual interest as a main driving force for change.

It is not about the policy, it depends upon the person who is teaching. If the teacher educator or teacher is interested in teaching environmental education, we can introduce it in our topics whenever we find an opportunity – we can teach certain chapters relating it to the environment. (*Medha, Interview 2*)

This view reinforces Nammy's perspective (below) that a lot of the changes he has made in his teaching had been triggered by personal interest and not policy changes. He was also of the view that often EE relies on one motivated teacher or teacher educator and that the program typically falls through if and when that person leaves the program.

Nammy: Yes like when we went camping with [a particular organisation] it was because of one person's support. There was no government initiative or support and today when he is retired there is no one to carry it forward. Of course the management wants to continue

> but the other person in charge does not have so much initiative to carry it forward.

Researcher: but this new person stepped into his place [role].

Nammy: no he was appointed and he does not have that much interest … it is just part of his responsibilities. (*Nammy, Interview 3*)

A prime issue then seems to be the lack of an educative process pertaining to policy development and implementation. Blue drew attention to this point when asked about that which she thought was most important for her as a teacher educator.

> We need to be educated; we need education. (*Blue, Interview 10*)

The only tangible effect of the policy changes seemed to be the added impetus given to Eco-clubs. Eco-clubs had been set up to increase environmental activities amongst school clubs. As part of this movement schools were provided with grants (approximately Rupees 5000 according to Medha, Interview 2) to organise environmental activities. Eco-clubs mainly function after school hours and students join in on a voluntary basis. Some of the activities conducted included tree planting, cleaning the school premises, maintaining the school gardens and organising drawing/Nammynting competitions. Teacher educators referred to the fostering of these Eco-clubs as one of the most concrete benefits of policy changes. Efforts made by these Eco-clubs were probably more visible as teacher educators could actually see the students involved and make some noticeable changes.

> [In] every school the [education] department has made it compulsory that there should be one Eco-club … Each Eco-club should hold so many activities every year, records should be maintained and one conference will be called, every school student has to participate in that, so higher level competitions are held – taluka level, then district level, then state level competitions will be held for the students and this honouring will be done for the winners by the department of education. (*Medha, Interview 2*)

While Eco-clubs may be a fine initiative to garner momentum for EE programs in schools there is need for research on these programs, their impacts and usefulness because at the time of the interviews, it was hard to ascertain what real impact they actually had on environmental views and understandings. The main initiative provided by the government seems to be monetary and there were no clear indications of the type of leadership and directives on the kind of activities to be conducted under the aegis of these Eco-clubs. There seemed to be a superficial approach to it and the potential held by these Eco-clubs at bringing grass root level changes was not being fully harnessed. So while activities like tree planting can bring about awareness on the need for more trees it need not necessarily build on students' sense of belonging to the environment or foster feelings towards nurturing these trees. Blue elaborated on this in one of her conversations with me regarding the 'Van Mahotsava' [tree ceremony] held every year as part of the Environmental Day celebrations.

> Every year they [some local celebrity or politician] plant a tree. No one waters it, it dies. Next year they come and plant a new tree in that same hole. It goes on every year … (*Journal Entry 5*)

These teacher educators had not earnestly devised new strategies to teach EE. Rather as described in the previous section they relied rather heavily on traditional teaching strategies – mainly lectures (in fact, giving examples about the environment or nature was the main mode of integrating EE in their daily teaching practices). The most popular mode of integrating EE into daily teaching practices was by giving examples or talking about it (as indicated below):

> Except when I take example from the content, the textbook when I am teaching them. I usually say whatever value is there … while giving example I tell them about it, knowingly or unknowingly we might integrate it but it is not a requirement in the syllabi. (*Kala, Interview 11*)

> Wherever it is possible for me to do it, I give examples. Sometimes I plan for those examples and sometime without planning, because I am interested in the subject the examples automatically come to me. (*Muleedhara, Interview 9*)

> No, not because of all these things [changes in policies] but out of my own interest when I am teaching. [Subject] is a Content-cum-Methodology subject, so I have to tell about the content also while not directly teaching the content. So I give examples from the content and while doing that I take examples of the environment so that I can discuss about environmental issues and matters with the pupils. (*Axmi, Interview 5*)

> Whenever there is an opportunity I emphasise the protection of the environment, how degradation is taking place and what are the measures taken up by the government … I draw examples from whatever is conducive to drive the point home. (*Anjalie, Interview 1*)

Teaching therefore seemed to be synonymous with telling. When asked about their own experiences in teaching EE one of the teacher educators replied:

> By only teaching. There is a set curriculum, just go and tell them [student teachers], they will just go and by-heart (memorise) it and they will do it. (*Blue, Interview 10*)

Another popular mode of teaching was reading and then dictating notes.

> In the classroom also – teaching means in the case of some teachers – is reading. It is just oral presentation of ideas or asking students to note down, mark in the textbooks. (*Bhargava, Interview 9*)

Only one of the teacher educators was involved in an extracurricular activity in the past, as a National Cadet Corps (NCC) officer, which involved organising camps. He tried to integrate environmental awareness activities into his teaching as part of the camp program.

> Whenever there is scope we ran programs and tell the students about the importance of surroundings and all that. And on Gandhi Jayanti every year I make the student's clean the campus. To create awareness of the environment we did a National Run program – we created banners and there was a 2 km run. Such activities are organised. (*Nammy, Interview 3*)

However, he did not continue any of these activities as a teacher educator in the institution due to a lack of time and scope.

Elaborating on the teaching strategies, Poornima discussed the following 'techniques':

> Poornima: First of all we identify the topic wherever it is possible and wherever there is an opportunity to integrate – such topics will be identified. Then we identify the plug points – wherever the environmental issue can be fused into that. Then we fuse the environmental issue along with the main content or main theme of the topic. In what way is it connected to the environment, what can be highlighted and what should be highlighted?
>
> Researcher: And how do you do this, what kind of teaching styles do you use?
>
> Poornima: through lectures, in some situations we ask students to give answers or responses by asking some questions. (*Poornima, Interview 4*)

Kala justified lecturing as the main teaching method because EE was a new topic and so according to her the students lacked the ability to work independently.

> I use lecturing mainly … sometimes group work or paid work is given, because all the things cannot be done. What happens is that this [environmental education] is a new thing to them, they have not studied in their degree classes, we cannot give much discussion because they don't know how to proceed … yes mostly we only have to give them the input and few questions we will ask between about that, sometimes they answer and many a times they don't answer. (*Kala, Interview 11*)

Again, as Poornima (Interview 8) stated, taking students out of the class was out of the question; so even activities like 'nature-games' were done inside the class with the teacher educator explaining the game and students observing it. A typical class (as observed many times throughout this project) has students sitting in rows while the teacher stands in the front talking and giving notes. Many such classes featured a handwritten transparency on an overhead projector with little attempt made to involve the students [P.O. 1–9]. Of all the classes observed, there was only one in which the dominant approach was not lecturing.

Throughout the interviews and classroom observations, the teacher educators consistently stated that they had not received any directives to make any changes in their teaching or approach to curriculum development, there were no initiatives provided to bring about change, there was no professional development opportunities to explore different teaching strategies not were there any incentives or pressures to make the changes; and so there seemed to be a general lack of change.

> My views about environment have been the same before the Supreme Court judgement and after. I still have the same feelings … In teaching – whatever views I express in my teaching before the judgement, I still express the same views. Nothing has changed, just the communication styles. Ideology is the same. (*Chidambar, Interview 7*)

Barriers to Implementation of EE

Previous research has shown that despite having a predisposition towards teaching EE, teachers may not follow through because of existing barriers (May, 2000). This section of the chapter summarises the barriers that teacher educators face in their daily teaching which hinders their implementation of EE in their classrooms.

Darling-Hammond et al. (2005, p. 447) identified some key problems with traditional teacher education. The following is a list of those problems and how they are manifested in India. Some other barriers experienced by teacher educators at this particular institution have also been identified and explained below.

Superficial curriculum. These teacher educators perceived that the curriculum was not in tandem with the changes prescribed by the new policies. As is clear from the data, their curriculum had remained unchanged for about 12 years. All these teacher educators emphasised the constraints that the rigid syllabus placed on them. The lack of flexibility was seriously felt. They were unable (and perhaps unequipped), to make changes due to the perceived pressure of completing the syllabus on time. As was noted in earlier chapters, this rigidity was driven by the fact that centralised exams are the main assessment tools for the students.

> Burden of the syllabus – that is the main thing that stops us all … yes and when we have to do environmental education it is a burden. Because we have to make use of our time for teaching this concept, so we have to remain in some areas [delve deeper into the topic]. That is natural otherwise we could go in a hurried way [move on with the topic and finish the syllabus on time]. So the burden of the syllabus is the main reason at all levels. (*Poornima, Interview 4*)

149

Having to finish the syllabus in a limited time placed a lot of stress on these teacher educators who felt that they had no time to even try and work around some of the problems.

> No [we don't work around these problems] ... there is no time. (*Poornima, Interview 4*)

Inadequate time. In this case the length of the program [10 months] and the amount of time allotted to each subject were seen as major problems (D.A. 2). In keeping with the pressures of the syllabus the time provided was inadequate according to these teacher educators. Both the teacher educators and student teachers struggled with this issue.

> Now what is happening is that both staff and students are running after time and they are over burdened. The students are really stressed with more writing assignments and they are scared of assignments. And even staff don't find time for co-curricular activities, they complain later on. (*Anjalie, Interview 1*)

Given this scenario, it is not surprising that in this institution the students and teacher educators did not prioritise EE. It is merely seen as an add-on, a co-curricular activity that had to fit in based on the time constraints. Inadequate time and the accompanying stress to complete the syllabus were major issues for these teacher educators. This point was exemplified by Leena's example – he is allocated 40 instructional periods to complete the syllabus but was of the view that he needed (and used) many more periods to actually complete it – which meant he was always under stress due to a lack of time.

> The thing is that we have to complete it within 40 instructional hours. Of course we will exceed, more than 70 periods we will take ... so that is according to the syllabus. Of course we all exceed. I usually take 70–80 periods. (*Leena, Interview 8*)

Another issue that adds to the stress of time for participants was the duration of the course. As highlighted in Chapter 8, these teacher educators saw this as a major hindrance to providing quality education. Although considered to be a one-year course, the actual instructional time is less:

> Our course is only 10 months duration and nearly two months are lost in teaching practice, the curriculum is over-burdened. We are supposed to teach 100 hours to complete a paper but in reality we don't get 100 hours. At the most we may get 80 hours, sometimes we have to forgo co-curricular activities and teach from 9.30 am – 5 pm – all theory classes. So that is a big problem to us. If instead the course is really of full one-year's duration we can organise such activities. (*Anjalie, Interview 1*)

Fragmentation. The view that EE is an offshoot of science education also created barriers in implementation because it was perceived that it restricted training and education opportunities exclusively to science teacher educators. Therefore, for those teacher educators who did not hail from a science background it was highly likely that they lacked exposure to EE. By restricting educational opportunities, these teacher educators from non-science backgrounds were, in effect, marginalised. Viewing EE as a part of science education further compartmentalised it for them; especially if they carried the notion that science is a tough subject.

So you train everyone, all teacher educators. Why do they want only science educators, why do they want only Principals to attend the refresher courses (*Kala, Interview 11*)

Also it is considered a part of Science... and it is then difficult in comparison to other subjects. Because in environmental education you talk about carbon cycle, food chain, biosphere, those things and the students feel it is most difficult... so student attitude is a problem. (*Anjalie, Interview 1*)

This need for training for all was extended to students too. Teacher educators like Bhargava and Chidambar felt that EE should be made compulsory in teacher education.

It should be present as a compulsory subject because if it is present as a compulsory subject – naturally all will learn ... all students will go for that and study about that and at least some percentage of students will develop interest in that particular area – environmental education. So that lack of compulsion maybe another barrier. (*Bhargava, Interview 9*)

It should be made a core subject. (*Chidambar, Interview 7*)

Uninspired teaching methods: Traditional views of schooling. Traditional lecture and memorisation continued to dominate. As elaborated in earlier sections all the classes (except one) used the traditional lecture methods with teacher educators providing notes, which students later memorised for their examinations. Student teachers worked in isolation with little involvement with the community and seemed to master chalkboards and textbooks instead of computers and web-based learning. Their pre-service education was not necessarily in line with what they were expected to do in their classrooms. Although teacher educators mentioned the use of other strategies in their teaching, none were visible in their practices. Informal conversation with the teacher educators also reaffirmed the fact that lecturing was the main strategy with the aim of transmission of knowledge.

Apart from the above five barriers, teacher educators at this institution pointed to other restraints they encountered while trying to implement EE.

Education/Training. These teacher educators believed that education, or the lack of it, was a key barrier. They saw policy makers as disconnected from the realities of the classroom (a somewhat curious position considering that which the data suggests about their own connection to schools and teachers). They called for the education of policy makers – namely the government officials and bureaucrats who, according to them, drafted policies without actually having worked in the field.

> The top people … like those who are implementing the government policies –
> the curriculum, responsible for education, Secretaries – the IAS officers, they
> should be educated first, the Head of Education should be educated first – if
> you don't know anything then you cannot implement [the policies] on me.
> (*Blue, Interview 10*)

> Maybe policy makers are not thinking of practical aspects. Of course they have
> brought policy but what further they have to do – what type of curriculum
> they have to bring about, what type of training materials they have to develop,
> so regarding the practical implementation of that policy they are not thinking
> about. They are not thinking about the resources they have to provide.
> (*Bhargava, Interview 9*)

There was a common view that there was not a coherent national program and that therefore signalled a weak attempt to implement policies. Underpinning that there was a strong view for a nationally driven policy that pushed for uniform reform across the country.

> In India what happens is that we make a lot of policies, problem is with the
> implementation. We have to make a nation-wide program and that program has
> to be implemented. (*Nammy, Interview 3*)

These teacher educators saw a lack of 'training' as a major hindrance. In this study that point kept coming across as a major factor that affected these teacher educators teaching of EE.

> And the government and department of education have to provide training to the
> teachers in this respect. See even though there is scope to teach environmental
> education in the content and syllabus many teachers are not making effective
> use of this and that is only because of lack of training, which creates a barrier.
> If that is removed and the teachers make a commitment then I think teachers
> can play a very important role. (*Nammy, Interview 3*)

> I feel that training of teachers and teacher educators is required because they
> should be familiarised with the various concepts of environmental education
> and how to bring about the integration, so such things they should know. For
> this reason training is important. (*Bhargava, Interview 9*)

Some of them said that while they may be aware of the environmental concepts, they did not know much about EE. They felt that they lacked the skills to integrate EE into their teaching. This lack of knowledge attributed to their lack of confidence in dealing with the subject.

> I don't have the knowledge about that particular field [environmental education], that's why I am afraid of that. Basically we should know the concepts- then only can we enter the field. (*Poornima, Interview 4*)

Once again the need for education was felt – training was seen as the main source of increasing their knowledge and competencies to teach EE.

> Yes, training and even basic knowledge is required about the environment, about environmental education, what are the techniques, strategies which we should understand first then only we have to enter the field. (*Poornima, Interview 4*)

> So they know about environment … but they [teacher educators] don't know how to teach it, environmental education they may not know. Except if they conduct programs [training programs], then they will know that. (*Kala, Interview 11*)

Even when training was provided it was through a one-day workshop with no access to on-going professional development for these teacher educators. According to Leena (Interview 8), the one-day workshop on EE that was offered was not followed up by any other activity or educational opportunity. As so much of the research into professional development illustrates, such one-shot workshops do not provide sustained benefits to participants.

Attitude. According to these teacher educators their students lacked the 'right attitude' towards education in general and seemed to confine their thinking and interests only to their area of specialisation.

> And attitudinal changes should be taken, like for everything you need the proper attitude … [Students] are not much interested, because after SSLC [year 10] we go in for subject specialisation, so we feel that if I do commerce, then my area, my world is commerce. Whatever is happening [elsewhere] is not my concern. So lack of concern is an issue, why I should do – that attitude. (*Kala, Interview 11*)

According to one of the Teacher Educators' changes in the political situation and cultural climate of the country accounted for the lack of interest in the environment, which in turn had caused disdain towards EE.

> A lack of interest related to environment or environmental education on the part of common people and political aspects – because all should happen through political things only. So maybe a lack of importance for environmental education and all people think about improving economically and the standard of living. So with those intentions the concepts and aspects of environmental

education have been forgotten... we think of our own comforts, we should have a vehicle, AC [air-conditioning] – it's very hot, what adverse effects it has on the environment – no one goes to think about that. (*Bhargava, Interview 9*)

This emphasis on economic development over environmental well-being and the ensuing rush to 'modernise' appears (from participants' perspective) to have created a disconnect with culture and age-old traditions of living sustainably.

Culturally too many changes are taking place. Like as I gave the example of Tulsi [refer to Chapter 5], most of Hindu houses here now live in flats [apartments], they don't have the plant and they don't go for worshipping. So culturally too much of changes are taking place, the younger generation are not very much exposed to the culture in comparison to the older generation – maybe that gap is creating less interest towards the environment ... part of the reason is that maybe they not have elders [due to the trend toward nuclear families] – grandparents who can tell about the culture. Parents are very busy – both maybe working. (*Bhargava, Interview 9*)

Language barrier. The prevalence of English as the major language was a barrier, especially for those students and teacher educators who were not well versed with it. An inability to speak English fluently creates a heavy reliance on text and pre-made materials, which hampers chances of intuitively integrating EE into their teaching.

When they are teaching that is the biggest problem, speaking and teaching in English so then they are always concentrating on the language rather than the content of what they are teaching. (*Kala, Interview 11*)

Lack of information. Teacher educators saw information dissemination as another important issue that affected their practice of EE. As noted in Chapter 8, these teacher educators did not feel as though they were involved in the policy making process. To make matters worse – they also did not feel that they were being kept abreast of the latest policy changes.

Leena: See any policies and programs we should be immediately notified. The information should be disseminated to all the B Ed colleges.

Researcher: so it doesn't happen right now? How do you get information?

Leena: no, by the media ... and they will not send any circulars, any notifications to the colleges. I mean all the teacher educators are neglected ... one thing is that we should be informed – in any government plans we can be included; our opinions should be included. (*Leena, Interview 8*)

This lack of information meant that (as mentioned in the previous section), these teacher educators were not aware of many of the policy changes. There was then a gap between what they taught their students in the teacher education institutions and what their student teachers experienced once they started working as full time teachers.

> And the new programs – they try to originate new programs for schoolteachers. See there is a yawning gap between what we do in the college of education and what takes place in the classroom at the school level. And my students are ill equipped at the secondary school level right now. Because a number of new programs have been implemented at the school level and here we are not training them for that, because the department does not give us enough funds or enough training or pass on information. (*Anjalie, Interview 1*)

Neglect. The above gap between the teacher education program and classroom teaching points to a shortage of educational programs designed to orient teacher educators towards major policy changes. These teacher educators accused the authorities of neglect and felt that the authorities – particularly in the government – were not interested in their work.

> In the government – especially the education department – we don't get any guidance, they never bother how the college is functioning, what are the problems, what are the inputs. We send out college magazine regularly to them, not even once – [in more than a decade] – have I received a letter from the director – commending my job, complimenting my job or criticising my job – Nothing … no appreciation, no criticism, they are not even bothered to discuss any problems. (*Anjalie, Interview 1*)

Lack of resources. The resources available to this particular teacher education institution were very limited. For example, access to even simple resources was limited:

> Leena does not have any documents – I had to get them through the Principal. She has the exam papers, but she could not use the photocopier without the Principal's permission. Even if she has to take a single copy, she needs to take permission from the principal. I asked her about how she gives out information or prepare handouts, worksheets etc. for her students. Well she handwrites one copy – rarely uses a computer to type – and then gives it to one student. That student makes a copy for herself and passes it on to the others – so it is like a chain reaction. But the students have to do it on their own. (*R.J. 5*)

In terms of resources, the library was under stocked. It had very few new books on EE. As described in earlier chapters the institution did not subscribe to any of the national or international journals of EE. There were only two computers available for teacher educators to use – one in the Principal's room and the other in the administrative office (R.J. 1). Naturally these teacher educators did not make much use of these computers. Internet access was limited and teacher educators naturally saw this as a barrier in accessing latest information and research.

> If we have Internet connection for all of us, that is good. (*Leena, Interview 8*)

There weren't enough quality teaching materials available.

> If we have to teach the subject, sometimes the teachers find it difficult, sometimes pupils find it difficult, because not many books are there on environmental education. Here and there a few books might be there, but nothing exclusively on environmental education. Not many good books are available … no resources or materials are passed down. (*Anjalie, Interview 1*)

> The main problem is a lack of study materials is a problem, poor knowledge in connection with the environment. (*Chidambar, Interview 7*)

The lack of resources was directly attributed to a lack of funding for the institute. This particular college of education was a semi-aided institution [as explained in Chapter 5], which means that the government paid a few of the teacher educators' salaries. All administrative and resource costs were to be borne by the management (which often had to cut corners to make ends meet):

> I am not computer savvy myself but I understand that you can pass on information very quickly and you can use it in the classroom, give power point presentations and all that will really help. But the problem is that one has to go for investment and the management is not ready to invest immediately lump sum money. (*Anjalie, Interview 1*)

Privatisation of teacher education. Privatisation of the education sector and withdrawal of government support had seriously damaged smaller semi-aided institutions like this one. They were not fully privatised and so could not increase their fees to accommodate more staff and resources. They did not receive enough grants and assistance from the government, which created further issues:

> You see our parent body – the institution – is not at all interested in teacher education course. Not at all interested in improving teacher education course, in solving the problems we have right now. In India teacher education is most problematic front today because of unscrupulous managements, a lot of privatisation, easily giving permission to start a college and under educated teacher educators. A lot of hurdles and problems are there in teacher education. So it has become difficult to maintain standards. There is a lot of deterioration of standards in teacher education courses in India … 10 people have to work for 20–30 people, they are overburdened. (*Anjalie, Interview 1*)

The for-profit attitude, according to this teacher educator, was seriously harming teacher education institutions. Teaching and learning had moved from being a noble profession to being a moneymaking business, which meant that profits were of paramount importance.

> And people will invest money if there are returns, the management will invest money if there are returns, and otherwise they will not invest. So education has become a kind of industry now to earn money ... profit and loss. (*Anjalie, Interview 1*)

At this institution, staff was underpaid [they received approximately half the salary of a UGC[1] paid staff] and do not receive any retirement benefits, leave benefits or provident benefits. Further to this, staff was recruited on a yearly contract basis, which offered much less security than the other UGC paid staff who were permanent employees.

> So we have a sector of unorganised and untrained teachers and lecturers ... unmotivated. So you cannot expect a 100% commitment from them. Of course in my college they work very well because they are all our own products [i.e., most of the teacher educators at this institution were students of this institution]. (*Anjalie, Interview 1*)

Lack of research. Another major barrier is the absence of research at this teacher education institution. Teacher educators did not have access to the latest journals in the field of teacher education or EE nor were they involved in any research studies themselves. According to Anjalie, this restricted their views of teaching; limiting their vision for what it might mean to be a teacher educator.

> I have been telling them that – to do a bit of research, to do a PhD and all that, but they are not interested because the salaries are very low. They will spend a lot of amount [on the PhD] and after doing this what are the avenues, can I get a promotion, can I get a good salary. Automatically people think about the practicalities, so then when they think that way they feel it is of no use – why should I spend ... even after that I may not be promoted, I may not get government salary, hardly at the most my salary may be increased by 200–300 rupees, so why should I do that – its quite natural ... [you only do research] for your satisfaction. (*Anjalie, Interview 1*)

It is clear then that this particular teacher education institution faces numerous barriers when it comes to implementing EE. It suffers from a lack of time, resource and finance and not surprisingly then lacks the ability to develop an EE program; especially as it has very little outside support.

Support for successful implementation of EE. According to Darling-Hammond (2006, p. 41) some common features of a good teacher education program include:

'a common, clear vision of good teaching; well-defined standards of practice and performance; a strong curriculum taught in the context of practice, explicit strategies developed to help students confront their own assumptions and learn from their own experiences; strong links between schools and university based faculty; and, research guided methods applying learning to real problems of practice'.

While the previous section dwelt on the problems and barriers that prevented these teacher educators from implementing EE, the following section seeks to understand the kind of support necessary in order to work around these barriers. This section considers those things could be done in terms of building a way forward. It discusses these teacher educators' perspectives and suggestions for helping to improve their future teaching of EE.

Strong curriculum. In order to be successful, teacher educators need 'access to strong curriculum and the materials with which to learn it, technology supports for learning and inquiry; reasonable class sizes, safe, clean facilities; and, equitable opportunities to benefit from all of these' (Darling-Hammond et al., 2005, p. 444). As described earlier these teacher educators had been relying heavily on a curriculum that remained unchanged in over 10 years. There is little doubt that 'modernising' the curriculum would be an important way of advancing possibilities for EE in this institution.

De-compartmentalisation of EE. These teacher educators felt that de-compartmentalisation of their work could make a difference:

> ... [we're] not expected to do it, since you are in charge of that [whatever their subject and designated responsibilities] you do it – that's the attitude, we have been given certain charges [responsibilities] so we are concerned only with that. So if any program comes under environment, she [the environmental education specialist] will be in charge of that along with that club. (*Kala, Interview 11*)

Through departmentalisation, these teacher educators felt isolated and uncomfortable in asking for assistance. More so, they were of the view that any request for assistance would be denied as it did not fall within the purview of their department. Therefore, creating a sense of belonging beyond the narrow confines of the department was seen as one way of positively addressing the situation.

> I think others also should be given a chance ... others who are not into environmental education will not be knowing more about it because they will be concentrating on their own field, so for others also such training should be given, so that they can incorporate the aspects of environmental education in their teaching also. (*Axmi, Interview 5*)

Incentives.   Appreciation of their work was another important way of supporting them. Providing teacher educators with incentives, motivating them to show initiative and encouraging their efforts could inspire them.

> At least some rewards or honouring, identification or recognition that this type of work is going on, this is because of the initiatives of this teacher or teacher educator. Like that some kind of recognition is needed. Providing incentives and all may not be in our hands and that may not be practically implemented but this is better. (*Poornima, Interview 4*)

Quality resources.   Access to quality resources, which include up to date teaching materials, a well-stocked library with recent books and journals would obviously be a step forward. These teacher educators needed access to better resources particularly better teaching materials – recent books and journals for referencing. At the time of this study, the only teaching material being used was the syllabus and one module published by NCERT. Providing them with good quality teaching resources would offer them insights and suggestions for different teaching strategies and activities for EE.

> Maybe some facts, information, pictures, CD's related to environmental aspects, knowledge about what is happening in other countries, other places related to environment – such resources if they are sent, then maybe we can have a show, a film show or something like that. This can help the students and me also. (*Axmi, Interview 5*)

Access to the latest technology would enhance both the teaching and learning experiences in their classrooms. Computers and the Internet in the classroom if supported with adequate training could make web-based learning a reality and put them in touch with other educators and educational materials. Access to audio-visual resources and the time to be able to use them would clearly enrich their classrooms. A well-equipped library would also work towards the same goal and make the latest research accessible to both the teacher educators and their students. Providing students with more opportunities to use a well-stocked library would also assist in honing their research skills. At the time of this research, students had access to the library for only 2 scheduled periods a day, which teacher educators like Leena [Interview 8] considered inadequate.

Better working conditions.   These teacher educators, as discussed earlier, sometimes taught classes with 100 students, the classrooms they worked in were hot and stuffy with a couple of fans to deal with temperatures in excess of 40 degrees Celsius, and they did not always have equal access to whatever little benefits the government or NGO's had to offer. It is impractical to expect them to work productively; leave alone innovatively under such appalling conditions.

Another important issue in improving working conditions is to improve salaries in order to make teaching a more lucrative profession. This could ensure that teaching attracted qualified, motivated teachers who chose teaching as a profession and didn't stumble upon it or pick it up for lack of other alternatives.

Collaborative professional development networks. Providing teacher educators with possibilities for interaction with other teacher educators from other colleges could also provide them with opportunities to learn from, and with, others who are working on similar issues. Leena thought that having a network of teacher educators to support each other would be helpful.

> And there should be a workshop – I mean there should be a get together of all the teacher educators of environmental education in a year. That will be good because we can discuss many things. (*Leena, Interview 8*)

This is in line with a call to form 'communities of learning' or 'professional learning communities' in order to prepare teacher educators from across different faculties to work in unison (Darling-Hammond, 2012; Darling-Hammond et al., 2005; Shagrir, 2011) – in this case on the implementation of EE. The collaborative work of individuals from various institutions could provide teacher educators with opportunities to learn, co-construct knowledge, acquaint themselves with knowledge developed by others and to continuously engage with research and development (Shagrir, 2011).

Drawing on Smith's views, Shagrir (2011) extended this notion of working and learning together suggesting it was a far better approach to professional learning than forms of induction that mainly rely on transmitting information, habits and routines. Therefore opening the doors of communication between teacher educators and policy makers is another avenue of support available to them. Providing them with first hand information and seeking their expert opinion could help keep them develop a sense of ownership about policy changes and associated requirements for curriculum development and practice.

Offering educational opportunities to all teacher educators could clearly help overcome the biggest hurdle that these teacher educators encountered; the feeling of being unprepared to teach EE. The education of teacher educators according to Cochran-Smith (2003, p. 25) needs to be conceptualised as a 'process of continual and systematic inquiry wherein participants question their own and others' assumptions and construct local as well as public knowledge appropriate to the changing contexts in which they work' thus providing them with a way to think about education as a process of change. This approach however would only work if teacher educators saw a 'potential in a future they construct in which expertise is defined as more than being a teacher in a teacher education programme' (Loughran, 2010, p. 289). As mentioned in earlier sections, these teacher educators did not see themselves as more than teachers in a teacher education context. They felt inadequate, lacked confidence and the know-how in teaching EE. Appropriate guidance, training and support, they contended, would enable them to teach EE better. It would enable them to move beyond their own experiences as students and student teachers. In teacher education colleges and schools, providing good settings for teacher learning would mean offering 'lots of opportunities for research and inquiry, for trying and testing, for talking about and evaluating the results of learning and teaching' (Darling-Hammond, 2008, p. 337).

> If training is given, if I am given a chance then whatever I have been taught or whatever information has been given – I will use it in my classroom. (*Axmi, Interview 5*)

> If government is supporting such [teacher educators], giving financial support and moral support specially – really we can work hard in that and we can make the people aware of it, so many things can be done is what I feel. (*Blue, Interview 10*)

Education is clearly important in helping to learn about policies and its impact in classrooms. This was particularly important to teacher educators like Kala who felt it was necessary in order to stay in touch with the realities of classroom teaching.

> … whatever they teach us that could be taught to our student teachers and those student teachers could go and implement directly in the schools. Because they are the ones who have direct contact with the children. We don't have that contact, we are in the colleges only – we don't have a direct link with the school children. So our students can be taught, can be oriented and they can bring about the change, implement it in the school level. Such programs [training] will be better. Like the syllabus, giving us some orientation or refresher courses, or conducting workshops for teacher educators. (*Kala, Interview 11*)

One of the suggestions offered was to have an environmental resource person who would visit the college of education and offer support.

> And even they should send resource persons to us so that we will know the latest developments that are taking place in the field of environmental education. In this way we can bridge the gap to some extent especially for the institutions or schools. (*Arya, Interview 6*)

Monetary support. Lastly, these teacher educators called for more financial support to the institution so that it could organise more 'environmental programs'. Grants were needed to fund the training program and information sessions that would increase teacher educators' knowledge about the environment. Ironically they did not really seek much help in improving their pedagogy and approach towards EE.

If we want to organise a 2–3 day program, who will spend the money? That is very important – the institution should be financed or the university should take the initiative. (*Bhargava, Interview 9*)

In short these teacher educators listed numerous avenues for support in helping them improve their implementation of EE. It is noteworthy that none of them shied away from the thought of integrating EE in their teaching. What they needed was adequate support to enable them to do so, and as a consequence, could be a conduit to achieving India's ambitious target of ensuring every child in every school experiences EE.

SUMMARY

Darling-Hammond (2006, p. 189) stated that 'continuously interweaving the demands of the subject matter with the needs of the students so as to shape the curriculum towards the child and the child's interests toward the curriculum is rather like sculpting a double helix of teaching and learning'. The teacher educators in this study struggled with moulding this double helix because of time pressures, insufficient educational expertise, inadequate resources and issues associated with the bureaucracy. The numerous policy changes failed to reach these teacher educators and there had been little change in their practice of EE as a result of these policy changes or the Supreme Court mandate. As the data makes clear, these teacher educators were simply continuing the way they had before the new policies had come into play. In other words student teachers at this institution were not being adequately prepared to implement the Supreme Court ruling – to provide EE in all schools across India.

These teacher educators largely blamed the system for this situation. They felt hampered by a curriculum that had failed to keep pace with the reforms, leaving them with little flexibility to innovate. The changes in National policy had not brought about any change in their own syllabus and they recognized the inconsistency between what they were teaching their student teachers and what their student teachers were expected to do in their own classrooms. (What's more, they did not work closely with local schools and communities to help bridge this gap.)

These teacher educators did not feel particularly motivated to change openly stating that they needed a push in order to take action. They reported numerous barriers to change, chief amongst them being a lack of education at every level – their pre-service teacher education, their in service education as schoolteachers and now the same lack of educative processes as teacher educators.

They blamed the political situation and fast changing cultural climate of the country with its increased emphasis on economic development (often at the cost of the environment) as a major reason for the lack of take up of policy reform. However, if provided with the necessary support there were clear signs of a willingness to learn about how to better implement EE in India; a challenging task in an equally challenging environment.

NOTE

[1] At the time of the interview UGC staff members were being paid approximately Rupees 18,000 with benefits whilst management staff were being paid Rupees 10,000 with no benefits (Anjalie, Interview 1).

SECTION 4

MAKING SENSE OF THE STORIES:
NEED FOR REFORM

SYNTHESIS

> This is the colourful and fragrant spring of environmentalism. Ideas emerge
> with each blossom. Over the next decades, these trees will change their shapes,
> grow new branches, and display new leaves. (Thomashow, 1996, p. 64)

India is currently in the throes of an awakening towards its environmental problems
caused by the ongoing and rapid development it is experiencing. This study in fact
was triggered by the growing concern for the rapid environmental degradation in
India and by the formulation of important policy documents in response to this
degradation. The aim of study (as stated in Chapter 2) has been to understand
participating teacher educators' experiences in implementing Environmental
Education in India. The following were the main objectives of the study:

1. to determine the ways, in which EE is understood, negotiated, determined and
   implemented by teacher educators in India;
2. to understand the organisational culture of teacher education in India and its role
   in implementing EE in context of the culture of teacher education; and,
3. to ascertain the characteristics – the qualities, issues and problems – that enable
   and/or constrain the development and implementation of EE in Teacher Education.

The preceding two discussed the findings from the research. This chapter
synthesizes these findings and highlights the major issues that emerge as a
consequence. Each of the above objectives makes up a section of the chapter and
together offers an integrated set of ideas that helps to explain the data in a more
integrated and holistic fashion. The final section builds on these ideas to make
a statement about EE in Teacher Education in India and discusses some of the
implications that emerge from this research.

At this point it is important to reiterate that the aim of this research was not to
look for findings that could be generalised across India and the teacher education
sector. In Shagrir's (2011, p. 82) words the intention was 'to explore contemporary
experiences in distinct contexts', to understand teacher educators' experiences,
to identify the main factors that influence the implementation of EE in teacher
education, and to further develop issues and concerns that need to be pursued in
future research as a consequence of the learning from this project. The outcomes
from the research as framed through the aims are now examined in detail.

THE WAYS, IN WHICH EE IS UNDERSTOOD, NEGOTIATED, DETERMINED AND IMPLEMENTED

This section discusses the different approaches to EE and how it is conceptualised at this particular teacher education institution in India. It specifically examines how the teacher educators who participated in the study at this institution understand EE, how they negotiate its implementation given the myriad demands on their time and attentions and how then they further determine the aspects and features of EE that they will likely implement in their own practice.

While examining the above objectives some of the key features apparent in the data are:

1. The lack of prioritisation of EE in India. This means that while EE is finding its place in policy documents, in this case it has not been prioritised in terms of implementation.
2. EE tends to be seen merely as an offshoot or branch of Science Education and has to yet establish itself as a field in its own right.
3. There is an overemphasis on Sustainable Development, which leads to a neglect of other key factors such as nature education.
4. There is a severe lack of educational opportunities to help prepare teacher educators to implement EE.
5. EE is also seen as a means of solving a problem rather than an area of study that is taken up for its own worth.

The rest of this section deliberates on each of these topics and sheds light on the findings in relation to them.

Lack of Prioritisation of Environmental Education

Bonnett (2006) lists two approaches to EE. One is 'environmentalism' where education actively promotes tangible and positive environmental behaviours. The other is an 'action competence' approach which promotes exploration and engagement in environmental issues through firsthand experiences and critical/ contextual analysis of those experiences. However, what this study suggests is the need for a fusion of these two approaches whereby the metaphysical aspects of the underlying issues might be dealt with. This would require thinking about the intrinsic motives that fuel how we think about 'ourselves and the world'. In so doing, the issues would be less about policy implementation and more about the meaning behind the policies. The reason for this approach is based on the question: 'What are we seeking to achieve through these policy reforms?' In attempting to comprehend how EE is understood and conceptualised at this particular institution in India the data (as particularly evident in the results), it appears to largely being paid 'lip service'. (Issues of policy formulation/implementation are further examined in a later section of this chapter that underscores the constraints and hurdles to EE in

India.) In India generally it could well be concluded that education is perceived by many as carrying a lower priority. For example, there was a decline in budget allocation for education from 3.13% in the 2004–05 to 2.84% in 2009–10. Despite an increase in the financial value of the funds available to the education sector, this figure falls short when compared to the allocation vis-à-vis the total budget (Kapur, 2011). Within the Education sector, teacher education and schools receive much less attention than fields like medicine and engineering – perhaps illustrating differences in values and societal aspirations. This view is particularly evident at the institution in this study where the medical college run by the same educational board had state of the art facilities, while the teacher education college had very limited resources.

Within Education, EE further slides down the priority list due to the pressures and demands of other 'important' and 'compulsory' subjects. These teacher educators were not sure about how effectively they thought their student teachers were being prepared to teach EE. They pointed to a lack of emphasis in the curriculum and lack of appropriate attitude and motivation amongst students as major issues. However, the interviews and classroom observations also pointed out that most teacher educators simply referred to environmental issues by way of giving examples during their lectures but were not substantive in terms of an underpinning EE stance. There was a clear lack of deeper understanding of EE and most teacher educators confirmed this when they talked about their own lack of confidence in the field. This was one of the main reasons why EE was not prioritised in their own teaching practices – as seen in the classroom observation data. While all the teacher educators discussed the need to prioritise EE they were unsure of how to go about doing that. As the data highlighted, most thought that giving examples was the only way they could infuse environmental topics into their teaching. The findings revealed a complete lack of outdoor educational opportunities for these Teacher educators and their students adding to the limitations they were confronted by – and perhaps inadvertently reinforced – in implementing EE.

Environmental Education as Science Education

The history of EE, as discussed in detail in the Literature Review (Chapter 2), can be traced back to Nature Education and a call for increased scientific and technological education to stem the increasing environmental crisis (Palmer, 1998). By the 1960s, there was greater recognition of the need to provide education to create awareness of the threats to human species and to stimulate thinking and discussion (Gough, 2006). The Tbilisi conference (UNESCO & UNEP, 1977) set the following goals for EE which are widely used to frame the field:

1. to foster clear awareness of, concern about, economic, social, political and ecological interdependence in urban and rural areas;
2. to provide every person with opportunities to acquire knowledge, values, attitudes, commitment and skills needed to protect and improve the environment; and,

3. to create new patterns of behaviours of individuals, groups and society as a whole towards the environment.

As is clear in the above goals EE was conceptualized as a more holistic approach; one that could cut across fields and disciplines. Issues of social equity, justice, security and peace are closely related to environmental wellbeing. Political, economic and social agendas have been dictating what teachers need to know and how they build capacity, including their skills and disposition (Grant, 2008). These are overriding factors in environmental decision-making whether under the auspices of EE, Education for Sustainable Development or Education for Sustainability.

Placing EE/Education for Sustainability under the umbrella of Science Education has often been an overarching approach. For example Fien and Maclean (2000) made a call for science to be at the core of the Education for Sustainability paradigm. However, in recent times there have been strong calls to broaden EE and Education for Sustainability to encompass issues of social equity, justice and security. Reliance on Science rather than social and community learning, in other words situating EE in complete isolation of the community falls short of the goals of EE – community involvement is paramount to EE (Singh, 2011). According to Schusler et al. (2009, p. 124) environmental action can only be fostered by co-creating environmental and social change, by building 'individuals' personal capabilities for further participation, contributing to personal and community transformation.' Hart (2003) also stresses that EE, as a social issue, is far more important than EE as Science.

One of the shortcomings pointed out by UNESCO (2002) in the current education system is the gap in dealing with wider issues in the sustainability paradigms. For example, UNESCO points out the lack of links made between people's health, their individual and collective actions and the health and sustainability of ecosystems. There is a wide gap in how teacher educators, key stakeholders and environmental educators operate and a significant amount of work is needed in order to be able to produce graduates capable of pursuing environmental education for a sustainable future (Cutter-Mackenzie & Tilbury, 2002, p. 30).

In this study the overwhelming feeling amongst the teacher educators involved in this study was that EE is viewed as a branch of Science (as was apparent in the results). As discussed in those chapters, this was problematic for these teacher educators and they felt seriously hampered in their roles and abilities to access information. Those teacher educators that did not come from a Science background believed that they did not have the skills or knowledge to teach about the environment. At the same time they also felt that there were no expectations for them to teach about the environment either. A closer look at the syllabus for the EE units taught at this institution showed a heavy reliance on teaching Environmental Science concepts as indicated in Chapter 5 with issues like pollution and conservation of natural places given high priority. Since most of these Teacher educators did not have a Science educational background (as indicated in Chapter 5) they did not feel confident with the subject matter to teach EE. They felt disempowered to teach EE due to this lack of Science education. These teacher educators saw EE as an offshoot of Science and did not appear to be cognizant of the goals of EE mentioned above.

Overemphasis on Sustainable Development

Sustainable development is a highly problematic term riddled with internal contradictions especially around the way it is interpreted (Bonnet, 2006). It seems to have taken the focus away from nature and experiences that nurture love and passion for the environment. It seems to assert that the central issues now revolve around saving/preserving/conserving the environment and regulating the consumption of its resources. Jickling (2001, p. 168) affirms this while describing two problems with the term sustainability. The first is the promotion of education as a 'tool in the service of some ideology' making it 'somehow justifiable to implant learners with the guiding principles of sustainability'. This according to Jickling amounts to indoctrination. The second problem according to Jickling is the 'one-dimensional nature' of the sustainability agenda, which is characterised by its inability to provide epistemological breadth to help us understand what else needs to be done to live well on this planet. The term 'sustain' means 'keep going continuously' which when presented as the ultimate aim of EE is seriously flawed (p. 169).

An activist approach towards EE or Education for Sustainability where universities are seen as 'perfect places for instilling the idea of sustainability in young minds' and for 'stemming environmental pollution and degradation' (Jain & Pant, 2010, p. 236) does little to promote the love and concern that Sobel (2008) considers crucial in developing environmental stewardship. Portraying students as 'Saviours' of planet Earth and the only hope towards allaying a disastrous future, in other words adopting a doomsday approach, spells a very negative attitude towards environmental education. Knowledge, bereft of experiences that develop deep commitment and connection to the environment and allow love to take root and flourish – hold no meaning. In John Burrough's words, 'Knowledge without love will not stick, but if love comes first, knowledge is sure to follow' (Sobel, 2008, p. 12).

The heavy emphasis on Sustainable Development at the institution in which this study was conducted brings with it all the issues briefly outlined above. Teacher educators (as indicated in Chapters 6 & 7) identified themselves with the Sustainability paradigms which then took away (as described above) from the experiences that helped grow long lasting passion and love for the environment. When questioned about their views on economic development versus environmental protection, these teacher educators almost unanimously vouched for economic development even if it came at the cost of the environment. As evidenced throughout the data (particularly in Chapter 7) Teacher educators held the view that economic development was the key to solving India's poverty problems and with advances in Science and Technology, the environmental aspects could then be solved.

Sustainable Development in this context is based on a near total emphasis on seeing the environment as a resource that needs to be preserved so that it can serve future generations of humans. On the one hand, this goes against the grain of the cultural ethos and tradition of Indian civilisation (as described in the Literature Review and the Conceptual Framework chapters). On the other hand, it asks the current generation to stem its growth/development/needs in order to save some for the future generations. At the Stockholm conference, the then Prime Minister of India, Indira Gandhi, emphasised that poverty and need were often the greatest polluters (Rangarajan, 2009). For a generation of people scrambling to meet its current needs, preserving the environment for the future can be a lot to ask. This is also the issue that critics have raised with the Sustainable Development movement, which has been planting its roots in India.

There have been some movements that emphasize Sustainable Development in India and this is exemplified by the fact that India's only journal in the field is called the Journal of Education for Sustainable Development. Sustainable Development according to a commonly used definition is 'development that meets the needs of the current generation without compromising the needs of the future generations' (World Commission on Environment and Development, 1987, p. 43). The question however is: 'How does one decide how much development is enough for the current generation and how much is needed to be preserved for the future generations?' This definition quantifies the environment into resources; something out there to be used. According to Sauve (2004, p. 146) we've reached a point where humans are mainly managing the environmental resources and education is mainly to foster this management and to be an instrument to inform the people and prepare them to support changes determined by experts and world leaders.

Inadequate Educational Opportunities

For EE to be successfully implemented a strong foundation and ongoing educational support is important; whether it is for the teachers or the teacher educators. Findings from other studies indicate teacher education as the weakest link in the chain (McKeown, 2000; Plevyak et al., 2001). These studies indicate a weakness in how these teacher education institutions fail to provide a solid, in-depth EE program to their student teachers. Adequate educational experiences are crucial in building Teacher educators' knowledge and confidence to implement EE. This plays a vital role in shaping their professional identities and how they understand EE.

Results in the current study reveal that at this particular teacher education institution the participating teacher educators lacked educational opportunities, which therefore undermines capacity building. This combination of a lack of conceptual knowledge along with a perceived lack of competence meant that EE existed only at the periphery. They dabbled with it a little bit – mainly by giving examples about the environment during their lectures. None of them talked about or displayed deeper or stronger involvement and connections with EE. They appeared to lack inspiration and not one of them talked passionately about the environment or how they implemented thinking and action in their classrooms. There was no mention of how environmental issues, particularly within their local communities, were being taken up at the institution. These teacher educators seemed to be waiting for someone else to take action for them, for some external force to come and set things up for them – it might be then harshly inferred that they could then just follow suit. It could well be suggested that this lack of power/agency is at the heart of why EE is being sidelined at this institution – one then wonders if it is the same at other similar institutions in India, thus exacerbating the situation at a national level.

Environmental Education as a Means to Solving a Problem

Environmental education when seen as a way of bringing an end to the prevailing environmental crisis is heavily flawed. Sobel (2008) describes this as a top-down mindset, which starts from a problem or a concept and moves to impose something in order to solve this problem. An example he gives is where we teach children about the 'horrors of rain-forest destruction' in order to encourage them to save the fast disappearing rainforests (p. 19). The act of saving these rainforests needs to be preceded by opportunities to cultivate healthy relationships with trees; 'Talking to trees and hiding in trees precedes saving trees' (p 19). Similarly, pretending to become animals in play, imitating their nature and calls precedes the urge to save them. As detailed in the literature review, ancient Indian systems have always been inextricably linked to the environment and its preservation. Viewing the environment as a problem and a hindrance to development and prosperity goes against the grain of the cultural identities of these teacher educators and shows the immense influence of developmental propaganda on them. Culturally, these teacher educators have discussed being nature worshippers and following the rituals around this that their respective religions propagate. However, they simultaneously seemed to espouse the belief that material riches and more access to consumables were synonymous with happiness and a better quality of life.

The curriculum that these teacher educators work with views environmental issues as problems that need to be solved. As discussed in Chapter 5 it is a part of a unit that discusses the problems that the Indian education system faces. It is taught along with other problems hindering the progress of education in India (e.g., its huge population and gender discrimination). Teacher educators (as indicated in Chapter 7) appear to see education as a major means of solving India's environmental problems, this places an onus on future generations as saviours of the environment. This thinking would clearly influence student teachers' exposed to this kind of EE.

Overview of First Objective

Overall then, within this institution these teacher educators understood EE on a superficial level with limited opportunities to engage at an organised or a deeper

173

level. They mainly interact with it as a branch of Science and as something that needs to be done in order to solve rising environmental problems. A lack of educational experiences in Science or a Science background coupled with inadequate in-service training appeared to hamper their ability to implement EE in their daily practices.

These teacher educators also lacked the vision to see themselves as agents of change. This reinforces Darling-Hammond's (2005, p. 451) claim that most teacher educators see themselves simply as 'teachers of teachers' and lack enough preparation for the task of educating teachers which leads them to teach their courses as general subjects without integrating the necessary pedagogical approaches to teaching these subjects. This is a major hurdle facing effective implementation of EE at this particular institution. The fact that EE is relegated to a sub-section of Science Education and that Science Education itself is accessible to a limited few, contrasts against a more holistic, all pervasive approach as espoused by Hart (2003), is a major issue for these teacher educators.

ORGANISATIONAL CULTURE AND ITS INFLUENCE ON IMPLEMENTATION OF EE IN TEACHER EDUCATION

While teaching in today's contexts is a highly demanding job, teacher education is all the more challenging because of the very high expectations it carries to educate the next generation of teachers. Teacher educators are expected to prepare 'a wide range of individuals to become teachers who can in turn enable an enormously diverse group of students to meet much higher standards than have ever before been expected of education systems' (Darling-Hammond, 2006, p. 8). Teacher educators today not only have to prepare teachers to deliver a curriculum or teach a textbook but also ensure 'learning for students with a broad assortment of needs' (Darling-Hammond L., 2006, p. 8). Such high hopes and expectations for teachers and teacher educators have led to a call for an increased focus on teacher education to improve the overall quality of teachers. According to Powers (2004), while attempting to best implement EE it is imperative to understand the perspectives of teacher educators (i.e., those who teach pre-service teachers). This section aims at deciphering the role of these teacher educators and how they see themselves in their profession. It discusses the role and influence of the organisation and its influence in the context of the culture of teacher education. In this section, in relation to the objectives of the study, the following are highlighted:

1. Teacher educators' professional identities were limited to seeing themselves as 'teachers of teachers.'
2. Lack of 'agency' and 'empowerment' tended to prevail.
3. Poor working conditions with few opportunities for professional development and support were apparent.

Their mainly technocentric eco identities were not 'in sync' with their cultural identities – creating a distance between their professional and non-professional self. The rest of this section discusses each of these features in more detail.

Teacher Educators or Teachers of Teachers?

Teacher educators at this institution did not see themselves as more than 'teachers of teachers' as has been evidenced in Chapters 8 and 9. This is somewhat problematic; as their interpretation of their role appeared to carry little more than the need to teach to a textbook or modules in this case and rushing towards finishing the prescribed syllabus. This meant that these teacher educators followed a structure similar to that which they experienced or practiced as teachers in a school. The entire setup of the institution was based on a high school model with students starting the day as one big cohort with students going through classes taught mainly through traditional lecture formats (as detailed in Chapter 5). In the afternoon, students dispersed into smaller groups for the 'specialised' subjects.

The structure of the institution and its teaching meant that the teacher educators continued to model themselves as teachers and did not make any distinction between identities as Teachers and Teacher educators. As mentioned in the data chapters they tended to continue to do what they were doing earlier – only the audience had changed. This meant that their focus was more on teaching the subject content and student teachers were left to grapple with the pedagogical aspects on their own. This reaffirms Darling-Hammond et al.'s (2005) assertion that teacher educators do not pay particular attention towards integrating pedagogical approaches while teaching subject matter. They tended to focus on content and failed to make a link between content, learning processes and the learning context. However, Pedagogical Content Knowledge (PCK) which includes a teacher's ability to 'anticipate and respond to typical student patterns of understanding and misunderstanding within a content area, and the ability to create multiple examples and representations of challenging topics that make the content accessible to a wide range of learners' has been proven to be an equally important aspect of teacher preparation (Grossman, Schoenfeld, & Lee, 2005, p. 201). As this study illustrates, focusing mainly on content knowledge does not fully prepare student teachers or build their capacity to teach in ways that are in accord with views of practice as comprising specialised knowledge, skills and abilities (Loughran et al., 2012).

As will be discussed in detail in section 3 of this chapter these teacher educators were under a lot of pressure to finish their syllabus. An end of year examination was the main form of assessment and so most of the teaching was geared towards preparing students to write these examinations. As described in Chapter 9, these exams are conducted by external bodies which means students have to be prepared in all sections of the prescribed course to ensure that there are no questions that are 'out of the syllabus'. Teacher educators are then consumed by the need to complete their syllabus so that their students score well. They are afraid that if questions from the uncovered syllabus appear on these exams they would have to face numerous complaints from the students. Also the institution's ranking and prestige depends heavily on the results of these exams and having students perform poorly in these exams would harm the prestige factor in terms of status for higher scoring students. This reinforces Hart's (2003, p. 1) research findings that point to teacher educators' struggles 'to answer questions of purpose, immersed as they are in the schizophrenic rush to meet both curriculum standards and pupil needs' and in this case also the demands of the institution.

Lack of Agency and Empowerment

The situation (above) follows on from the issue raised in the first section of this chapter related to these teacher educators' lack of 'agency' or lack of 'empowerment'. They appeared so bound by the curriculum that they seemed to have difficulty seeing beyond it. Teachers have been perceived as decision makers and collaborators, both educators and activists and teacher educators the ones that help shape these visions. If teachers have to be equipped to play all the above roles then it is evident that their teacher educators should be prepared to do the same (Cochran-Smith M., 2003). However, little has been done to help these teacher educators see themselves in the same light, let alone to prepare them to help their students see themselves in the above roles.

At this institution (as mentioned by one of the participants), there was not a single instance in his 28 years as a teacher educator that he had been asked about his views or opinions. As a consequence, they tended to see themselves as people who were just doing what they were being asked to do without any input in terms of their own opinions. They consistently insisted (as detailed in Chapters 8 and 9) that they had a lack of 'voice'. A direct result of this was the fact that these teacher educators did not think they had the 'power' to change anything and tended to expect change to be driven by external agents. Chapters 8 and 9 offered instances of them stating that they would be happy to do or teach a new topic including EE if someone told them to do so. This hints at this lack of agency.

Teacher educators' professional agency can be defined as the 'capacity to meaningfully construct and display their professional identity within socially defined contexts, in other words their capacity to negotiate and renegotiate professional identities within their local work practices' (Hokka, Etelapelto, & Rasku-Puttonen, 2012, p. 86). This means that teacher educators need to be able to negotiate and carry out their own intentions, while staying within the social and contextual constraints and challenges of resources and other obstacles. As this present study demonstrates, these teacher educators were clearly not able to manage their situation in that way.

As highlighted in the Literature Review (Chapter 2), teacher educators in Indian society are often seen as 'Guru's gurus' and command a lot of respect. They, as elsewhere, have tremendous impact on society by the sheer number of students they can touch in the span of their career. Therefore, Environmental reforms that touched these teacher educators would have far reaching impacts. It would seem fair to assert that given the advantage of students they could influence, these teacher educators' might find it important to have a greater sense of agency; which begs the question: 'How do we bring teacher educators to the forefront of the system and engage and involve them in decision-making that directly impacts their practice?'

Poor Working Conditions and Lack of Professional Development Opportunities

Learning to teach is increasingly being understood as a life-long phenomenon, a process that happens throughout the lifespan of an individual (Cochran-Smith, 2003; McDiarmid & Clevenger-Bright, 2008). At one end of the continuum is the 'apprenticeship of observation' (Lortie, 1975) that individuals experience as school students and then pre-service teachers. The learning to teach journey continues when they become teachers in schools and perhaps even later into experiences as teacher educators (McDiarmid & Clevenger-Bright, 2008, p. 137). There is clearly a need to move beyond learning to teach as learning through observation and experience alone and to enhance teachers' capacity for learning about teaching in new and meaningful ways, especially given the rising high expectations for teachers. Ranges of forces – policy initiatives being one amongst many – have been driving these high expectations.

An emerging issue is how teacher educators might be helped to build capacity and find ways to push the 'boundaries' of the box in which they are enclosed. Professional Development has a role to play and this is how teacher educators might be further educated about recent developments in the field and helped to gain a sense of the issues with which they need to grapple. This is particularly important if enhancing teacher educators' ability to take on an ecological approach to their work is to be achieved – which encompasses such things as curriculum development and renewal and reflective practitioner-based research (J. Fien & Maclean, 2000).

As indicated in Chapters 8 and 9 none of these teacher educators had been exposed to EE as part of their own educational journey whether at the undergraduate or post graduate levels. They had not received any training or professional development experiences as part of their pre service or in service experiences as schoolteachers. Except for one of the Teacher educators, none of the others had received any training as Teacher educators. In short none had been exposed to the content knowledge or the pedagogical aspects of teaching EE.

According to Darling-Hammond (2005), if academics in schools of education do not see themselves as Teacher Educators, rather as specialists in subjects (in this case History, Geography, Biology, Chemistry and so on), then there is a major systemic problem. It has been established that teachers generally teach in the 'the way that they were taught,' and their long 'apprenticeship of observation' (Darling-Hammond, 2006, p. 194) has an ongoing influence on their practice. While these Teacher educators discussed their knowledge of different strategies, none of those strategies were particularly evident in their teaching. Only one of the classroom observations by the researcher noted the use of role-play (one session) all other classes were traditional lectures. However, even the teacher educator who conducted the role-play class refused to allow access to a different class claiming that she was not prepared. This could be interpreted as suggesting that the earlier class was, in a way, an attempt to 'satisfy the observer' and not a normal aspect of practice.

Teaching using the transmission model can neither produce strong thinkers and problem solvers, nor address the diverse experiences and needs of student teachers (Darling-Hammond, 2006, p. 9). Giving examples, telling and showing students what to do works on the premise that 'learning is simple and uncomplicated and experiences of teacher educators can be transplanted into students of teaching' (Loughran, 2008b, p. 1178). There is therefore an urgent need for teacher educators to understand the interplay between teaching and learning and to focus on much more on the nature of pedagogy.

One way of developing such a focus is to provide teacher educators with opportunities for self-reflection. For the participants in this study, they had no time to pause and reflect on their practice. Teacher educators need opportunities to talk about their practices, what they have been doing over the years and why they have been approaching practices in a particular way. Such questioning of, and understanding the 'why' of practices is at the heart of pedagogy of teacher education. Currently these teacher educators appear unable to decipher how 'what they know should apply to teaching or to coordinate their work with that of other faculty who work with prospective teachers' (Darling-Hammond et al., 2005, p. 451). Providing a stress free environment for student teachers and a forum with no fear of being criticised would be a step in that direction. Appropriate professional development could provide these teacher educators with a window of opportunity that might lead to further pathways for growth and development and an understanding of the value of developing a pedagogy of teacher education. It is not surprising that successful policy reform cannot happen in isolation – it must be teamed up with long-term collaborative professional development, especially for teacher educators that are expected to deliver such reforms.

Some initiatives (to be detailed in Chapter 11) could include developing Collaborative communities with an inquiry stance toward educating these teacher educators in ways similar to that suggested by Cochran-Smith (2003). In her view, instead of having one teacher educator as a 'teacher' and the others as 'students' there is a community of teacher educators all learning from each other. This would involve developing networks amongst teacher educators from both within the institution and from across other universities. Such an approach would encourage learning and promote constructive collaboration. Darling-Hammond (2005, pp. 453–454) stated that the formation of such 'Collaborative Communities' has been neglected in higher-education institutions. Institutions like the one in which this study was conducted would certainly benefit from such an initiative. However, building and sustaining these Collaborative Communities is largely dependent on strong leadership with energy, enthusiasm and administrative skills to steer them. This study has revealed the tussle in which the institutional administration and government bodies are engaged.

As discussed in Chapters 5 and 9, the teacher education institution in this study is a semi-government institution, which means that technically the University Grants Commission (Government of India) pays the faculty salaries while the management pays for other resources and is responsible for other day to day expenses which it covers using student fees. However, at the time of this research only three faculty members were being paid through UGC. As mentioned in the Chapter 5 this means that there is a big discrepancy between what the UGC staff are paid in comparison to the rest of the teacher educators. In effect most of the teacher educators at this institution worked for very poor salaries despite their high qualifications – all of them had at least one, in most cases two postgraduate qualifications. As will be further discussed in Section 3 these teacher educators worked in a poorly resourced environment, had little or no access to any state benefits, worked long hours with little appreciation from higher authorities. At a basic level providing these teacher educators with help to develop their professional selves and build their confidence in teaching (EE – in this case) would certainly be a step in the right direction.

Interestingly, while all of the participants in this study were highly educated none of them were qualified to teach EE. As has been well illustrated in other studies, strong background knowledge in content areas – while not the sole determining factor – plays an important role in enhancing teacher confidence and student learning outcomes (Howard & Aleman, 2008).

Challenges to Teacher Educators' Identity

As a result of being 'non-interchangeable, distinctive human beings' teacher educators are prone to hold a 'conception of personhood that informs their sense of purpose' (Hansen, 2008, p. 22). While not necessarily being overtly obvious an individual's persona plays a role in influencing how they function and are seen to operate. Therefore, persona as an aspect of identity clearly creates images of the way a role is understood and seen through the societal interactions of work and the roles of that work.

The significant role of teacher educators' ecological or eco identities in shaping their overall implementation of EE is another aspect of the findings of this study that have been brought into sharper focus. As explored in Chapter 7 these teacher educators' eco identities were largely prone to be technocentric or anthropocentric. This was clear in their responses about issues associated with the environment and economic development. At various points during their interactions with the researcher, these teacher educators illustrated a leaning towards economic development – even at the cost of environmental development. Chapter 7 discussed these teacher educators' stance with regard to this issue because although the environment was important and they felt that it should be preserved/conserved, development was equally important. They felt that, while it is not right to sacrifice the environment for economic development, it was also not right to compromise economic development for the sake of the environment. Most espoused great faith in scientific and technological advances and the ability to resolve/defuse environmental problems. Economic development was however held in high regard by these teacher educators as a means to stem India's large-scale poverty and to bring India on par with other 'developed' nations.

As noted in Section 1 (above) all of these teacher educators had great faith in the idea of 'Sustainable Development', which they believed would create development without compromising the quality of the environment; views which appear to concur with the United Nations documents (4th International Environmental Education Conference Delegates, 2007; UNESCO, 1992, 2002; World Commission on Environment and Development, 2004), but which equally carry ethical implications for Sustainable Development as highlighted by Sauve (2004) who contended that: to see the environment as a reservoir of resources for development, conservation practices are unavoidable to constraints to sustainable development; the human relationship to environment is one of management; development is associated with sustained growth in a new world of economic order; education (as a communication and training process) is an instrument to promote sustainable development; following this "new vision of education", the "populace" will be "informed" and "prepared to support changes" determined by experts and world leaders (p. 146). As is evident through this research project, global influences have been strong in shaping these teacher educators' views of the environment and its interplay with development and are now reflected in interesting ways in their identities. Spivak (1994) would most likely describe this situation as Neocolonism in full bloom. The environment with all its rich living and non-living elements, cultures and values cannot be relegated to being just a bundle of resources solely meant to fuel economic and material development. Education on the other hand cannot simply be positioned as a means of spreading this agenda (Jickling, 1992). This is especially true when considered in light of the fact that there is little evidence about growing economic development bringing economic relief to India's poor. Magasaysay award winning Indian journalist P. Sainath (2011) pointed out that in the 16 years from 1995–2010 poverty and crop failure led to more than a quarter of a million Indian farmers committing suicide. 30% of India still lives below the poverty line, which is taken to be less than Rupees 28.65 per capita daily consumption in cities and Rupees 22.42 in rural areas (IBN Live India, 2012). Both of these figures translate into less than a dollar a day. According to a study the number of people in the lowest income bracket has increased by over 9% from 2005–2010. On the other hand the number of rich households grew two times faster than projected growth up to 2007 (Goyal, 2011).

This situation provokes thinking about the amount of development needed to bring India on par with other developed countries and if/how that would make a difference to the quality of life for the general populace. It seems fair to suggest that these teacher educators, with the influence they can have on their students, their qualifications and long term exposure to education, should really be in a position to critically examine and debate the issues of environment versus development. However, as this research has shown, there appears to be a lack of critical thinking and questioning in favour of a simple alignment with the international perspective of Sustainable Development.

Perhaps this case for economic development can be traced back to India's colonial roots. Although all the teacher educators described their culture and Indian'ness as a major influence on their personal lives, their eco identities did not seem to be in tune with their cultural identities. As a consequence, there seems to be a sense of dissonance between their identities as teacher educators and their identities as individual members of the society. This could also help to account for why they seemed so swayed by the developmental agenda.

In considering a postcolonial influence, it could be that the stereotypical 'general western culture' could be seen as favouring materialism and instant gratification, with the system supporting an aggressive, competitive, 'me-first' society leading to a sense of purpose for maximisation of personal material wealth as an overarching goal (Hillcoat, 1998). That of course is in sharp contrast to the ancient Indian philosophies of 'karma' which is loosely translated as fate, destiny, deeds, and 'moksha' which is loosely translated as final deliverance (Haigh, 2008, p. 236).

These Indian philosophies are based on putting others before self, doing work as a duty without worrying about the fruits and accumulating good deeds so that one has a better re-birth with the ultimate aim to attain 'moksha' which delivers one from the cycle of birth and rebirth. Clearly there is a contradiction then between current trends to value money over anything else and the traditional Indian thinking reflected in the way the environment is viewed as sacred and to be protected: 'All living beings are members one of another so a person's every act has a beneficial or harmful influence on the world' (Gandhi as cited in Mallik, 1962, p. 24). Yoga, meditation, vegetarianism, self-sustainability, and non-violence – namely simple living and service were highly regarded and sincerely recommended by Gandhi.

The end of colonial rule resulted in a bitter experience for most Indians, and millions died or were rendered homeless in the 'Partition' of India and Pakistan, in what has been termed the largest migration in human history. In 1947 India was a poor, industrially underdeveloped state, totally plundered of its wealth by the colonial rulers. The era between the 1950s and 1980s was marked by socialism and nationalism, led by rulers with strong leanings towards the USSR and Marxism. Nationalism became an excuse for selling shoddy, substandard products and for a tight control over state enterprises. It was the era of bureaucrats and gave rise to high levels of corruption – still evident in government institutions in India today. The lack of amenities and quality goods led to a strong affiliation with 'imported' goods.

Anything that had a 'Made in the U.S.A.' sticker, or any European destination for that matter, tended to be highly coveted.

In the period starting from 1990, economic restrictions were gradually removed and the country moved towards a free market economy. This open market economy brought in foreign investment and a deluge of high quality goods. Suddenly average Indians were exposed to a windfall of choices and all that was missing was the capital necessary to buy; all of which has been sated by the growth of the Internet in the last years of the decade (Kamdar, 2007; Luce, 2006).

This comparatively easy access to goods led to intense consumerism and a change in the Indian psyche. Living and accumulating good deeds for the next birth were replaced by 'instant gratification', and success measured in the 'goods' and 'brands' that one accumulated. Spivak (1994) described this shift as 'epistemic violence' whereby local indigenous culture was taken over by western ideologies. In many ways it is only by means of simultaneous reclamation of indigenous histories and cultures that a forward-leading path might genuinely be forged (Childs & Williams, 1997).

Western societies have been consumerist for a long time and there is now a growing realisation about the importance of stemming this consumerism and preserving the environment (Hillcoat, 1998). Sadly, in India environmental restrictions or concerns are often considered as hurdles or obstacles to the fulfilment of 'dreams'. Having suffered through an era of tight governmental regulations the common view that Indians now want the freedom to exercise their choices without have to 'worry' about anything prevails.

According to Childs and Williams (1997) post colonialism intersects with globalisation in many ways. Critics like Spivak (1994) in fact consider globalisation to be another form of colonisation with the added benefit that there is no need to build the infrastructure, develop the systems and incur administrative set-ups. Capitalism according to her has globalized (rather than localised) its mode of production.

During colonisation there was migration of workers (often forced) and during globalisation there is migration of work. Lack or discriminatory enforcement of labour laws, a totalitarian state, and minimal subsistence requirement of the work force have helped in providing 'cheap-labour' for the global industries. There is a need to place the historically marginalised parts of the world at the centre rather than the periphery of the education and globalisation debate (Tikly, 2001). As stated above, the rich-poor divide is growing both locally and globally. Spivak links imperialism and neo-colonial practices – 'the contemporary international division of labour is a displacement of the divided field of nineteenth-century territorial imperialism. Put simply, a group of countries, generally first-world, are in the position of investing capital; another group, generally third-world, provide the field for investment' (Spivak, 1994, p. 158). The notion of 'development' has been tweaked to involve indiscriminate violation of the environment such that raising concerns about the environment is deemed to be anti-development thus harming the progress of the country. (The protesters of the Narmada Dam (as detailed in Chapter 2) are a case in point.)

Postcolonial influences have had a tremendous effect on the education system, which appears to have suffered from continuing hegemony of western forms of knowledge/power and the spread of western consumer culture. The postcolonial system has created postcolonial elites – highly selective and elitist educational policies have been the norm since colonial times – who cater to their own interests and often continue stratification along the lines of ethnicity, gender, class and particularly in India – caste (Crossley & Tikly, 2004). In recent times another major area of interest has taken over – political gains and mileage. This could be one of the reasons why Sustainable Development is the new mantra for pushing the economic agenda – as mentioned earlier there is no consensus on how much development is needed to meet the needs of the current generation. Political parties with huge self-interests in a country like India seem free to manipulate the extent of development to meet their own agendas.

Teacher educators are not immune from the influences of this mindset. In effect, they are also deeply influenced by the consumerist 'revolution' that has overtaken India. Their views on EE are inevitably shaped by their own education and beliefs while at the same time experiencing ongoing identity challenges. As Richert contends, 'the ability to take moral action requires that teacher [educators] learn to act with intent. This means that teachers need to locate expertise inside, rather than outside, themselves' (Richert, 1997, p. 79).

Locating expertise inside would translate not only into a need to look at their own personal practices but also embedding the practices and curriculum in indigenous knowledge. The 1992 Earth Summit in Rio advocated indigenous knowledge as playing a positive role in developing and responding to environmental issues and risks. This has led to a deviation from earlier negative perceptions on indigenous knowledge towards acknowledging the purposeful and pivotal role it can play in EE. Using local knowledge in education can potentially stimulate and facilitate transformation of school curricula, which in turn can bring about 'situated learning' rich in relevance to local contexts and delving deeper into local environmental problems (Van Damme & Neluvhalani, 2004).

Consumerist mentality tends to foster over-consumption and disregard for the degradation of the environment that is caused. Such apathy towards environmental concerns has led to a rapid deterioration of the environment and accelerated the depletion of India's natural resources. This, coupled with India's burgeoning population, has placed undue stress on the environment. The Mithi River is one such example. In 2005 one of the worst floods that devastated Mumbai city was caused by the breakdown of its natural water carrying system – the Mithi River. Once used for transport and fishing, this river now carries tons of industrial and municipal wastes and its course altered due to urbanisation – all of which can be directly attributed to the unchecked and unregulated growth of the city (Citizens of Mumbai, 2007; Patil, 2006).

As the teacher educators in this study live in a post-colonial India, their traditional philosophies and views of the environment are constantly being challenged by a different set of values and these contradictions play out in unusual ways in terms of their developing identities and commensurate ability to influence (or not) the nature of educating for an environment that was once sacred but now under threat.

CHARACTERISTICS OF EE IN TEACHER EDUCATION IN INDIA

As discussed in the Literature review there have been calls to make teacher education the 'Priority of Priorities' (Tilbury, 1992). This view persists today as teacher education continues to attract considerable attention, particularly in the field of EE. There is limited research into teacher educators' experiences in implementing EE. Studies like those conducted by McKeown-Ice, Powers, Tilbury and Cutter-Mackenzie point to similar features, issues and problems in the field. This present study is at the forefront of research into teacher educators working with EE in an Indian context. This study draws attention to the particular characteristics and attributes that impact the implementation of EE. However, for the Teacher Education Institution itself, there is particular resonance with issues and concerns that other 'developing' countries faced in the 1990s (Darling-Hammond, 2005).

This section of the chapter draws the research together by discussing the main hurdles and key issues for EE in Teacher Education in India. First there is a discussion of the enabling factors that provide teacher educators with the impetus and motivation to work with EE. Secondly, the section elaborates on the issues, problems, constraints and hurdles that these teacher educators personally faced which hampered the development and implementation of EE in their daily practice. The entire section therefore draws attention to some of the key characteristics that play a significant role in how EE is approached within teacher education in India through the following:

1. Quality – quality of teaching, innovation in teaching strategies, connecting teaching to existing research and using research to further enhance their teaching.
2. Issues around lack of resources, inspiration and motivation to address issues of quality.
3. Problems of access to training, research, motivation, inspiration and prioritisation, policy-practice gap.

Attitude to Development and Implementation of EE

One of the main drivers of EE development for the teacher educators in this study was the perceived necessity to gear their teaching to integrating EE. This was partially influenced by their strong connections to their age-old traditions, which were heavily infused by beliefs of nature preservation, worship and interconnectivity between humans and the environment. As Chapters 7 and 8 highlighted, these teacher educators were ready to learn and be taught about how to teach EE and were seeking opportunities to understand EE better and were keen to participate in Professional Development to build their understanding. Interestingly, their student teachers seemed to come from similar traditional backgrounds[1] and so it seems reasonable to suggest that their home environments had exposed them to similar traditions and beliefs about the environment. Hence, these student teachers could well be equally receptive to a more 'all-encompassing' approach to EE. Therefore, at a base level there was likely to be motivation for development and change. However, that alone is not sufficient for change to actually occur.

Constraints on Development and Implementation of EE

As the data clearly illustrates, there were numerous constraints/hurdles and barriers that were evident throughout this research program and they have been partly canvassed in the previous chapter. They are now considered in more detail.

Scarce resources.   As discussed in Section 1 of this chapter, there was a clear lack of prioritisation of EE at every level – governmental, political and organisational. All the data chapters point to a massive lack of resources at this particular institution; at a level not able to be fully comprehended when considering this work from a Western perspective of resourcing. For example, the College of Education had two old computers, neither of which were easily accessible to staff and not accessible at all to students. There was one closely guarded photocopier in the office and only a handful of books in the library with very few being recent additions. What that meant was that these teacher educators and student teachers struggled to find resources that would support their learning and help them to be appropriately informed. There were few (if any) avenues open to them to be abreast of the latest developments or changes in thinking about and constructing EE. They had no access to journal articles that detailed and described recent studies; they were not up to date with new theoretical concepts and developments or new policies and generally had a lack of knowledge of global happenings in the field. It is of little surprise then that none of these teacher educators were involved in any research studies; which reinforces Cutter-Mackenzie's (2009) findings about educational research and lack of impact on teacher educators and their teaching practices. It would seem reasonable to suggest that these participants had a shallow understanding of EE in teacher education (McKeown-Ice, 2000; Powers, 2004) as a consequence of their lack of contact with the research literature. Further to this, these teacher educators worked long hours on a meagre salary and many did not have Internet at home. Some were 'technologically challenged' and did not even have an email account let alone the skills to use the Internet to source information. Given that most lived and worked in a small town their access to computers and libraries containing books relevant to EE could be described as limited at best.

This lack of resources seriously affected how EE was implemented in this particular Teacher Education institution. A key criterion for effective implementation of EE is to take it outdoors. Prominent researchers perceive a serious gap in the ability to foster love and passion for the natural environmental if confined to the four walls of a classroom. Sobel (2008) advocated the need to provide first hand experiences in the outdoors and innovate teaching approaches for nurturing this love for the environment before being asked to save it. Chawla (1999) emphatically stressed the need to move outside classrooms and forge boundaries. However, as noted previously, given the lack of resources at this particular teacher education institution this was often not practical thus reinforcing the restriction of teaching within the four walls of the classroom. Added to this was the large class sizes and the traditional classroom layout of old wooden desks in serried ranks, further minimizing the likelihood of innovative teaching approaches; the space controlling the teaching and learning rather than facilitating.

Inflexible/uninspiring curriculum. Rigidity is not confined to the classroom. Chapters 8 and 9 pointed to these teacher educators' constant rush to meet students' needs, complete the syllabus and prepare students for the examinations – all within a very short time frame (10 months). The pressure to cram a complete teacher education program into one year was a major issue. All of the teacher educators in this program considered this pressure as being their greatest challenge. They found it almost impossible to meet the expectations of the program in the short time span. There was little (or no) room for innovation and they had been teaching the same curriculum for more than 10 years. Added to this 'burden of the curriculum' was the 'burden of rigid assessment'.

University wide examinations are the main form of assessment at this particular teacher education institution and they created a great deal of stress for student teachers and also the teacher educators whose performance was linked to their student's results on these exams. In a brusque criticism of this approach Singh (2011, p. 114) stated that, 'if you want to change student learning, then change the methods of assessment.' Quality in EE is based on the need for 'thoughtful thinking through of situations', it is difficult to see how that might be encouraged when the entire system is geared towards one round of examinations.

Professional development. While this issue has already been discussed in Section 2, it warrants further mention as it is a pressing problem for these teacher educators. Globally teacher educators face multiple demands with a serious dearth of curriculum that addresses their needs and policies that support their ongoing learning (Cochran-Smith M., 2003). This lack of exposure to EE as part of their own educational journeys at the undergraduate or post graduate level and the continuing lack of educational opportunities seriously hampers implementation of EE. Addressing the lack of appropriate Professional Development is clearly a key issue arising from this study.

Policy-practice gap. There has been a barrage of policy documents flooding the Indian education system, particularly in the last decade (see Chapter 2). However, policies devoid of consultative processes with end users do not translate into meaning in practice. As described by Babbage (2008), policies drafted by government officials who are not familiar with the daily grind of teaching in classrooms inevitably leads to a lack ownership by practitioners. Darling-Hammond (2005, p. 451) described how teacher education exists in a 'highly politicised regulatory environment in which standards for accreditation, licensing, and certification are substantially governed by political bodies rather than by the profession itself', thus the 'key levers are more complex and difficult to manage'. So although these teacher educators agreed that the policies were set with the best intentions, they did not identify with them. This gap between policy and practice (i.e., teacher education practices and teacher education compliance) therefore creates a barrier to change and an impediment to implementation of policy in meaningful ways. Thus the difference between rhetoric and reality is starkly evident in the results of this study. Policy changes triggered by the Supreme Court's directives were intended to bring about sweeping changes in EE in India and help stem India's growing environmental problems. There was a firm belief in the need for change and to drive home the importance of EE in India's education system. While the judiciary and government authorities at the highest level recognised the need for change in education to encompass EE unfortunately it does not appear to have 'filtered down through the system'.

In short, answering the research questions have led me towards discovering a gaping hole in an under resourced system in India in which teacher educators' identities, approach to practice and somewhat contradictory and personal and professional understandings and practices of EE combine to confound the intention of the Supreme Court's directive.

NOTE

[1] Based on field notes derived of informal interactions with these student teachers and the observations that they all started their first lecture with a prayer, they all wore saris and they all were very traditional in their thinking about EE in the curriculum.

SECTION 5

BRINGING THE STORIES TOGETHER: TRADITIONS NURTURE FUTURES

CONCLUSION

To avoid appearing to be impractical or unreasonable, we often fail to penetrate below the surface of things to deeper causes. As a result we offer aspirin-level solutions to potentially terminal illnesses. Until we see the crisis of sustainability as one with roots that extend from public policies and technology down into our assumptions about science, nature, culture and human nature, we are not likely to extend our prospects much. (Orr, 1992, p. 1)

It is apt to reiterate at the beginning of this section that this book is not a comprehensive look at EE in India or the world. It is an individual, close and concise effort to view trends and debates within the larger field of Teacher Education and EE within an Indian context. In its focus of on EE in India, this study examined teacher educators' experiences of implementing EE in India. As has been consistently highlighted throughout this study, there is no doubt that there is an urgent need for EE reform in India.

The major concerns that emerged through analysis of the data illustrate that teacher education in this particular institution in India is in need of urgent reform if teacher educators are to be the agents of change central to policy priorities and mandates. While the policy reforms are a right step in the right direction, the study illustrates that policy alone has not changed the field of EE.

The study points to the lack of 'agency' and 'voice' in these teacher educators, which severely limited the intended impact of policy reform. While teacher educators unambiguously saw EE as an important and necessary part of the overall teacher education experiences for their student teachers, they lacked sufficient incentive, motivation and encouragement to implement EE in an appropriate and meaningful way. Given the tremendous personal and professional pressures and demands on their time, worldviews of EE and ability to manage and control their practice, their ability to negotiate and implement EE in their daily practices is severely limited.

Organisational imperatives and structures undoubtedly play an important role in the implementation of EE. However, this study has revealed the gaping hole in these structures exacerbated by serious lack of professional support. As is evident in this study, these teacher educators are not bereft of recognition of the need to better incorporate EE into their practice; they just do not appear to have sufficient skills, knowledge or confidence to do so.

Being embedded in the cultural ethos of India also suggests that these teacher educators are challenged by traditional knowledge and modern consumerist hopes and expectations leading to technocentric views premised on near total faith that development will offer a way out of poverty. It creates a tension between tradition and prospects for the future in a modern world.

TRADITION VERSUS FUTURE

Tagore (2010) explained that the cultural construct of the Indian society has, over centuries, built the feeling that a mere individual cannot do much and, basically, it is the karma of an individual to live his/her life without stirring things up too much. Suffering and indignity is a result of actions from our past lives and have to be meekly accepted. The cycle of life and birth is seen as the only way of getting out of past misdeeds as well as social and religious disabilities. Tagore asserted that, 'The habit of submitting to conditions into which one is born as predestined and inevitable is the strongest link in the chain of our political servitude' (p. 14). India in recent years has been undergoing changes that have, in a many ways, torn through these long held beliefs. There is greater acknowledgement of cause and effect. As illustrated in Chapters 6 & 8 this particular teacher education institution could be viewed as being caught in a time warp, somehow trapped between the lost Colonial World and the new emerging Indian world. While the external forces of change have significant influence both personally and professionally on the teacher educators caught in the system, it is not difficult to see how feelings of helplessness could become a form of protection from a world in which contradiction appears at almost every turn.

Mckeown-Ice (2000) pointed to a shallow approach to EE, dealing more with awareness, knowledge and learning. This seems to be the case here too with traditional knowledge and views challenged by ever increasing everyday events and situations. In her book 'India Divided' Vandana Shiva (2005) advocates 'swadeshi' as a means to end globalisation. 'swadeshi', loosely translated, means relying on one's own country/place for one's needs. This call for boosting the 'swadeshi' movement could equally be extended to development. In other words 'Swadeshi Development' could be juxtaposed with 'Sustainable Development' and could help challenge (or at least contain) the consumerist wave sweeping across India. India's rich past can and should enrich its future rather than be seen as something that needs to be cast away in order to build the future.

Any attempts to move forward though clearly needs to involve seriously pushing the boundaries of teaching and learning which requires ongoing opportunities for teacher educators to seek support and scaffolding if they are to be seen as the ushers of reforms. In the same vein progress cannot be achieved unless we shed our colonial hangovers and appreciate our indigenous heritage.

This study highlights the paucity of research in EE in teacher education in India; it is still in its nascent stages. This study is the first major qualitative study in EE in India and provides an in-depth view of teacher educators' experiences in implementing EE in India. It is hoped that this study might promote other studies that could capitalise on these findings and seek to determine how, as a consequence, real change might be facilitated.

There is clearly a need now for a more comprehensive study that extends this research in ways that opens up the field to more generalizable outcomes so that implementation plans might be more meaningful than hopeful. Further to this, as few studies have been conducted into teachers' and school students' experiences with EE as part of their school education in light of the policy reforms, such research could add to the impetus for serious change.

It is clear that, in the specific context of the participants in this study, there is clear evidence that EE is poorly understood and determined by teacher educators in India. EE clings to the fringes of these teacher educators' practice as it is neither prioritised nor implemented in ways that might make a significant difference at this particular institution. An exploration of the extent to which the participating teacher educators' identities influenced their practice of EE in the organisational culture of teacher education pointed to a sense of dissonance between these teacher educators' professional, cultural and ecological identities.

In conclusion if teacher educators are to bring about much needed change in the EE as laid down by the policy reforms imposed by the Supreme Court of India, more needs to be done to enable, inspire and support them to do so. By not prioritising teacher educators' pedagogical needs and strengthening Teacher Education itself, ambitious policy reforms have little meaningful impact. This study reveals a major gap between policy, practice and implementation that unless seriously addressed will confine the hopes and expectations of change in EE in teacher education to the realms of rhetoric rather than reality.

APPENDIX 1

B.Ed. Degree Examination
(Non-Semester Scheme)
EDUCATION – 6
Area of Specialisation : Environmental Education

Time : 2 Hours   Max.Marks : 50

Note : There are two sections in the question paper. Both are compulsory.

SECTION – A

Note: Answer the following questions in about THREE pages each.

1. a) (i) Explain the principles of Environment.

    (ii) "Earth is a Miracle Planet" Elucidate.

                                                                                          5+5

OR

    b) (i) Explain the significance of carrying capacity ofthe environment.

        (ii) Discuss the principle of 10% law of energy with two examples.

                                                                                          5+5

2. a) (i) Explain the flow of energy through non-living components.

        (ii) Explain the material flow in Carbon Cycle.

                                                                                          5+5

OR

    b) (i) Discuss the distribution pattern of different types of natural resources.

        (ii) Explain how modernisation has led to environmental degradation.

                                                                                          5+5

3. a) (i) Explain the importance of Environmental Education.

    (ii) Discuss the role of exhibition in teaching of Environmental education.

                                                                            4+6

                                    OR

    b) (i) Discuss the need for active role of teachers in promotion of environmental education.

    (ii) Explain how you would organise eco-club in your school.

                                                                            5+5

                              SECTION – B

Note: Answer any FOUR in about a page each.   4x5=20

4. a) Explain the legislative measures in relation to Environmental Protection.

    b) Explain any two food pyramids.

    c) Discuss the problem of over population.

    d) What is Eco-friendly Life Style?

    e) Describe the consequences of water pollution.

    f) Explain the nature of evaluation in environmental education.

                              * * *

APPENDIX 2

Proposed Semi-structured Interview Questions:

1. What have been the major influential factors in your decision to become a teacher / teacher educators.
2. What have been your experiences with nature as part of your growing up years? What have been your experiences with nature and being outdoors?
3. Please tell us about any special memories with families and friends and experiencing nature.
4. What is your understanding of the term 'environment'? How would you define it? How do you feel about the environment?
5. What are your views about the environment and environmental issues?
6. Are there any unique features of India's environment? What are they? What are the major environmental concerns facing India today?
7. Are you involved in any environmental groups or activities? Tell me about that.
8. How do you feel about the following statements:

    - The environment is a resource to be used by human beings.
    - Economic growth should and must continue, even if it results in damage to the environment.
    - The environment should be protected, even if it results in a reduction in economic growth.
    - The environment should be preserved and protected, no matter what the cost.

9. What are your views about environmental education in India?
10. How do you feel about the implementation of environmental education in India?
11. Tell us about your personal experiences in inculcating / implementing environmental education.
12. Tell us about your students' experiences in implementing environmental education in their classrooms.
13. Have you received any training in environmental education as a teacher or teacher educator? Tell me about that?
14. How would you rate your knowledge about the environment and environmental education? Where would you place yourself on a scale of 1–10?
15. Do you feel that a particular belief / commitment is needed to teach environmental education effectively?
16. How do you think your particular cultural background has aided / restrained your views and your teaching of environmental education?
17. What are your views about the Supreme Court mandate on environmental education?

18. What kind of support do you receive from outside agencies – central / state / local / institutional?
19. Are there ways in which you could be better supported by the above agencies?
20. What are the positive / enabling factors that help you in implementing environmental education? How do you maximise them?
21. What are the negative / constraining factors in implementing environmental education? How do you work around them?
22. How have recent changes in policy / curriculum affected you?
23. Are there any changes that you have seen / made in your curriculum/teaching methods / styles in light of these policy changes?
24. Is there a particular strategy / strategies that you have used to incorporate environmental education in your teaching?
25. Have there been any rules / policies / guidelines from your institution that have influenced your environmental teaching practices?
26. Do you feel that you receive enough support / initiatives from the institution for implementing environmental education? How do you think this can be improves?

APPENDIX 3

Interview Facesheet   Date & Time: _____

Name of Interviewee: _____

Pseudonym: _____

Gender: _____   Age: _____

Religion: _____

Languages spoken: _____

Place of birth: _____

Experience as a teacher: _____

Experience as a teacher educator: _____

Experience with TMA Pai: _____

Current teaching speciality: _____

Current Research: _____

Educational Qualifications: _____

APPENDIX 4

Post Interview Comment Sheet (adapted from Cutter-Mackenzie, 2003, pp. 268–269):

Participant – pseudonym, description:

Setting:

Difficulties encountered (methodological or personal)

Personal feelings about the experience:

Insights and reflections:

APPENDIX 5

Observation Notes Sheet:

Class layout – sketch

General Notes:

- Teaching Strategies – Chalk n talk, group, inquiry
- Environment themes / issues – what issues or themes they talk about?
- Personal connection / relations – do they talk about themselves – are they living what they are saying, their env'al beliefs and identities?
- What is the student's role in the class – passive or active participants?
- Where culture and tradition fits – how it manifest itself into practice?
- How is the policy being implemented?

Post Observation comment sheet:

What was the dominant approach?

What did the teachers do?

What did the students do?

How do I feel about it?

How does it relate to my experiences as a student / teacher?

How have things changed over the decade since I was at Uni?

REFERENCES

4th International Environmental Education Conference Delegates. (2007). *Moving forward from Ahmedabad...: Environmental education in the 21st century*. 4th International Environmental Education Conference. Retrieved December 6, 2009, from http://www.tbilisiplus30.org/FinalRecommendations.pdf

Babbage, K. (2008). *What only teachers know about education: The reality of the classroom*. Lanham, MD: Rowman and Littlefield.

Baez, A. V. (1987). Education and conservation strategy. In A. V. Baez, G. W. Knamiller, & J. C. Smyth (Eds.), *The environment and science and technology education* (Vol. 8, pp. 37–46). Oxford, UK: Permagon Press for ICSU Press.

Barnett, J., Matthew, R., & O'Brien, K. (2010). Global environmental change and human security: An introduction. In R. Matthews, J. Barnett, B. Mcdonald, & K. O'Brien (Eds.), *Global environmental change and human security* (pp. 1–32). Cambridge, MA: Massachusetts Institute of Technology.

Barrow, C. (2012). Socioeconomic adaptation to environmental change: Towards sustainable development. In J. Matthews, P. Bartlein, K. Briffa, A. Dawson, A. Vernal, T. Denham, ... F. Oldfield (Eds.), *The Sage handbook of environmental change* (Vol. 2, pp. 426–446). London, UK: Sage Publications Ltd.

Barta, P., & Pokharel, K. (2009, May 13). Megacities threaten to choke India. *Wall Street Journal*. Retrieved from http://online.wsj.com/article/SB124216531392512435.html

Batra, P. (2005). Voice and agency of teachers: Missing link in national curriculum framework 2005. *Economic and Political Weekly*, 4347–4356.

Beijaard, D., Meijer, P., & Verloop, N. (2004). Reconsidering research on teachers' professional identity. *Teaching and Teacher Education, 20*(2), 107–128.

Bennett, J. (2012). *Little green lies : An exposé of twelve environmental myths*. Ballan, Victoria: Connor Court Publishing.

Berry, A. (2004). Confidence and uncertainty in teaching about teaching. *Australian Journal of Education, 48*(2), 149–165.

Bogdan, R., & Bilken, S. (2007). *Qualitative research: An introduction to theories and methods*. Boston, MA: Pearson A & B.

Bohannan, P. (1995). *How culture works*. New York, NY: The Free Press.

Bonnet, M. (2006). Education for sustainability as a frame of mind. *Environment Education Research, 12*(3–4), 265–276.

Bronfenbrenner, U. (1979). *The ecology of human development: Experiments by nature and design*. Cambridge, MA: Harvard University Press.

Brown, L. (2011). *World on the edge: How to prevent environmental and economic collapse*. Washington, DC: Earthscan.

Bryner, G. (2011). *Protecting the global environment*. Colorado, CO: Paradigm Publishers.

Bullough, R. V. Jr. (1997). Practicing theory and theorizing practice in teacher education. In J. Loughran & T. Russell (Eds.), *Teaching about teaching: Purpose, passion and pedagogy in teacher education* (pp. 13–31). London, UK: Falmer Press.

Bussey, M., Inayatullah, S., & Milojevic, I. (2008). *Alternative educational futures: Pedagogies for emergent worlds* (pp. 235–252). Rotterdam, The Netherlands: Sense Publishers.

Carson, R. (1964). *Silent spring* (Colonial ed.). London, UK: Readers Union.

Census of India. (2011). *Size, growth rate and distribution of population*. New Delhi, India: Government of India. Retrieved from http://www.censusindia.gov.in/2011-prov-results/data_files/india/Final_PPT_2011_chapter3.pdf

Center for Environment Education. (Ed.). (2007–2008). *Center for environment education: Annual report*. Ahmedabad, India: Center for Environment Education.

Center for Environment Education. (2012). *The green teacher*. Retrieved November 2, 2012, from http://www.greenteacher.org/

Chawla, L. (1999). Life paths into effective environmental action. *Journal of Environmental Education, 31*(1), 15–26.

Chhokar, K., & Chandrasekharan, S. (2006). Approaches to environmental education for sustainability in India. In J. Chi-Kin Lee & M. Williams (Eds.), *Environmental and geographical education for sustainability: Cultural contexts* (pp. 1–359). New York, NY: Nova Science Publishers.

Chhokar, K., & Pandya, A. (2005). Samvardhan: An experiment in education for sustainable development. *The Declaration: Bi-Annual Report, 7*(2), 20–24.

Childs, P., & Williams, P. (1997). *An introduction to post-colonial theory.* Hertfordshire, UK: Prentice Hall Europe.

Chin, P. (1997). Teaching and learning in teacher education: Who is carrying the ball? In J. Loughran & T. Russell (Eds.), *Teaching about teaching: Purpose, passion and pedagogy in teacher education* (pp. 117–130). London, Washington, DC: The Falmer Press.

Citizens of Mumbai. (2007). An appeal to save Mumbai from floods or water logging. Retrieved Febraury 23, 2010, from http://www.petitiononline.com/mumbai07/petition.html

Cochran-Smith, M. (2003). Learning and unlearning: The education of teacher educators. *Teaching and Teacher Education, 19*, 5–28.

Cochran-Smith, M., & Lytle, S. L. (1999). Relationships of knowledge and practice: Teacher learning in communities. In A. Iran-Nejad & C. D. Pearson (Eds.), *Review of research in education* (Vol. 24, pp. 249–305). Washington, DC: AERA.

Conca, K., & Dabelko, G. (Eds.). (2004). *Green planet blues: Environmental politics from Stockholm to Johannesburg* (3rd ed.). Colorado, CO: Westview Press.

Cotton, D. R. E., Warren, M. F., Maiboroda, O., & Bailey, I. (2007). Sustainable development, higher education and pedagogy: A study of lecturers' beliefs and attitudes. *Environmental Education Research, 13*(5), 579–597.

Creswell, J. (2007). *Qualitative inquiry & research design: Choosing among five approaches* (2nd ed.). Thousand Oaks, CA: Sage.

Creswell, J. (2008). *Educational research: Planning, conducting, and evaluating quantitative and qualitative research.* New Jersey, NJ: Pearson Prentice Hall.

Crossley, M., & Tikly, L. (2004). Postcolonial perspectives and comparative and international research in education: A critical introduction. *Comparative Education, 40*(2), 146–156.

Cuff, D., & Goudie, A. (2009). *The Oxford companion to global challenge.* New York, NY: Oxford University Press.

Cutter, A. (1998). *Integrated pre-service environmental education: The abandonment of knowledge* (Honours Honours Thesis). Gold Coast, Australia: Griffith University.

Cutter-Mackenzie, A. (2003). *Eco-literacy: The "Missing pradigm" in environmental education* (PhD). Brisbane, Australia: Central Queensland University.

Cutter-Mackenzie, A. (2009). *Eco-literacy: The "Missing pradigm" in environmental education.* Saarbruken, Germany: Lambert Academic Publishing.

Cutter-Mackenzie, A. (2010). Teaching for sustainability. In R. Gilbert & B. Hoepper (Eds.), *Teaching society and environment* (4th ed., pp. 348–363). South Melbourne, Australia: Cengage Learning.

Cutter-Mackenzie, A., & Tilbury, D. (2002). Meeting commitments for a sustainable future. In B. Knight (Ed.), *Reconceptualising learning in the knowledge society* (pp. 17–34). Flaxton, Queensland, Australia: Post Pressed.

Darling-Hammond L. (2006). *Powerful teacher education.* San Francisco, CA: Jossey-Bass.

Darling-Hammond, L. (2008). Knowledge for teaching: What do we know? In M. Cochran-Smith, S. Feiman-Nemser, J. McIntyre, & K. E. Demers (Eds.), *Handbook of research on teacher education: Enduring questions in changing contexts* (3rd ed., pp. 1316–1323). New York, NY: Routledge.

Darling-Hammond, L. (2012). *Creating a comprehensive system for evaluating and supporting effective teaching.* Stanford, CA: Stanford Center for Opportunity Policy in Education.

Darling-Hammond, L., Pacheco, A., Michelli, N., LePage, P., Hammerness, K., & Youngs, P. (2005). Implementing curriculum renewal in teacher education: Managing organizational and policy change. In L. Darling-Hammond & J. Bransford (Eds.), *Preparing teachers for a changing world: What teachers should learn and be able to do* (pp. 442–479). San Francisco, CA: Jossey Bass.

206

Day, C. (2007). School reforms and transitions in teacher professionalism and identity. In B. Townsend & R. Bates (Eds.), *Handbook of teacher education: Globalization, standards and professionalism in times of change* (pp. 597–612). Dordrecht, The Netherlands: Springer.

Denzin, N. K. (2001). *Interpretive interactionism.* Thousand Oaks, CA, London, UK, & New Delhi, India: Sage.

Diamond, J. (2005). *Collapse: How societies choose to fail or survive.* Australia: Allen Lane-Penguin Books.

Earth Summit. (2012). *The future we want: Rio + 20 outcome document.* Retrieved October 28, 2012, from http://www.earthsummit2012.org/

Eckersley, R. (1992). *Environmentalism and political theory: Toward an ecocentric approach.* Albany, NY: State University of New York Press.

Edwards, A. (2010). *Thriving beyond sustainability: Pathways to a resilient society.* Gabriola Island, Canada: New Society Publishers.

Ferreira, J., Ryan, L., & Tilbury, D. (2006). *Whole-school approaches to sustainability: A review of models for professional development in pre-service teacher education.* Canberra, Australia: ARIES

Ferreira, J., Ryan, L., Cavanagh, M., & Thomas, J. (2009). *Mainstreaming sustainability into pre-service teacher education in Australia.* Canberra, Australia: ARIES.

Fien, J. (2006). A letter from the future: UNESCO and the decade of education for sustainable development. *Australian Journal of Environmental Education, 22*(1), 63–70.

Fien, J., & Maclean, R. (2000). Teacher education for sustainability: II. Two teacher education projects from Asia and the Pacific. *Journal of Science Education and Technology, 9*(1), 37–48.

Fien, J., & Trainer, T. (1993). Education for sustainability. In J. Fien (Ed.), *Environmental education: A pathway to sustainability.* Geelong, Victoria: Deakin University.

Gabriel, N. (1996). *Teach our teachers well: Strategies to integrate environmental education into teacher education program.* Boston, MA: Second Nature.

Gadgil, M. (2007). Social change and conservation. In J. Pretty, A. Ball, T. Benton, J. Guivant, D. Lee, D. Orr, … H. Ward (Eds.), *The SAGE handbook of environment and society* (pp. 485–500). London, UK: SAGE Publications Ltd. doi:http://dx.doi.org/10.4135/9781848607873.n34

Garbett, D., & Ovens, A. (2012). Being a teacher educator: Exploring issues of authencity and safety through self-study. *Australian Journal of Teacher Education, 37*(3), 44–56.

Gornall, J., Wiltshire, A., & Betts, R. (2012). Anthropogenic drivers of environmental change. In J. Matthews, P. Bartlein, K. Briffa, A. Dawson, A. Vernal, T. Denham, … F. Oldfield (Eds.), *The Sage handbook of environmental change* (Vol. 1, pp. 517–536). London, UK: Sage Publications Lts.

Goueli, S. (2003). *Environmental education in an Egyptian university: The role of teacher educators* (PhD). Alberta, Canada: University of Alberta.

Gough, A. (2006). A long, winding and (rocky) road to environmental education for sustainability in 2006. *Australian Journal of Environmental Education, 22*(1), 71–76.

Goyal, M. (2011). Talk of inclusive growth, rich getting richer, faster: Report. *The Economic Times.* Retrieved from http://articles.economictimes.indiatimes.com/2011-02-01/news/28424869_1_mckinsey-households-income

Grant, C. (2008). Teacher capacity: Introduction to the section. In M. Cochran-Smith, S. Feiman-Nemser, J. McIntyre, & K. Demers (Eds.), *Handbook of research on teacher education: Enduring questions in changing contexts* (3rd ed., pp. 127–133). New York, NY: Routledge.

Grossman, P., Schoenfeld, A., & Lee, C. (2005). Teaching subject matter. In L. Darling-Hammond & J. Bransford (Eds.), *Preparing teachers for a changing world: What teachers should learn and be able to do* (pp. 201–231). San Francisco, CA: John Wiley & Sons.

Gu, Q. (2007). *Teacher development: Knowledge and context.* London, UK: Continuum.

Guha, R. (2006). *How much should a person consume: Thinking through the environment.* Delhi, India: Hachette India.

Haigh, M. (2008). The sattvic choice. In M. Bussey, S. Inayatullah, & I. Milojevic (Eds.), *Alternative educational futures* (pp. 235–252). Rotterdam, The Netherlands: Sense Publishers.

Hammersley, M., & Atkinson, P. (2007). *Ethnography: Principles in practice.* New York, NY: Routledge.

REFERENCES

Hansen, D. T. (2008). Why educate teachers? In M. Cochran-Smith, S. Feiman-Nemser, J. McIntyre & K. Demers (Eds.), *Handbook of research on teacher education: Enduring questions in changing contexts* (3rd ed., pp. 5–9). New York, NY: Routledge.

Hart, P. (2003). *Teachers' thinking in environmental education.* New York, NY: Peter Lang Publishing Inc.

Heilbronn, R. (2008). *Teacher education and the development of practical judgement.* London, UK; New York, NY: Continuum International Publishers.

Hillcoat, J. (1998). Consuming passions: Educating the empty self. *Australian Journal of Environmental Education, 14,* 57–64.

Hokka, P., Etelapelto, A., & Rasku-Puttonen, P. (2012). The professional agency of teacher educators amid academic discourses. *Journal of Education for Teaching: International Research and Pedagogy, 38*(1), 83–102.

Howard, T., & Aleman, G. (2008). Teacher capacity for diverse learners: What do teachers need to know? In M. Cochran-Smith, S. Feiman-Nemser, J. McIntyre & K. Demers (Eds.), *Handbook of research on teacher education: Enduring questions in changing contexts* (3rd ed., pp. 157–174). New York, NY: Routledge.

Human Development Report Office. (2011). *Human development index.* Retrieved October 30, 2012, from http://hdr.undp.org/en/statistics/

Hungerford, H., & Simmons, B. (2003). Environmental educators: A conversation with Paul Hart. *Journal of Environmental Education, 34*(4), 4–12.

Hunter Lovins, L., & Cohen, B. (2011). *Climate capitalism: Capitalism in the age of climate change.* New York, NY: Hill and Wang.

IBN Live India. (2012). *India's poverty line now lowered to Rs 28 per day.* Retrieved June 4, 2012, from http://ibnlive.in.com/news/indias-poverty-line-now-lowered-to-rs-28-per-day/240737-3.html

International Conference Environment and Society: Education and Public Awareness. (1997). *Declaration of Thessaloniki.* Paper presented at the International Conference Environment and Society: Education and Public Awareness, Thessaloniki, Greece.

International Union for Conservation of Nature and Natural Resources (IUCN). (1980). *World conservation strategy: Living resource conservation for sustainable development.* Retrieved October 31, 2012, from http://data.iucn.org/dbtw-wpd/edocs/WCS-004.pdf

IUCN. (1971). *Learning to change the future.* Retrieved November 25, 2012, from http://cmsdata.iucn.org/downloads/cec_history_30sept08_draft.pdf

Jain, S., & Pant, P. (2010). Environmental management systems for educational institutions: A case study of TERI university, New Delhi. *International Journal of Sustainability in Higher Education, 11*(3), 236.

Jickling, B. (1992). Why I dont want my children educated for sustainable development. *Journal of Environmental Education, 23*(4), 5–8.

Jickling, B. (2001). Environmental thought, the language of sustainability, and digital watches. *Environment Education Research, 7*(2), 167–180.

Jickling, B., & Spork, H. (1998). Education for the environment: A critique. *Environment Education Research, 4*(3).

Joshi, M. (2005). *ESD in India: Current practices and development plans.* Paper presented at the International Conference on Education for Sustainable Development. Kuching, Sarawak, Malaysia, Sarawak Development Institute, Kuching, Sarawak, Malaysia.

Kamdar, M. (2007). *Planet India.* New York, NY: Scribner.

Kapur, A. (2011). *Analysis of state budgets: Elementary education.* Retrieved July 4, 2012, from http://www.azimpremjifoundation.org/pdf/state-budget.pdf

Kaur, A., & Bhati, M. S. (2012). Environmental education in teacher education. *Indian Streams Research Journal, 2*(4), 1–4.

Kemp, D. (2004). *Exploring environmental issues: An integrated approach.* London, UK: Routledge.

Khirwadkar, A., & Pushpanadam, K. (2007). Education for sustainable development: Implications for teacher education. *International Forum of Teaching and Studies, 3*(3), 5–13.

Khoshoo, T. N. (1987). Environmental education: The Indian experience. In A. V. Baez, G. W. Knamiller, & J. C. Smyth, (Eds.), *The environment and science and technology education* (Vol. 8, pp. 25–26). Oxford, UK: ICSU Press.

Khoshoo, T. N. (2010). Introduction. In U. D. Gupta (Ed.), *My life in my words* (pp. 1–6). New Delhi, India: Penguin Books Ltd.

Khoshoo, T. N., & Moolakkattu, J. S. (2009). *Mahatma Gandhi and the environment: Analysing Gandhian environmental thought.* New Delhi, India: The Energy and Resources Institute (TERI).

Krapivin, V. F., & Varotsos, C. A. (2007). *Globalization and sustainable development: Environmental agendas.* Chichester, UK: Praxis Publishing Ltd.

Lacey, G. (2011). *Sufficient for the day. Towards a sustainable culture.* Boxhill, Victoria: Yarra Institute Press.

Lofland, J., Snow, D., Anderson, L., & Lofland, L. (2006). *Analyzing social settings: A guide to qualitative observation and analysis.* Belmont, CA: Wadsworth/Thomson Learning.

Lortie, D. C. (1975). *School-teacher: A sociological study.* Chicago, IL: Chicago University Press.

Lotz-Sistika, H. (Ed.). (2009). *Utopianism and educational processes in the United Nations decade of education for sustainable development: A critical reflection.* The Netherlands: Wageningen Academic Publishers.

Loughran, J. (2008a). Enacting a pedagogy of teacher education. In J. Loughran & T. Russell (Eds.), *Enacting a pedagogy of teacher education* (pp. 1–15). New York, NY: Routledge.

Loughran, J. (2008b). Toward a better understanding of teaching and learning about teaching. In M. Cochran-Smith, S. Feiman-Nemser, J. McIntyre, & K. Demers (Eds.), *Handbook of research on teacher education: Enduring questions in changing contexts* (3rd ed., pp. 1177–1182). New York, NY: Routledge.

Loughran, J. (2010). *What expert teachers do: Enhancing professional knowledge for classroom practice.* Crow's Nest, Australia: Allen & Unwin.

Loughran, J. (2011). On becoming a teacher educator. *Journal of Education for Teaching, 37*(3), 279–291.

Loughran, J., & Northfield, J. R. (1996). *Opening the classrom: Teacher, researcher, learner.* London, UK: Falmer.

Loughran, J., & Russell, T. (Eds.). (1997). *Teaching about teaching: Purpose, passion and pedagogy in teacher education.* London, UK: Falmer Press.

Louv, R. (2010). *Last child in the wood: Saving our children from nature-deficit disorder* (Vol. Rev.). London, UK: Atlantic.

Luce, E. (2006). *In spite of the gods.* London, UK: Little, Brown.

Maathai, W. (2009). Preface. In P. Corcocan & P. Osano (Eds.), *Young people, education and sustainable development: Exploring principles, perspectives and praxis.* The Netherlands: Wageningen Academic Publishers.

Mallik, T. (1962). *Gandhi on the environment.* Ahmedabad, India: Navjivan Press.

Matthews, J., Bartlein, P., Briffa, K., Dawson, A., Vernal, A., Denham, T., ... Oldfield, F. (2012). Background to the science of environmental change. In J. Matthews, P. Bartlein, K. Briffa, A. Dawson, A. Vernal, T. Denham, ... F. Oldfield (Eds.), *The Sage handbook of environmental change* (Vol. 1, pp. 1–34). London, UK: Sage Publications Ltd.

May, T. (2000). Elements of success if environmental education through practitioner eyes. *Journal of Environmental Education, 31*(3), 4–11.

Mazur, L., & Miles, L. (2009). *Conversations with green gurus.* West Sussex, UK: John Wiley & Sons Ltd.

McDiarmid, G. W., & Clevenger-Bright, M. (2008). Rethinking teacher capacity. In M. Cochran-Smith, S. Feiman-Nemser, J. McIntyre, & K. Demers (Eds.), *Handbook of research in teacher education: Enduring questions in changing contexts* (3rd ed., pp. 134–156). New York, NY: Routledge.

Mckenzie, M. (2005). The post-post period and environmental education research. *Environment Education Research, 11*(4), 401–412.

McKeown, R. (2000). Environmental education in the United States: A survey of preservice teacher education programs. *The Journal of Environmental Education, 32*(1), 4–11.

REFERENCES

McKeown, R., Hopkins, C., Rizzi, R., & Chrystalbridge, M. (2002). *Education for sustainable development toolkit.* Retrieved January 10, 2010, from http://esdtoolkit.org

McKeown-Ice, R. (2000). Environmental education in the United States: A survey of preservice teacher education programs. *The Journal of Environmental Education, 32*(1), 4–11.

McKeown-Ice, R. (2005). *Guidelines and recommendations for reorienting teacher education to address sustainability.* Retrieved December 6, 2009, from http://unesdoc.unesco.org/images/0014/001433/143370E.pdf

McKeown-Ice, R. (2012). Teacher education 1991–2012: Reflecting on 20 years. *Journal of Education for Sustainable Development, 6*(1), 37–41.

McKeown-Ice, R., & Hopkins, C. (2002). Weaving sustainability into pre-service teacher education. In W. L. Filho (Ed.), *Teaching sustainability at universities: Towards greening the curriculum.* Germany: Lange Scientific.

Miles, R., & Cutter-Mackenzie, A. (2006). *Environmental education: Is it really a priority in teacher education?* Paper presented at the Australian Association of Environmental Education Australia.

Miles, R., Cutter-Mackenzie, A., & Harrison, L. (2006). Teacher education: A diluted environmental education experience. *Australian Journal of Environmental Education, 22*(1), 1–11.

Millenium Ecosystem Assessment Board. (2005). *Millenium ecosystem assessment report.* Retrieved December 6, 2009, from http://www.millenniumassessment.org/en/Condition.aspx

National Commission for Education Research and Technology. (2005). *National curriculum framework.* Retrieved November 24, 2009, from http://www.ncert.nic.in/html/pdf/schoolcurriculum/framework05/Currilular Areas.pdf

National Council for Teacher Education. (2009). *National curriculum framework for teacher edcuation: Towards preparing professional and humane teacher.* New Delhi, India: Member Secretary, National Council for Teacher Education Retrieved from http://www.ncte-india.org/publicnotice/NCFTE_2010.pdf

National Council of Teacher Educators. (2005). *Environmental education curriculum framework for teachers and teacher educators.* New Delhi, India: NCTE.

National Survey Sample Organization. (2012). 66th round of national sample survey. Retrieved October 29, 2012, from http://mospi.nic.in/Mospi_New/site/inner.aspx?status=3&menu_id=31

Nemerov, N. L., & Agardy, F. (Eds.). (2005). *Environemntal solutions: Environmental problems and the all-inclusive global, scientific, political, legal, economic, medical and engineering bases to solve them.* USA: Elsevier Academic Press.

Nielsen, R. (2005). *The little green handbook: A guide to critical global trends.* Melbourne, Australia: Scribe Publications Pty Ltd.

Organisation for Economic Co-operation and Development. (1995). *Environmental learning for the 21st century.* Retrieved November 27, 2012, from http://www.ensi.org/media-global/downloads/Publications/224/OECD_environmental_Learning1.pdf

Orr, D. W. (1992). *Ecological literacy: Education and the transition to a postmodern world.* Albany, NY: State University of New York.

Orr, D. W. (1994). *Earth in mind: On education, environment, and the human prospect.* Washington, DC: Island Press.

Orr, D. W. (2002). Four challenges of sustainability. *Conservation Biology, 16*(6), 1457–1460.

Orr, D. W. (2007). Ecological design and education. In J. Pretty, A. Ball, T. Benton, J. Guivant, D. Lee, D. W. Orr, … H. Ward (Eds.), *The Sage handbook of environment and society* (pp. 209–224). London, UK: Sage Publications Ltd.

Orr, D. W. (2012). *Ecological design intelligence.* Retrieved December 9, 2012, from http://www.ecoliteracy.org/essays/ecological-design-intelligence

Oulton, C. R. (1996). *Environmental education in the 21st century: Theory, practice, progress and promise.* London, UK: Routledge.

Palmer, J. (1998). *Environmental education in the 21st century: Theory, practice, progress and promise.* London, UK: Routledge.

Pande, A. (2001). Environmental education in rural central Himalayan schools. *The Journal of Environmental Education, 32*(3), 47–53.

210

Pandya, M. (2000). *Teacher education for environmental education in India.* Paper presented at the Third UNESCO Japan Seminar on EE in Asia Pacific Region. Tokyo, Japan.

Pandya, M. (2004). *Continuing professional development in EE.* Paper presented at the Eighth UNESCO Japan Seminar on EE in Asia Pacific Region. Tokyo, Japan.

Parthasarthy, M. A. (1987). Range, opportunities and applicability of non-formal environmental education. In A. V. Baez, G. W. Knamiller, & J. Smyth (Eds.), *The environment and science and technology education* (Vol. 8, pp. 349–354). Oxford, UK: Permagon Press for ICSU Press.

Patil, A. (2006). *The development and implementation of a teacher education model in environmental science for Indian certificate of secondary education (ICSE) schools* (PhD Doctoral dissertation). New York, NY: Columbia University. Retrieved from http://images.lib.monash.edu.au/er/theses/patil.pdf

Patton, M. (2002). *Qualitative research and evaluation methods* (3rd ed.). Thousand Oaks, CA: Sage.

Payne, P. (2001). Identity and environmental education. *Environment Education Research, 7*(1), 67–88.

Pepper, C., & Wildy, H. (2008). Leading for sustainability: Is surface understanding enough? *Journal of Educational Administration, 46*(5), 613–629.

Plevyak, L. H., Bendixen-Noe, M., Henderson, J., & Wilke, R. (2001). Level of teacher preparation and implementation of EE: Mandated and non-mandated EE teacher preparation states. *The Journal of Environmental Education, 32*(2).

Powers, A. (2004). Teacher preparation for environmental education: Faculty perspectives on the infusion of environmental education into preservice methods course. *The Journal of Environmental Education, 35*(3), 3–10.

Pretty, J., Ball, A., Benton, T., Guivant, J., Lee, D., Orr, D. W., . . . Ward, H. (2007). Introduction to environment and society. In J. Pretty, A. Ball, T. Benton, J. Guivant, D. Lee, D. W. Orr, ... H. Ward (Eds.), *The Sage of handbook of environment and society*. London, UK: Sage Publications Ltd.

Qablan, A., & Al Qaderi, S. (2009). How to change university faculty members' attitudes and behavior in the context of education for sustainable development. *Applied Environmental Education & Communication, 8*(3), 184–194.

Rajagopalan, R. (2011). *Environmental studies: From crisis to cure* (2nd ed.). New Delhi, India: Oxford University Press.

Rangarajan, M. (Ed.). (2009). *Environmental issues in India: A reader*. New Delhi, India: Dorling Kindersley (India) Pvt. Ltd.

Ravindranath, M. J. (2000). Living traditions. In D. Yencken, J. Fien, & H. Sykes (Eds.), *Environment, education and society in the Asia-Pacific: Local traditions and global discourses* (pp. 99–112). London, UK: Routledge.

Ravindranath, M. J. (2002). India. In J. Fien, D. Yencken & H. Sykes (Eds.), *Young people and the environment: An Asia-Pacific perspective* (pp. 65–77). The Netherlands: Kluwer Academic Publishers.

Ravindranath, M. J. (2007). Environmental education in teacher education in India: Experiences and challenges in the United Nation's decade of education for sustainable development. *Journal of Education for Teaching: International Research and Pedagogy, 33*(2), 191–206.

Richardson, V. (1996). The role of attitudes and beliefs in learning to teach. In J. Sikula, T. J. Buttery & E. Guyton (Eds.), *Handbook of research on teacher education* (Vol. 2, pp. 102–119). New York, NY: Macmillan.

Rodgers, C., & Scott, K. (2008). The development of the personal self and identity in learning to teach. In M. Cochran-Smith, S. Feiman-Nemser, J. McIntyre, & K. Demers (Eds.), *Handbook of research on teacher education* (3rd ed., pp. 732–756). New York, NY: Routledge.

Rosean, C., & Florio-Ruane, S. (2008). The metaphors by which we teach: Experience, metaphor, and culture in teacher education. In M. Cochran-Smith, S. Feiman-Nemser, J. McIntyre, & K. Demers (Eds.), *Handbook of research on teacher education* (3rd ed., pp. 707–731). New York, NY: Routledge.

Sainath, P. (2011, December 8). Some states fight the trend, but still.... *The Hindu*. Retrieved from http://www.indiatogether.org/2011/dec/psa-suidata.htm

Sarabhai, K. (1995). *Strategy for environmental education: An approach for India.* Paper presented at the North American Association for Environmental Education, Washington DC, U.S.A.

Sarabhai, K. (2007). Thirty years after tbilisi. *Journal of Education for Sustainable Development, 1*(2), 169–170.

Sarabhai, K. (2008a). The Ahmedabad declaration 2007: A call to action. *Journal of Education for Sustainable Development, 2*(1), 87–88.

Sarabhai, K. (2008b). Towards a handprint for sustainable development. *Journal of Education for Sustainable Development, 2*(1), 1–3.

Sarabhai, K., Raghunathan, M., & Kandula, K. (2000). *Status reports: India* (pp. 127–143). Ahmedabad, India: Center For Environmental Education.

Sauve, L. (2004). Sustainable development in education: Consensus as an ethical issue. In W. Scott & S. Gough (Eds.), *Key issues in sustainable development and learning* (pp. 145–146). London, UK: RoutledgeFalmer.

Schusler, T. M., Krasny, M. E., Peters, S. J., & Decker, D. J. (2009). Developing citizens and communities through youth environmental action. *Environment Education Research, 15*(1), 111–127.

Selby, D. (2006). The firm and shaky ground of education for sustainable development. *Environment Education Research, 30*(2), 351–365.

Shagrir, L. (2011). Professional development of novice teacher educators: Professional self, interpersonal relations and teaching skills. In T. Bates, A. Swennen, & K. Jones (Eds.), *The professional development of teacher educators* (pp. 55–70). London, UK and New York, NY: Routledge.

Sharma, V. M. (2010). Environmental pollutions: Ancient solutions in the light of sanskrit literature. In K. R. Gupta (Ed.), *Environmental education in India* (pp. 169). New Delhi, India: Atlantic Publishers and Distributors (P) Ltd.

Shiva, V. (2005). *India divided: Diversity and democracy under attack.* New York, NY: Seven Stories Press.

Singh, P. (2011). Developing a community of thinking: Assessment of environmental education. *Environment Education Research, 17*(1), 113–123.

Smyth, J. (2008). Environment and education: A view of a changing scene. In A. Reid & W. Scott (Eds.), *Researching education and the environment: Retrospect and prospect.* Oxon, England: Routledge.

Sobel, D. (2008). *Childhood and nature: Design and principles for educators.* Portland, Maine: Stenhouse Publishers.

Spivak, G. (1994). Can the subaltern speak? In P. Williams & L. Chrisman (Eds.), *Colonial discourse and post colonial theory* (pp. 66–111). New York, NY: New York Press, Columbia University.

Srivastava, L. (2009). Securing India's energy future: What does the world have to worry about? In N. Stacey, G. Boggs, B. Campbell, & W. Steffen (Eds.), *Prepare for impact: When people and environment collide in the tropics* (pp. 33–37). Darwin, Australia: Charles Darwin University Press.

Summers, M., Childs, A., & Corney, G. (2005). Education for sustainable development in initial teacher training: Issues for interdisciplinary collaboration. *Environment Education Research, 11*(5), 623–647.

Supreme Court of India. (2003). *M C Mehta-petitioner versus Union of India and Ors – respondents.* Retrieved from http://www.downtoearth.org.in/html/sc_directive.htm

Swaminathan, M. S. (1987). Education, environment and livelihood security. In A. V. Baez, G. W. Knamiller, & J. Smyth (Eds.), *The environment and science and technology education* (Vol. 8, pp. 13–24). Great Britain: ICSU Press.

Swennen, A., Jones, K., & Volman, M. (2011). Teacher educators: Their identities, sub-identities and implications for professional development. In T. Bates, A. Swennen, & K. Jones (Eds.), *The professional development of teacher educators* (pp. 138–155). London, UK & New York, NY: Routledge.

Tagore, R. (2010). *My life in my words.* New Delhi, India: Penguin Books Ltd.

Thomashow, M. (1996). *Ecological identity: Becoming a reflective environmentalist.* Cambridge, MA: The MIT Press.

Tikly, L. (2001). Globalisation and education in the postcolonial world: Towards a conceptual framework. *Comparative Education, 37*(2), 151–171.

Tilbury, D. (1992). Environmental education within pre-service teacher education: The priority of priorities. *International Journal of Environmental Education and Information, 11*(4), 267–280.

Tilbury, D. (1994). The international development of environmental education: A basis for a teacher education model? *International Journal of Environmental Education and Information, 13*(1).

Tilbury, D. (2004). Rising to the challenge: Education for sustainability in Australia. *Australian Journal of Environmental Education, 20*(2), 103–114.

U. S. Bureau of Census. (2009). *World population: 1950–2050*. Retrieved November 6, 2009, from http://www.census.gov/ipc/www/idb/worldpopgraph.php

UNDESD. (2007). UN decade of education for sustainable development: The first two years. *Journal of Education for Sustainable Development, 1*(1), 117–126. doi:10.1177/097340820700100120

UNEP. (1972). *Declaration of the United Nations conference on the human environment*. Retrieved November 25, 2009, from http://www.unep.org/Documents.Multilingual/Default.asp?DocumentID= 97&ArticleID=1503

UNEP. (2012a). *GEO 5 – Global environmental outlook: Environment for the future we want*. Kenya, Africa: UNEP.

UNEP. (2012b). *Global environment outlook 5: Summary for Asia and the Pacific Region on the eve of Rio+20*. Retrieved November 12, 2012, from http://www.unep.org/geo/pdfs/geo5/RS_AsiaPacific_ en.pdf

UNESCO, & UNEP. (1977). *Tbilisi declaration*. Retrieved March 15, 2010, from http://www.gdrc.org/ uem/ee/tbilisi.html

UNESCO. (1975). *International workshop on environmental education: The Belgrade charter*. Retrieved March 15, 2010, from unescodoc.unesco.org/images/001/0001777/017772eb.pdf

UNESCO. (1992). *Agenda 21*. Retrieved November 15, 2009, from http://www.un.org/esa/dsd/agenda21/ index.shtml

UNESCO. (2002). *Education for sustainability, from Rio to Johannesburg: Lessons learnt from a decade of commitment*. Paris, France: UNESCO.

UNESCO. (2005a). *Draft international implementation scheme*. Retrieved December 6, 2009, from http://portal.unesco.org/education/en/file_download.php/e13265d9b948898339314b001d91fd01draft Final+IIS.pdf

UNESCO. (2005b). *Guidelines and recommendations for reorienting teacher education to address sustainability*. Retrieved Febraury 23, 2010, from http://www.unescobkk.org/fileadmin/user_upload/ apeid/Conference/papers/McKeownGRTETASPaperV2.doc

UNESCO. (2005c). *United Nations decade of education for sustainable development*. Retrieved November 9, 2009, from http://www.unesco.org.en.esd

UNESCO. (2007). *The Ahmedabad declaration*. Retrieved November 1, 2012, from http://portal.unesco.org/geography/en/ev.php-URL_ID=9451&URL_DO=DO_TOPIC&URL_ SECTION=201.html

UNESCO. (2011). *Wolrd data on education – India*. Retrieved November 1 2012, from http://unesdoc.unesco.org/images/0021/002113/211302e.pdf

UNESCO-UNEP. (1992). UNCED: The earth summit. *Connect, 17*(2), 1–8.

United Nations Educational Scientific and Cultural Organization. (1997). *Educating for a sustainable future: A transdisciplinary vision for concerted action*. Retrieved September 4, 2009, from http://www.unesco.org/education/tlsf/TLSF/theme_a/mod01/uncom01t05s01.htm

Van Damme, L., & Neluvhalani, E. (2004). Indigenous knowledge in environmental education processes: Perspectives on a growing research arena. *Environmental Education Research, 10*(3), 353–370.

Varma, P. (2005). *Being Indian*. New Delhi, India: Penguin Books.

Wali, M. (1987). A holistic view of human ethics. In A. V. Baez, G. W. Knamiller, & J. Smyth (Eds.), *The environment and science and technology education* (Vol. 8, pp. 27–28). Oxford, England: ICSU Press.

Weiner, M. (1991). *The child and the state in India : Child labor and education policy in comparative perspective*. Princeton, NJ: Princeton University Press.

Wilson, H. (2008). The last word: An interview with Marilyn Cochran-Smith. *Journal of Advanced Academics, 19*(4).

Wolcott, H. (2008). *Ethnography: A way of seeing* (2nd ed.). Plymouth, England: AltaMira Press.

World Bank. (2003). *WDR 2003: Sustainable development in a dynamic world: Transforming institutions, growth, and quality of life*. Retrieved November 11, 2012, from http://wdronline.worldbank.org/ worldbank/a/c.html/world_development_report_2003/abstract/WB.0-8213-5150-8.abstract

REFERENCES

World Bank. (2009). *India country overview 2009*. Retrieved June 21, 2011, from http://www.worldbank.org.in/WBSITE/EXTERNAL/COUNTRIES/SOUTHASIAEXT/INDI AEXTN/0,,contentMDK:20195738~menuPK:295591~pagePK:141137~piPK:141127~theSite PK:295584,00.html

World Bank. (2010). *Development and climate change*. Retrieved November 11, 2013, from http://wdronline.worldbank.org/worldbank/a/c.html/world_development_report_2010/abstract/ WB.978-0-8213-7987-5.abstract

World Bank. (2012). *India: World development indicators*. Retrieved June 4, 2012, from http://data.worldbank.org/country/india

World Commission on Environment and Development. (1987). *Our common future (The Brundlant report)*. Oxford, England: Oxford University Press.

World Commission on Environment and Development. (2004). Towards sustainable development. In K. Conca & G. D. Dabelko (Eds.), *Green planet blues: Environmental politics from Stockholm to Johannesburg* (3rd ed.). Colorado, CO and Oxford, England: Westview Press.

World Wide Fund (WWF). (2008). *Living planet report 2008*. Retrieved October 30, 2009, from http://assets.panda.org/downloads/living_planet_report_2008.pdf

Yale University. (2012). *Environmental performance index*. Retrieved October 28, 2012, from http://epi.yale.edu/

Yencken, D., Fien, J., & Sykes, H. (Eds.). (2002). *Environment, education and society in the Asia-Pacific: Local traditions and global discourses*. New York, NY: Routledge.

Young, Z. (2002). *A new green order? The world bank and the politics of the global environment facility*. London, UK: Pluto Press.

Zavestoski, S. (2003). Constructing and maintaining ecological identities: The strategies of deep ecologists. In S. Clayton & S. Opotow (Eds.), *Identity and the natural environment: The psychological significance of nature* (pp. 297–315). Massachusetts, MA: Massachusetts Institute of Technology.

CPSIA information can be obtained at www.ICGtesting.com
Printed in the USA
LVOW01s1505021015

456698LV00005B/41/P

9 789463 002158